DESIGNING WOMEN

FILM AND CULTURE

A SERIES OF COLUMBIA UNIVERSITY PRESS
EDITED BY JOHN BELTON

Picturing Japaneseness: Monumental Style, National Identity, Japanese Film
    Darrell William Davis

*Attack of the Leading Ladies: Gender, Sexuality, and Spectatorship in Classic
    Horror Cinema*
    Rhona J. Berenstein

This Mad Masquerade: Stardom and Masculinity in the Jazz Age
    Gaylyn Studlar

Sexual Politics and Narrative Film: Hollywood and Beyond
    Robin Wood

The Sounds of Commerce: Marketing Popular Film Music
    Jeff Smith

Orson Welles, Shakespeare, and Popular Culture
    Michael Anderegg

*Pre-Code Hollywood: Sex, Immorality, and Insurrection in American Cinema,
    1930–1934*
    Thomas Doherty

*Sound Technology and the American Cinema: Perception, Representation,
    Modernity*
    James Lastra

Melodrama and Modernity: Early Sensational Cinema and Its Contexts
    Ben Singer

*Wondrous Difference: Cinema, Anthropology, and Turn-of-the-Century
    Visual Culture*
    Alison Griffiths

Hearst Over Hollywood: Power, Passion, and Propaganda in the Movies
    Louis Pizzitola

Masculine Interests: Homoerotics in Hollywood Film
    Robert Lang

Special Effects: Still in Search of Wonder
    Michele Pierson

DESIGNING

WOMEN

CINEMA

ART DECO

AND THE

FEMALE FORM

LUCY FISCHER

COLUMBIA UNIVERSITY

PRESS   NEW YORK

Columbia University Press
Publishers Since 1893
New York   Chichester, West Sussex
Copyright © 2003 Columbia University Press

Columbia University Press wishes to express its appreciation for assistance given by The Richard D. and Mary Jane Edwards Endowed Publication Fund of the University of Pittsburgh toward the cost of publishing this book.

Library of Congress Cataloging-in-Publication Data
Fischer, Lucy.
Designing women : cinema, art deco, and the female form / Lucy Fischer.
p. cm. — (Film and culture)
Includes bibliographical references and index.
ISBN 0–231–12500–3 (cloth : alk. paper) — ISBN 0–231–12501–1 (paper : alk. paper)
1. Art and motion pictures. 2. Art deco. 3. Women in motion pictures. 4. Women in art.
I. Title. II. Series.

PN1995.25.F57   2003
791.43'657 — dc21   2002041711

Columbia University Press books are printed on permanent and durable acid-free paper.

Printed in the United States of America
Designed by Linda Secondari

c 10 9 8 7 6 5 4 3 2 1
p 10 9 8 7 6 5 4 3 2 1

An earlier version of chapter 4 appeared as "Greta Garbo and Silent Cinema: The Actress as Art Deco Icon." in *Camera Obscura* 16.3 (2001): 83–111 (all rights reserved; used by permission of the publisher). The same version (and title) was also included in Jennifer Bean, ed., *A Feminist Reader in Early Cinema* (Durham, N.C.: Duke University Press, 2002), 476–98. An earlier version of chapter 5 appeared as "Designing Women: Art Deco and the Musical" in Peter Buhler, Caryl Flinn, and David Neumeyer, eds., *Music and Film* (Middletown, Conn.: Wesleyan University Press, 2000), 295–315.

In memory of Marienbad, Austria,

its razed synagogue, and Resl, Pepp, and Lolo Fischer

CONTENTS

ACKNOWLEDGMENTS

I am beholden to a variety of individuals and institutions for assistance on this project.

First, I would like to thank several people at my home institution, the University of Pittsburgh. I am indebted to the work of numerous research assistants: Louise Malakoff, Jessica Mesman, Jessica Nassau, Allana Sleeth, and Kirsten Strayer. I would also like to thank Andrea Campbell of the Film Studies Program for her help on this project, and Jim Burke and Joe Kapalewski of Photographic Services for their care in filming objects from my own collection. My Chair, David Bartholomae, allowed me to take a research leave of absence (on very short notice) and my Dean, John Cooper, made that leave a practical possibility. I received a Type II Research Grant from the university that enabled me to purchase numerous illustrations for the book, and I was a recipient of support from the Richard D. and Mary Jane Edwards Endowed Publication Fund.

I would like to credit the National Endowment for the Humanities, which supported my work by awarding me a Fellowship for University Professors in the spring of 2002. I am grateful as well to several individuals (and former colleagues) at the Museum of Modern Art who assisted with my research: Charles Silver in the Film Study Center, as well as Mary Corliss and Terry Geeskin in the Film Stills Archive. Several other individuals facilitated the procurement of images for this volume: John Findling of Indiana University Southeast, Tim Wilson at the San Francisco Public Library, Marcia Schiff at the Associated Press, Beverley Perman at Sevenarts, Ltd., Silvia Ros at the Wolfsonian, Katharine Oakes at the British Film Institute, and Jill Bloomer at the Cooper-Hewitt National Design Museum, Smithsonian Institution. My gratitude further extends to several curators who invited me to lecture on aspects of my research early on: Bill Judson of the Carnegie Museum of Art in Pittsburgh and John Hanhardt of the Guggenheim Museum in New York City. And thanks to Jennifer Bean, who solicited part of my work on this project for an article in *Camera Obscura*, and to David Neumeyer and Caryl Flinn, who included a different segment of the book in a volume on music and film.

Jennifer Crewe, my editor at Columbia University Press, has been a pleasure to work with—always helpful, encouraging, knowledgeable, and quick with an answer to a query. John Belton, the series editor, is a truly astute reader, managing to ask the precise questions that you should have asked yourself. He provided many insightful comments and suggestions for the manuscript's revision. I would also like to thank Roy Thomas for his "eagle eye" in editing the text.

Finally, I would like to thank my husband Mark and my son David for their love and patience over the years that this manuscript has been in the making. Not only did they have to deal with my writing a book (and its attendant familial stresses) but, given my penchant for Art Deco collecting, they had to tolerate the incursion of my "research" into the geography of our domestic landscape. I have depended upon (and treasured) their indulgence.

DESIGNING WOMEN

INTRODUCTION

A Method to My Madness

Sometimes I imagine that I was born in the 1920s or 1930s. In fact, I was not. I can only entertain this fantasy because of my lifelong immersion in the movies and the vivid world they created for me. As it happens, much of that universe was replete with the allure of Art Deco.

My attraction to the style began with a love of film musicals. Initially, I believed it was only the dance, music, and romance of the films that I adored—be it the fluid grace of Fred Astaire and Ginger Rogers or the dizzying camp of Busby Berkeley's vertiginous production numbers. With time, however, I realized that my fondness for the genre transcended these factors and attached equally to costumes, décor, and theatrical mise-en-scène.

The roots of this predilection are complicated. On one level, Art Deco was, for me, simply synonymous with movie glamour. But on another level, I am sure that my love of Deco has more eccentric autobiographical, and even psychoanalytical, derivations. My parents and their circle courted, married, and furnished homes in the 1930s, which raises questions as to whether my interest in Art Deco evokes some Freudian "primal scene." Thus, I grew up under the extended influence of an Art Deco domestic milieu—whether in the form of the female figural lamps and tall decorative pedestals in the apartment of my mother's friend or the clothes I saw in old family photographs. While my mother largely eschewed the Style Moderne, she nonetheless participated in the period's attendant Orientalism—in her love of chinoiserie and "Chinese Chippendale" furniture, an appreciation I admit inheriting.

Furthermore, I grew up in Manhattan, an architectural wonderland of the Art Deco style. As a child, the skyline I habitually viewed included the majestically

Myth, memory, history—these are three alternative ways to capture and account for an allusive past, each with its own persuasive claim.
—Warren Susman (1984:151)

FIGURE I.1

The auditorium and stage of
Radio City Music Hall. (Courtesy Museum of Modern Art)

austere Empire State Building as well as the jewel-capped Chrysler Building. As
a film spectator, I occasionally attended shows at Radio City Music Hall, an inter-
nationally regarded Art Deco shrine (fig. I.1). For everyday film viewing, I went to
neighborhood theaters like Loew's 72nd Street, built in 1932. While I have no personal recollection of the site, when I began work on this project I came across a
photograph of its interior and realized it had been furnished in the lushly exotic
décor of the time (which in this case included a huge statue of Buddha and a modernist ladies room).

My first scholarly engagement with the Art Deco style came through an article
I wrote on the films of Busby Berkeley (Fischer 1976). At the time, however, I over-
looked the films' settings to consider, instead, the symbolic content of their form,
especially their obvious kitsch and somewhat offputting stereotypical vision of
Woman. It was quite a while before I realized that part of what drew me to these
films (despite their misogyny) was the design movement they reflected.

I became aware of my interest in Art Deco through a seemingly unrelated passion—a love for collecting that struck me when I moved from New York City to a small Pennsylvania college town. Bereft of my usual urban haunts and pursuits (and, quite frankly, feeling displaced), I sought to discover what might constitute "fun" for me in this new alien locale. It turned out to be a quest for flea markets and "antique" shows. At first, as though under some incomprehensible force, I found myself purchasing old kitchen implements (rusted ice tongs, old wooden milk bottle cases, and the like). Perhaps I entertained some fantasy of turning "rural" with the move. This stage, thankfully, passed (though some of its prizes remain as unwanted debris in my overcrowded basement). My turn to Deco objects came through the intervention of others who executed pilgrimages to my new Pennsylvania abode with antique purchases in mind. A friend from graduate school came to visit one weekend and looked for old Fiesta Ware table settings. Though I then found this form of pottery clumsy and ugly (and caused a tiff by saying so), I suspect that the Deco aesthetic had already begun to insinuate itself into my mind (and pocketbook). Later, after I moved to Pittsburgh, the visit of my husband's cousin from Los Angeles—a West Coast "swap meet" veteran—turned delightful with a trip to the local antique shop, where she waxed poetic over a low-priced Art Deco lamp she noticed. She did not purchase it, however, for fear of breaking it on her return trip home. Within days of her departure, I inexplicably found myself at the shop again, buying the lamp for myself (fig. I.2). Once my awareness of such objects had been piqued, it never waned, and over the years I became increasingly obsessed with acquiring Art Deco glassware, pottery, jewelry, light fixtures, and the like. Especially fascinating to me were objects bearing the traces of the Art Deco Woman—an icon utilized as the base or column of candlesticks, candy dishes, ashtrays, and lamps or as an etched or bas-relief figure in the surfaces of glass, bronze, and silver (see fig. I.3).

By now, my life is overrun with such objects, which have proliferated to a level that almost defies explanation. More and more, when I have occasion to watch the final moments of *Citizen Kane*, I picture myself as an aged matron in a bourgeois "Xanadu"—or imagine my posthumous self leaving behind crates of junk for my friends, relatives, and offspring to scavenge. This book is an attempt to lend some method to my madness—to confess, tame, rationalize, and perhaps justify my guilty pleasure. (Significantly, Van Nest Polglase, the art director for Welles's film, had once worked in the Art Deco mode on the Astaire/Rogers musicals.)

Clearly, in grappling with my Art Deco mania I am struggling with a remnant of the past; and as the opening epigraph indicates, there are three methods for so doing. This book will draw on them all. Certain sections will focus on the

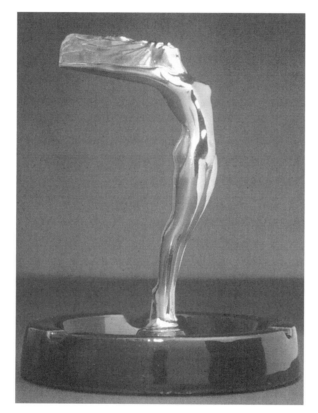

mythic elements of the style—its association with youth, glamour, modernity, exoticism, stardom, and femininity. Other segments will concentrate on *historical* aspects of the mode—the genealogy of its style, its relation to preceding art and design movements, its bonds with the movies, its ties to consumerism in the twentieth century, its links to the New Woman. Finally, this introduction invokes the question of *memory*, as I seek, on a more intimate level, to comprehend what Art Deco means to me.

COLLECTING AND RECOLLECTING

Art Deco artifacts . . . [are] floating signifiers without clear referents. —Mark Winokur (1996:199)

I will approach the subject of memory through a brief meditation on my fixation with Art Deco objects (jewelry, housewares, ornamental pieces, and the like), especially those which incorporate the figure of Woman. Such a deliberation will be highly personal, since it is a truism of the theory of collecting that what one acquires is ultimately the self. As Jean Baudrillard states, "A given collection is made up of a succession of items, but the final term must always be the person of the collector" (1994:12). In a sense, by "outing" my habit I am violating what Baudrillard sees as one aspect of the paradigm, a tendency for collecting to have an "aura of the clandestine, of confinement, [of] secrecy . . . all of which give rise to the unmistakable impression of a guilty relationship" (9). On the other hand, Susan Pearce finds the female collector far more comfortable than the male in admitting her obsession (1995:203).

In reading the literature on collecting, I came to realize, with some horror, that in many respects I follow a typical pattern. In my devotion to the pastime I am like one in three Americans (Pearce:159); and in my predilection for decorative objects, I am quintessentially female (Belk 1995:98; Pearce:201–202). Were I male,

I would evidently be more likely to covet militaria or machines (Pearce:212–13). Furthermore, the ascendancy of collecting in my life followed two important personal losses—another classic feature of the syndrome (Belk:144). In my case, it was the involuntary uprooting from New York (the city of my birth and upbringing) and the death of my father, which followed shortly thereafter. Thus, as Russell Belk remarks, collecting can be both "compensatory [and] security-seeking" (144). The particular choice of my collection "theme" (Art Deco design pieces) has its own logic as well since the mode has particular associations with the early modern urban center and is often deemed the "skyscraper style." By acquiring its vestiges, was I not on some level miniaturizing and agglomerating a bit of Gotham for myself? Furthermore, my father, though a small businessman by trade, was an artistic individual who did oil painting and made jewelry. As an Austrian émigré, he also was associated in my mind with a certain European sophistication. He grew up in Marienbad, an elegant spa town, and his family owned a shop (Fischer and Deutsch) that sold jewelry and decorative objects to visitors. Again, in my focus on the artifacts of the Style Moderne (a movement that was born on the Continent in the era of my father's youth), might I not have been, in some oblique fashion, addressing a parental void? Related to loss is the sense that collecting seeks to defy time. John Elsner and Roger Cardinal remark that collections "gesture to nostalgia for previous worlds" (1994:5), and Susan Pearce notes how the "material nature of objects means that they . . . alone, have the capacity to carry the past physically into the present" (170–71).

Beyond such traumatic issues as separation and death, theorists have linked collecting to broader notions of childhood. Werner Muensterberger asks: "What else are collectibles but toys grown-ups take seriously?" (1994:31). Now, as I peruse the Art Deco "ladies" that overrun my home (on lamps, candlesticks, planters, letter openers, glassware), I recall with a start that I was an inveterate doll fan as a girl. My family made fun of how I slept with numerous ones lined up beside me in the bed, virtually crowding me out. I can recall the thrill of being given a "Saucy Walker" who could stroll with me through the apartment, and the disappointment of not being given a "Tiny Tears" whom I might have fed. When I refused to go to school in the first grade, my mother "sweetened the deal" of my return by promising to order for me a nurse doll that was available through the Curity Bandage Company. I can still remember the suspense of waiting for her arrival by mail. Could it be that the ubiquitous presence of Art Deco ladies in my current household is an adult "spin" on my childhood dolls? Many theorists, in fact, see collectibles not simply as simulacra of childhood paraphernalia but as objects with a certain affective power to comfort, palliate, and compensate the grown-up—as do

FIGURE I.2 (*Opposite*)
My first Art Deco lamp.
(Author's collection. *Photo:*
Joe Kapalewski, University
of Pittsburgh)

FIGURE I.3
The Art Deco Woman as
decorative ashtray. (Author's
collection. *Photo:* Joe
Kapalewski, University
of Pittsburgh)

"transitional" objects the young. As though to cement the connection between my present love of Art Deco and my former affection for dolls, I recall that I currently own a book entitled *Glamorous Movie Stars of the Thirties Paper Dolls* by Tom Tierney. Each page of the volume presents the figure of an actress clothed in undergarments accompanied by drawings of several of her famous screen outfits that one can cut out and attach to her body with tabs (be it a dress for Jean Harlow designed by Adrian for *Dinner at Eight* [1933] or one created for Carole Lombard by Travis Banton for 1934's *Twentieth Century*). I recall having many such books as a child, though the figures to be outfitted then were mostly comic book characters like Katy Keene or Veronica.

But my fascination with Art Deco ladies is not merely a replay of the protomaternal instincts I showered on my girlhood dolls. For clearly, these decorative figures represent mature females with an emphatic (if abstract) sense of sexuality. (I should note that I am too old to have collected Barbies, so my childhood dolls were all of the innocent, prepubescent type.) I am reminded here of Jean Baudrillard's notion that collections have about them "a strong whiff of the harem" with the owner positioned as "the sultan of a secret seraglio" (1994:10). Counter to Baudrillard's gender implications, however, it is intriguing to note that Pearce finds the Vamp image one that is frequently collected by women, who see her as a progressive figure of "availability and change" (202). Significantly, Pearce finds this urge often manifests itself via women's interest in 1930s fashions, cosmetics, and movie memorabilia, through which they enact "a clear element of self-identification" with the Hollywood star and "the kind of universal seduction symbol she was" (201). Hence, my impulse to relate the Art Deco "Vamp" to the cinema is one envisioned by collection theory. Furthermore, as a woman whose childhood was lived in the constrained 1950s, I may have found, in the Art Deco female, a subversive emblem. As Belk notes: "Collections can say things about us that it would be socially unacceptable to express aloud" (90).

From its earliest days, the cinema has been associated with magic. Parker Tyler, for example, named his 1947 study of film *Magic and Myth of the Movies*. Likewise, it seems hardly accidental that one of the medium's seminal directors was Georges Méliès, a man first known as a stage prestidigitator. Even in our own era, film is probably most venerated for its fantastic "special effects"—a variation on its magical potential. Certainly this supernatural aura plays a part in drawing all spectators to the movie screen, but I have had a particular fascination with the subject. Another of my early essays concerned the image of woman in the turn-of-the-century "trick" film (Fischer 1979), so when I was asked recently to write an article on experimental filmmaker Maya Deren, I found myself comparing her work with that of Méliès (Fischer 2001). Hence, I am not surprised to learn that collecting (which I tie to my love of the movies) has been seen to have a transcendental component. Muensterberger sees collectibles as having for their owners the power of "holy relics" and finds the impulse to acquire them as motivated by an "attempt to surround oneself with magically potent objects" (250, 10). I confess that this sense of enchantment informs my love of jewelry (be it Art Deco or otherwise). On the one hand, such baubles seem to have the power to transform and augment the body to which they are appended. On the other, it is possible to see the translucent gem stones that often decorate such ornaments (be they authentic or faux) as akin to mysterious amulets or crystal balls. Perhaps that is why pendants are often called "charms." On another note, Belk has spoken of the collector's tendency to "anthropomorphize" his collectibles, no matter what their genre—stamps, pens, or thimbles (76). By accumulating Art Deco figural pieces, I have literalized this impulse —amassing objects that already bear a quasi-human form.

Collecting in the modern era also has intriguing ties to consumerism since, in truth, it is a variation of that practice. Seen negatively, collecting is a means of asserting one's status in a materialist society that defines us by our possessions (Belk:87). The acquisition of expensive and rare items is the ultimate goal—to assure one's prestige or to engage in a strategy of economic investment. But collecting can also be viewed in a more positive and transgressive light. Belk sees it as a defiance of crass materialism, allowing the consumer to exercise "creative control in an otherwise alienated market-place" (15). Rather than shop in a conventional and predetermined fashion, collecting is more like "a treasure-hunt, an adventure, a quest, and a delight" (72). Furthermore, for him, "collecting epitomizes the sacralization of consumption in the contemporary world. The ritual of bringing [objects] into the collection decommoditizes, [and] singularizes" them (94). Belk also finds progressive the fact that many mass-produced items (like those I acquire from the Art Deco era) are now collectible, a natural outcome of a society in which consumer goods "have become the central focus of our dreams and desires" (139). Finally, Belk sees the modern collector as potentially heroic— a "savior of lost, neglected, or endangered objects" who struggles against "conspicuous waste" (81, 150). While I would not want to make such meritorious claims for my Art Deco collecting (which I am more likely to ascribe to a weakness of the flesh), it is interesting to observe that what I appropriate *is* often merely the flotsam and jetsam of another era. When on one occasion I took my mother with me to a flea market, she kept asking whether I was really going to buy the "junk" that I eyed. She assured me that what I was now willing to pay considerable money for had once been sold at Woolworth's and that *her* mother would never have let it in her house (and my grandmother was a Russian immigrant, not a high-toned blue blood). But the abject nature of the "objects of my affection" are not entirely surprising. As Pearce notes, collectors often find themselves attracted to things "for antisocial reasons, where the fascination lies in their worthlessness for other people" (172).

My mother's reaction to my Art Deco bric-a-brac, however, also raises the subject of kitsch, since much of the era's iconography (including its pink flamingos) has become the source of sardonic humor. For Susan Stewart, the kitsch object stands as an emblem of panache valued for its own sake. As she notes:

> Whereas objects such as hand tools had an original use value, the original use value of kitsch objects is an elusive one. Their value in the context of origin was most likely their contemporaneousness, their relation to the fluctuating demands of style. Hence kitsch and camp items may be seen as forms of metafashion. Their collection constitutes a discourse on the constant re-creation of novelty within the exchange economy. (1993:167)

Because they tend to represent a style, Stewart finds kitsch objects less revelatory of a collector's personal consciousness. As she remarks: "Kitsch objects are not apprehended . . . on the level of the individual autobiography; rather, they are apprehended on the level of collective identity. They are souvenirs of an era and not of a self, of collective identity" (167). Moreover, Stewart sees kitsch and camp associated with the cultural "feminine" through the latter's connection to notions of insignificance and inauthenticity. As she comments: "Fashion and fad take place within the domain of the feminine not simply because they are emblematic of the trivial. . . . Rather, the feminine-as-impersonation forms a discourse miming the discourse of male productivity, [and] authority" (168). Hence, again, my Art Deco collection bespeaks a sense of parody. As decorative pieces, they are quintessentially superfluous, and as objects which often represent women, they make clear the vagaries of style that subtend notions of consumerism, collecting, and femininity. Finally, Stewart observes how the complexity and contradiction of the kitsch item lies in its overembodiment. As she points out, its objects offer "a saturation of materiality . . . which takes place to such a degree that [their] materiality is [made] ironic" (167). Hence, despite its apparent overabundance of substance, "the kitsch object . . . marks the complete disintegration of materiality" (168). To some degree this notion comforts me since, as applied to the Art Deco female, it transforms a figure that apparently treats woman as sexual object into one that problematizes that very stance. Beyond this question, Stewart sees a democratic thrust to kitsch articles, since their unlikely valuation accomplishes a plebeian "popularization of the antique" (167).

In my acquisition of Art Deco artifacts, I enact another common aspect of collecting: the tendency to accumulate objects that have some professional association (Muensterberger:242). Thus, physicians often search for antique medical instruments, gardeners for vintage flower pots, and architects for old drafting tools. While I have not purchased much movie memorabilia (Shirley Temple tumblers, stereopticons, Charlie Chaplin dolls), I have, clearly, accumulated countless artifacts that represent a notable Hollywood "style." There is yet another connection between my collecting and the cinema. The habit has been seen by theorists to provide people with an "omnipotent sense of mastery" (Belk:19). As Pearce notes, "We can control our collections as we can few other matters in this world" (178). Thus, in acquiring, classifying, and displaying one's objects, the collector creates an alternative universe entirely determined by her rules, desires, and designs— much as a theatrical director controls the objects in a set. Hence, in recalling *Citizen Kane*'s final scene (the cluttered, antique-filled warehouse), we can imagine it not only as the enormous repository of a newspaper magnate's curio collection but also as the memorable domain of a film director's cinematic mise-en-scène. Finally, in writing this book I am clearly taking my collecting impulse to another level by "collecting" my thoughts about Art Deco and putting them down in written form. Thus, in the following chapters I analyze and contextualize my "obscure object of desire" and postulate its relevance to cinematic history and form.

1. THE ART DECO STYLE

Modernity and the Feminine

THE ART DECO AESTHETIC

In 1936, toward the end of an era ruled by the aesthetic of Art Deco, interior designer Winnifred Fales envisioned the future and asked what critics to come would make of the movement and the concepts for which it stood. Writing now, more than six decades later ("beginning at the end," as Fales anticipated), I find that her question still begs an answer. It is the purpose of this book to provide one—to ponder the "meaning" of Art Deco as it impacted the era's conception of cinema, womanhood, modernity, fashion, and consumerism. To accomplish this, however, I must first probe the term *Art Deco* itself, then explore and enumerate the mode's basic components—its design elements as well as its social-ideological imperatives. For as Roland Barthes has written, while "a little formalism turns one away from History . . . a lot brings one back to it" (1957:112).

The name *Art Deco* has come to signify a popular international trend that surfaced between 1910 and 1935 and affected all aspects of world design: fashion, crafts, housewares, jewelry, furniture, architecture, and interior decoration. What is both significant and problematic about the term is that, although its use is now ubiquitous, it was not coined until the 1960s—as an abbreviation of the hallmark Exposition Internationale des Arts Décoratifs et Industriels Modernes, staged in Paris April through October of 1925 (Duncan 1993:8).[1]

Today's furnishings: what report will they make of us to our descendants? . . . Beginning at the end, which of necessity will be the starting point of future generations attempting, from a study of its art forms, to reconstruct the social codes of the first half of the present century and discover "the ideas for which the period stands," what do we find expressed by the Contemporary mode?
—Winnifred Fales (1936:172)

---

1. Steven Levin (1991:5) says the term *Art Deco* was coined in 1966 for an exhibition in Paris (March 3–May 16, 1966) at the Musée des Arts Décoratifs. The catalog for the show was entitled *Les Années '25'—Art Deco/Bauhaus/Stijl/Espirit Nouveau.*

During the twenties and thirties, the movement was known as modernism or the Style Moderne.

In truth, Art Deco was never monolithic but had many branches and tributaries. As Eva Weber notes: "Of all the decorative arts styles, [it] was perhaps the most *eclectic*, drawing as it did on a wide variety of historical and contemporary sources" (1985:11; emphasis added). Because of this, scholars have disputed the precise meaning of the term. For some, it is pertinent only to a limited school of French design (tied to the 1925 exposition) and to the direct legacy of that movement. The *Grove Dictionary of Art*, for instance, cautions against using the designation to apply to much of the design work created in the United States in the 1920s and 1930s which was, it is claimed, more affected by Viennese contemporary style. On the other hand, that very same source notes how the French Art Deco school was itself originally impacted by such foreign influences as Vienna's Wiener Werkstätte and Russia's Ballets Russes.[2] Taking another stance, the *Encyclopedia Brittanica* recognizes the mode's porous boundaries and lists the following among Art Deco's myriad influences: Art Nouveau, the Bauhaus, Cubism, and the Ballets Russes.[3] Throughout this volume, I will invoke the term in this latter, broader sense to denote a design movement that, at points, connects with many others. On some level, Art Deco's alternate (but outdated) moniker is perhaps more indicative of the movement's wide, inclusive, and entangled roots.

In its insistent contemporaneity, Art Deco was identified with the machine age—both in its imagery and its graphics. As Muriel Draper writes in 1928: "Machinery has become a part of our acting-feeling-thinking lives. . . . Our eyes perceive its multiform design day and night. Cigarette-lighters, electric light bulbs, typewriters and telephones are commonplaces of our daily existence" (98). Deco's attitude toward technology contrasts strongly with that of its predecessor, Art Nouveau, which held sway from 1890 to 1914. That movement was highly identified with Nature as an oppositional stance to the Industrial Revolution (Gallagher 2000:105; Greenhalgh 2000:21).

Sometimes Deco's invocation of the mechanical was purely symbolic. As Katharine Morrison McClinton notes, one icon of Art Deco style was the abstract shape of the "backward diagonal lines of the racing car" as it "follow[ed] the direction of its movement" (1986:8). Similarly, an automobile radiator cap designed by

---

2. See entry on "Art Deco" in the online version of the *Grove Dictionary of Art* at www.groveart.com.

3. See entry on "Art Deco" in the online version of the *Encyclopedia Brittanica* at www.search.eb.com.

Harriet W. Frishmuth in 1925 is entitled "Speed" and depicts a winged woman in flight (Duncan 1993:133). And a bas-relief from the Hotel St. George in Brooklyn (fig. 1.1) depicts all means of mechanical conveyance: steamship, bus, train, even dirigible (Kaplan 1995:150).

At other times, Deco's homage to the mechanical was quite literal. Metal and glass lamps designed by Jean Perzel and Maison Desny in the late 1920s look more like machine parts than decorative objects (Duncan 1993:66–67). The same is true of a three-pronged silver candlestick designed by Jean Puiforcat (Arwas 1992:98). Similarly, a Cubist-style lamp created by Jean Goulden looks more like an industrial beacon than a home furnishing (Arwas:10). And a table base designed by Archibald Taylor in 1939 resembles an airplane propeller (Kaplan:328). Furthermore, the sophisticated look of certain machines (like home appliances) raised them to the level of museum pieces: for example, the sleek digital clock made by K. Weber in 1934; the travel irons designed by Richard Spencer in 1941; the coffeemakers (resembling chemistry beakers) created by Gerhardt Marcks between 1925 and 1930, and the gorgeous blue glass "Nocturne" radio crafted by Walter Dorwin Teague in 1935 (see plate 1) (Kaplan:148, 162, 277, 328).

Not only did Deco adopt a rhetoric of the mechanical, it utilized new modes of production. Weber remarks: "Art deco reflected the recent decades of rapid technological advance and an aesthetic appreciation of mechanical production. Art Deco fostered collaboration between the arts and industry, and relied as well on the mass production of its designs" (11). A good example of this tendency would be the work of French metal craftsman Edgar Brandt, who used industrial materials like steel and aluminum and employed stamping presses and autogenous soldering to repeat decorative motifs (Arwas 1992:93).

Characteristically, Art Deco was known for its simplified geometric and symmetrical patterns—traits associated with the machine age. As Winnifred Fales noted at the time: "Streamlining [is] now a commonplace in . . . design" (1936:156). This aesthetic is evident in Jean Desprès's tea service of 1925, a conglomeration of

FIGURE 1.1

Bas-relief from the Hotel St. George, Brooklyn, N.Y. (c. 1930); designer unknown. (The Mitchell Wolfson Jr. Collection, Wolfsonian-Florida International University, Miami Beach. *Photo:* Bruce White)

rectangles and monoliths (Duncan 1993:74). It is also visible in the chrome and blue glass candlesticks by Chase, with their square bases and globular midsections (fig. 1.2).Similarly, it is apparent in rugs designed by Ivan da Silva and Edward McKnight Kauffer in the 1930s, which seem indebted to the graphics of Piet Mondrian (Duncan 1993:53, 44). It is also present in jewelry pieces designed by Paul Brandt, Jean Fouquet, and Raymond Templier in the 1920s, with their assemblages of pure shapes, lines, and curves (Duncan 1993:172–73). Finally, a geometric sense is dominant in an Omega mantel clock of the 1920s, which is composed of a rectangle and triangles adorned with circles and squares (Duncan 1993:79). In its employment of basic forms, Art Deco again reacted against Art Nouveau—known for its romanticism, sentimentality, asymmetry, intricacy, and biomorphism. One magazine piece of April 1928, for example, decried "L'Art Nouveau . . . [for having] permitted itself to get into a frightful tangle with nature—water-lilies, tulips and fig leaves." On the other hand, the "authentic New Art of the present day rest[ed] on the solid foundation of basic integrity" (Teall:114). For Donald Albrecht, Deco's simplified mode was also a response against the excesses of the Victorian age: "Appreciation for the modern style went deeper than for just its graphic value. Many members of the generation born at the end of the nineteenth century welcomed it as an antidote to the Victorian clutter and fussiness of their parents' interiors" (1986:xi).

In keeping with Deco's stark high-tech façades, color was often reduced to the basics: black, white, and silver. Alastair Duncan notes that ebony, "with its jet black surface, buffed repeatedly to draw out its innate majesty, was Art Deco's favourite wood" (11). Similarly, an article in *Good Furniture and Decoration* magazine of 1929 waxes poetic about black glass used in the décor of Chicago's Saks Fifth Avenue (Robbins:94). In 1931 a *Harper's Bazaar* column proclaims "The Rising Tide of White Decors" (74), while an article by Kathleen Howard praises "White Accents" (35). Furthermore, Dorothy Todd of *House Beautiful* advises that "white-wash has a major significance in the new aesthetic" representing "a clear slate" (1929:474). Silver leaf factors into the elegant design of such pieces as Leo Fontan's wooden "petite commode" or Eileen Gray's "Canoe" *chaise longue*—both from the early twenties (Duncan 1993:23, 29). Interestingly, while in certain contexts colors were delimited to the white, black, and gray scale, in others (like kitchen and bathroom decoration) Deco championed bold and saturated tones like vermilion, fuchsia, or apple green (an issue to be discussed in chapter 3).

In its industrial orientation, Art Deco employed such synthetic materials as plastic (Bakelite, Lucite, Vitrolite, linoleum, and Formica) and metal (chrome, stainless steel, aluminum, and wrought iron). Winnifred Fales, for example, adores

FIGURE 1.2

Geometric candleholders by

Chase. (Author's collection.

Photo: Joe Kapalewski,

University of Pittsburgh)

the use of synthetic threads in a textile weave "that glistens like sunlight on water." She asks: "Can it be . . . cellophane! The identical shiny, transparent substance that wraps the bread, protects the lampshade, and adds glitter and gaiety to Christmas packages"(1936:43). The Deco style also drew heavily upon art glass in its designs, here preferring achromatism to the colorful stained panels of the Victorian age. As Alastair Duncan notes: "By etching, enameling or sandblasting the glass, the designer could orchestrate the light; by pressing or engraving it he could achieve sculptural effects; and by combining such processes, he could obtain any number of nuances. In place of the spectrum there was milkiness and limpidity" (1993:65) (also, see fig. 1.3). Such glass was used to craft a variety of decorative objects (lamps, statuettes, bowls, candlesticks, vases, and sliding panels). In Deco's appropriation of industrial methods, it attempted to combine craftsmanship with technology and merge artisanship with mass production.

Certain architectural tropes formed the hallmark of the Art Deco idiom. Appliances, decorative objects, or furniture (like bathtubs, tables, lamps, or beds) were

often mounted on platforms (fig. 1.3). For the sake of flexibility, furniture was frequently modular and, to achieve sleekness, "built-in." Recessed niches were created in rooms to house lamps or *objets d'art*. Screens were employed to interrupt the monotony of rectangular space.

Like modernism itself, Art Deco was tied to the city (versus Art Nouveau, which was linked to eternal Nature) and deemed by some the "skyscraper style." Deco's links to urban sophistication were trumpeted in its architectural use in prestigious office towers, nightclubs, hotels, restaurants, theaters, and apartment buildings (for example, such monumental sites as the Chrysler Building in New York City). Even in home design, Deco was connected to the metropolitan. As Curtis Patterson wrote in 1930: "We live today, generally, in city apartments. The rooms in a city apartment, recently built, present a new set of proportions to which the scale of classic interior architecture no longer applies" (94). Sometimes the notion of "skyscraper style" was taken quite literally. Thus a cocktail service designed by Norman Bel Geddes for Revere Brass and Copper Company mimics, in its chromium-plated outline, the staggered look of an urban skyline, as does the silhouette of a pitcher designed in 1928 for the Apollo Studio line by Louise Rice (Duncan 1993:77; Kaplan:329). Similarly, an elaborate bookcase designed by Paul Theodore Frankl in 1926 is called the "skyscraper" (Kaplan:329). Finally, a grille on the City Bank Farmers Trust Building in New York (1929–1931) sports a silhouetted frieze of a city scene (Duncan 1993:188).

In its bonds to modernity, Art Deco echoed various avant-garde movements — another sign of what Weber deems its "eclecticism." From Constructivism and Futurism, it inherited a love of the machine; from Cubism, a passion for stark geometric forms; from German Expressionism, a penchant for distortion. From Sergei Diaghilev's Ballets Russes (which opened in Paris in 1909 and stayed for many years), it borrowed a sense of theatricality — witness Dorothy Todd's dismissal of the 1925 Paris Exposition as fostering a "night-club vision of life" (470). While, on one level, Deco opposed Art Nouveau, it was also indebted to it — sometimes adopting and adapting the latter's rhetoric of sinuous lines, whip-lash curves, botanical forms, and female figures. According to McClinton, modernist pioneers like

THE ART DECO STYLE

Charles Rennie Mackintosh, Josef Hoffmann, Louis Sullivan, and Frank Lloyd Wright all drew upon the "austere side of Art Nouveau" for their development of an early Deco aesthetic (6).

While beholden to experimental modes, Deco was also palatable to the general public. As Mark Winokur observes: "Deco was accessible . . . in a way the various other modernisms were not. In fact, the value of Art Deco . . . resided in its ability to be avant-garde while circumventing completely the difficult-to-watch wrenchings of reality that were intrinsic to expressionism, surrealism, or cubism" (1996:199). In keeping with Deco's mass appeal, department stores such as Macy's hosted exhibitions of the new "applied arts" as early as the mid-1920s, and Lord and Taylor produced a show of the Style Moderne in 1928 (Weber:11; *Grove Dictionary of Art*). Here we are reminded of Andy Warhol's later statement that, eventually, "All department stores will become museums, and all museums will become department stores" (Solomon 2002:41).

Despite its resolute contemporaneity, Art Deco was influenced by traditional, and even primeval, forms. Specifically, it evinced a fascination with the "Ancient" and the "Primitive"—as rendered through a litany of tropes. From Egypt (where King Tutankhamen's tomb had been discovered in 1922), Deco embraced pharaonic imagery (e.g., sphinx heads, scarabs, and cats: see fig. 1.4). An article in *Harper's Bazaar* of 1928 displays women's accessories against a background of Egyptian females in profile ("Accessories . . . ," 110–11). From the broader Middle East, Deco recycled the Babylonian/Assyrian ziggurat structure—a pyramidal terraced tower whose successive levels are each smaller than the one beneath. So popular was this motif that an entire strain of Deco came to be known as "zigzag moderne" (Weber:12). As evidence of this, Hugh Ferris (1929) includes the ziggurat in his futuristic vision of the urban metropolis: "The ancient Assyrian ziggurat . . . is an excellent embodiment of the modern New York. . . . [M]ay we not for a moment imagine an array of modern ziggurats, providing restaurants and theaters on their ascending levels?" (98). From pre-Columbian Mexico, Deco drew upon the sunray image; and from Africa, the stylized mask and materials such as ivory and animal skins (especially zebra and tiger) (Weber:14, 19). Significantly, in this era, shipping lines like Cunard hyped "The Great . . . African Cruise" in its advertisements:

> There's a primitive something in us that tingles at the glamorous word . . .
> AFRICA. Tomtoms throbbing in the bush . . . the bark of a baboon . . . the
> calm majesty of the veldt . . . Africa's witching spell lays hold and gives one
> something to treasure, a richness of experience that is Africa's own. (Cunard
> Anchor Lines Advertisement 1930:170)

From Native America, Deco embraced the geometric patterns of traditional Indian pottery, jewelry, and basketry. Extending its romance with the Southwest, a 1931 article in *Harper's Bazaar* promotes tourism in Arizona and praises the Biltmore Hotel as "a bold architectural experiment" that "is a beautiful blend of modernistic and Indian design" (Barrett:88). Not surprisingly, magazine decorating columns of the era made a direct connection between the "Primitive" and the contemporary. As Elizabeth Otey remarks in the September 1935 issue of *Good Housekeeping*:

> Moderns have often gone back to primitive art for ideas. The results are more sophisticated than any primitive peoples have ever been able to produce, for the simple reason that we are consciously reproducing a shape or design that is pleasing in its simplicity whereas earlier craftsmen were striving for something new to them and crudeness was inevitable. (73)

Beyond Deco's attachment to the Ancient and the Primitive, it courted the historic and contemporary Exotic. Some designers even appropriated modern black forms—especially those of jazz (a subject to be discussed in chapter 5 on the film musical). Others looked toward the Orient—as had Art Nouveau previously—with a fondness for the legacy of Japan (Gallagher:10–11). Evincing such an influence, a woman's Deco compact designed by Charlton sports an enameled surface resembling a woodcut landscape print (Duncan 1993:174). Similarly, a vanity case designed by LaCloche is adorned with a traditional cherry blossom motif made of crystal and lapis (Duncan:169). Furthermore, Saks Fifth Avenue, Chicago, boasts of using Japanese wallpaper in its décor (Robbins:94), and an article in *House and Garden* features "A Japanese Garden Created in the Catskill Mountains" (1929:106–107). Significantly, in this period, ocean liners advertised travel to Japan. A Dollar Steamship Line ad explains to us: "Why [we] will linger enchanted in Japan":

> Whether the ricefields, terraced in broad low steps to the hilltops, are shimmering with flooded young green, peasant women knee-deep in work in them, or are golden brown with harvest-time, the rice already being thumped out on round stones, Fujiyama's peerless form, topped in snow-white, will stand forth like a phantom mountain from some fairy tale illustrated by an inimitable Japanese artist. (1929:59)

Deco's Orientalism also revealed, of course, a fascination with China. A 1929 Macy's advertisement highlights "Chinese Clay Figurines" in the store's Department of Oriental and Occidental Art. The text accompanying the ad has an almost *faux* scholarly tone to it:

In the Tang dynasty the making of mortuary pottery was a vast industry spreading over all China . . . Made long ago for interment with the dead, in order that the souls might be cared for after their departure, these lovely figurines have served their purpose, and are now rescued from the oblivion of ancient tombs, so that new generations may enjoy their beauty ("Chinese Clay Figurines" 1929:7)

By 1936, decorators speak of a design school called "Chinese-Modern," considered so important that it should be "classed as a distinct trend" (Fales 1936:159). Not surprisingly, the Dollar Steamship Line also stopped in China.

Deco's attraction to the Exotic was registered not only in its iconography (images of lotus flowers or cacti), but in the materials and palette it employed. Such rare woods as ebony, thuya burl, palmwood, magnolia, palisander, amboyna, East Indian laurel, and macassar were utilized; and shades like jade green were all the rage (Fales 1936:158). According to Fales, "Colored lacquers are another souvenir of the Orient which have been appropriated by modern craftsmen" (159).

For Winokur, Deco's appropriation of the Exotic managed to "styliz[e] the accouterments of ethnicity," while "maintain[ing] a safe distance" from them. It "aestheticized colonialism" and brought "a tourist's view of the world back to this country" (202). Quite fittingly, a Deco aesthetic was associated with the look of the very vehicles of modern travel: steamships, airplanes, and automobiles.

Deco's prominence was also tied to its strident consumer orientation (to be discussed more fully in chapters 2 and 3). The style imposed itself on all aspects of American culture: clothes, jewelry, interior decoration, architecture, graphics, housewares, and home appliances (irons, toasters, radios, lamps, radiators, and clocks). While Deco artifacts at the high end were available at such elegant stores as Tiffany, knock-offs were accessible in more pedestrian establishments. This

FIGURE 1.4

Egyptian Revival jewelry. (Author's collection. *Photo:* Joe Kapalewski, University of Pittsburgh)

egalitarian potential of the Art Deco style was recognized early on in the coverage of the traveling show that toured the United States from the 1925 Paris Exposition. Writing in the *New York Times* (of its booking at the Metropolitan Museum of Art in 1926), an anonymous reviewer labels one section of the piece "Beauty for All Classes," and notes that "even . . . bourgeois families [could] indulg[e] themselves" despite the fact that the "artists and artisans of France are indeed appealing to a luxurious taste." In another segment of the article entitled "Luxury is Democratized," the writer heralds an imminent "turn about" in the class appeal of the new French design style: "the materials of luxury are to find their level among the vulgarians of taste. A number of the best fabric designs in the modern field are done for and in cotton"—a cheaper material than silk ("French Decorative Art":10).

"STRANGE ANOMALY": ART DECO'S AMERICAN RECEPTION

People of good taste from every country and of every aesthetic creed visited the [Paris] Exposition, shuddered and turned away. But the commercial impulse was considerable and is still responsible for many of the little accidents which we see around us to-day. —Dorothy Todd (1929:470)

It is obvious from the literature of the period that Art Deco was associated, in the American mind, with Europe—Paris being the center of that Continental universe. Clearly, this perception arose for two reasons. The first was the importance of the famous 1925 exposition itself, which built upon the stellar reputation of such modernist European design movements as Austria's Wiener Werkstätte group. Not only was the 1925 Paris Exposition widely covered in the American press but, as alluded to earlier, some four hundred objects from the show were displayed at New York's Metropolitan Museum of Art in 1926, then sent to galleries in smaller cities (Sanford 1926:185). The second reason for the exhibition's strong association with Europe is that it included no American crafts or architecture.

Generally, the American response to Art Deco fell into two camps. One group saw the trend as being anathema to the American sensibility and therefore called for its rejection. Witness the plethora of pejorative terms that peppered various articles describing the Deco style: "disgusting," "horrible," "fantasmagoric," "ponderous," "incongruous," "exaggerated," "freakish," "stupid," "ugly," "eccentric," "bizarre," "vulgar," "trivial," "faddish," "distorted," "caricaturish," "undigested," "gross," "grotesque," and "accidental." Opposed to this group was another which advanced the acceptance of Art Deco, viewing America's dismissal of the mode as outdated. For these critics, Deco was associated with such positive terms as "modern," "voguish," "bold," and "original."

Controversy on this issue was registered as early as October 1925 in a review of the Paris Exposition in *Good Furniture Magazine*. Howell Cresswell describes the argumentative crowds that perused the cutting-edge exhibition, and seems to blame the artwork itself for the contentious atmosphere:

> A cry of "How beautiful and exquisite" is often followed parrot-like by fifty others who follow within hearing distance, while at the same stand an angry shout of "Horrible," "Disgusting" naturally causes a train of disapproval for another few minutes. Often it is a heated discussion. (187–88)

Writing about the exposition in *House and Garden* that same year, Richardson Wright proudly flaunts America's rejection of modernism. He reports that the "United States had no building and took no part [in the event] save for the visit of official delegates." He continues: "The reason why this country was not represented at the exhibition was simply the fact that there are not enough of our average people and artists interested in the modernist styles of decoration to justify our exhibiting." He concludes: "We are not inclined that way" (1925:77–78). He ends his piece by deeming the exposition "the most serious and sustained exhibition of bad taste the world has ever seen" (110).

In a similar vein, Arthur Wilcock of *Good Furniture Magazine* finds the exposition's artifacts "strange and exaggerated." He predicts that "none of the stuff shown will make any impression upon American taste," and that it "will not be taken up or bought to any extent by our discriminating people" (1925:260). Significantly, he explains the difference between American and European responses to the exposition by referencing their diverse experiences of World War I. As he notes, Americans "have not any of the upset mental attitude of the war, which the proximity of the war on its own soil has brought to the mentality and the mental outlook of the people over there" (260). Hence, he sees Europe's love of modernism as tied to their post-traumatic malaise.

A year later, in the February 1926 issue of *House and Garden*, Frank Alvah Parsons also decries Art Deco. As he writes:

> The lines of much of the modernist furniture, such as that displayed at the Exhibition [*sic*] des Arts Décoratifs in Paris last summer, are the first feature that repels me. They are distorted. There is a gross quality about the

curves of the legs and backs of chairs and tables. They lack subtlety. . . . They often seem to have been designed for the express purpose of caricaturing the ugly shapes of cripples and the afflicted. Here a chair looks like a hunchback. (72)

Similarly, in 1929, Dorothy Todd calls the trend a "decorative instinct run riot" and accuses it of reflecting "triviality, noise, extravagance—all the vices of contemporary society" (470).

Such conservative attitudes are also evident in American interior design manuals of the period. The chapter headings of Winnifred Fales's *A Simple Course in Home Decorating* (1927) are organized by traditional categories (e.g., "The French Periods in Decoration," "The Tudor and Jacobean Periods," "The Dutch Influence in England," and "Our American Heritage"). The only mention of contemporary design comes in the section on "Spanish and Italian Influence in Modern Decoration." In point of fact, the photographs included in this latter chapter depict antique reproductions. Furthermore, the author warns that

Furniture design is, or should be, a gradual evolution, not a series of fresh creations. Originality in this field is more successfully expressed through subtle modifications, the introduction here and there of a new detail carefully wrought in the same spirit as the original, or in efforts toward still greater refinement, than in attempts to produce something totally unlike everything which has gone before, as exemplified in the horrors of *l'Art Nouveau*. (1927:xvii)

In 1930, Curtis Patterson still finds "Modernism . . . a fighting word," and notes that a "decorator in the modern spirit bestows upon his client not peace but an argument" (95). As late as 1935, Helen M. Daggett dismisses the new mode in a lengthy tirade in her home decorating book:

Do not think that the style known today as "modernistic" is the thing to buy for your home: the style identified by the sharp, zig-zag lines, the points, angles and garish colors. This style cannot last very long, of course because it will not "fit in" gracefully with other types and periods of furniture. You will see this "modernistic" style in public places like the corner store . . . or in any place where a new fad is used for the purpose of attracting the attention of passers-by. But for use in the house in good taste—No! Such a style does not belong there! (1935:64–66)

While a positive reaction to modernism was slow to take hold in America, some critics embraced it early on. In a *Harper's Bazar*[4] article of 1928, Muriel Draper regrets that Americans, who are usually identified with progress, reside in houses based on plans "derived from Byzantium, Greece, Italy, France, England and Spain during the last thousand years" (98). As she muses:

> Strange anomaly—that eyes accustomed to the clean surfaces, delicate symmetry and controlled proportions of steamships, automobiles, and gas-tanks, should live amidst such a clutter of compromises as most contemporary interiors present. The simple lines and polished surfaces of the new furniture should be a welcome relief. (1928:98)

Similarly, a column in *House and Garden* predicts that "this country will doubtless soon sow its crop of Modernist houses" ("Bulletin Board" 1929:51). Again, noting an inconsistency in American attitudes, the author reports: "In public buildings we lead the world; [yet] in domestic work our architects are still content to follow traditional design and their clients content to live in a traditional house." For the author, it is "strange" that "a modern businessman who has enjoyed his radio in the evening, risen the next morning to eat breakfast cooked by electricity . . . chooses to live in a house of 18th century design, surrounded say, by furniture that he calls Early American" ("Bulletin":51).

By 1930 modernism had achieved some degree of popularity in the United States. In a *Harper's Bazaar* essay, Patterson proclaims that

> When these words reach the eye of the reader, the season of 1929–1930 in interior decoration will sleep with its fathers. It has been a vibrant year. It has seen the ultra-modern note of the twentieth century not only tolerated but, in degree and by the more fashionable, accepted. (94)

Patterson characterizes modernism's rise as "meteoric" and proclaims that "the School of New York [now] joins the School of Paris, of Rome, of Berlin, of Vienna" (95). Clearly, his linkage of these European sites makes clear how the Style Moderne was not seen as exclusively a French design mode.

While Fales's book of 1927 had decried modernism, her 1936 volume sings another tune. As she notes (in *What's New in Home Decorating*):

> Heretofore we have leaned heavily upon the past, endlessly repeating the traditional forms of the Old World in an effort to squeeze the ultimate trickle of inspiration out of the dry husks of antique art. But today our artist-

---

4. In November 1929 the spelling of the magazine changed to *Harper's Bazaar*.

designers are becoming alive to the decorative potentialities inherent in native themes. These themes—drawn from such diverse sources as machinery, skyscrapers, airplanes, shipping, bridges, Coney Island, cotton picking, and the American landscape—they are blithely interpreting in vibrant colors and dynamic forms and patterns which more truly express the quickened tempo of our harder working, harder playing, complex modern lives. (Fales 1936:1)

Even sections of Daggett's 1935 decorating guide—despite the previously quoted vitriolic harangue—acknowledge the possibilities of contemporary form:

The best in the modern of our day utilizes the many beautiful materials available today. New uses of woods, new metals, new textiles and woven materials, glass, cork, rubber and allied compositions, are all brought into action, and flowing through them all is the theme of simplicity, utility, serviceability, charm of line, beauty of color, and supreme comfort in use. While some examples may seem cold, hard and severe at first, their use soon proves them to be utterly comfortable and delightful in color and texture. (66)

As a result of this cultural ambivalence around modernism, design companies walked a tightrope in pitching products to the public. A 1929 advertisement for Stunzi Sons Silk Company has the equivocal tag line: "Modern . . . but embodying the arts of centuries."

If, however, there was one sector of American culture where Art Deco achieved decided prominence, it was the movies, an entertainment medium that, by the 1930s, drew between 60 and 90 million American viewers each week (Ware 1982:178). It would not be an overstatement to suggest that from the late 1920s through the mid-1930s, every aspect of film form was affected by the Style Moderne. In this regard, the cinema partakes of what Miriam Bratu Hansen deems "vernacular modernism." As she notes:

I take the study of modernist aesthetics to encompass cultural practices that both articulated and mediated the experience of modernity, such as the mass-produced and mass-consumed phenomena of fashion, design, advertising, architecture, and urban environment, of photography, radio, and cinema. I am referring to this kind of modernism as "vernacular" . . . because the term . . . combines the dimension of the quotidian, of everyday usage, with connotations of discourse, idiom, and dialect. (2000:333)

Such "vernacular modernism" clearly influenced set design, through the work of a series of art directors associated with movie studios: Van Nest Polglase at RKO, Stephen Goosson at Fox, and Cedric Gibbons at Metro-Goldwyn-Mayer. (Interestingly, Hugh Ferris, in describing the look of the modern city from atop a skyscraper, talked of its resembling "a film set" [16]). In addition to helping establish the on-screen mise-en-scène, Hollywood art direction had a great effect on American interior decoration. A November 1929 issue of *Harper's Bazaar*, for example, ran a feature entitled "Joseph Urban's Urban Apartment" that showed how the art director's abode (like his set designs) was clearly influenced by the Style Moderne.[5] Second, Deco also left its stamp on film costuming, especially for actresses, with artists like Adrian and Orry-Kelly working at MGM and Warner Bros. Third, even the posture of actors was used to create Deco-inspired designs. As Winokur notes, stars "became [through blocking] generic Deco works, [and] sculpturesque pieces" (204). This can, perhaps, best be understood by contemplating the choreographed stances of dancer Fred Astaire, whose bodily contour often resembled a modernist line drawing. This sense is echoed in a *Photoplay* article of April 1937 entitled "The *Outline* of Astaire" (Griffith 1971:242–43; emphasis added). Fourth, a Deco aesthetic informed the graphic idiom of many movie posters of the era, as well as the font and layout of studio logos (like those for RKO, Universal, and 20th Century-Fox). Finally, Deco had a tremendous effect on the architecture of American movie theaters, especially those elegant and luxurious spaces known as "picture palaces" (to be discussed further in chapter 7). Among the most famous, of course, was New York's Radio City Music Hall (created by Donald Deskey in 1932 and restored in the 1990s; see fig. I.1). In part, the influence of Art Deco on the movies may have had to do not only with its broad international recognition but also with the number of European émigrés working in Hollywood, who brought with them a sense of Continental style. Here one thinks of directors like Jacques Feyder, Edgar G. Ulmer, F. W. Murnau, Victor Sjöström, Benjamin Christensen, Mauritz Stiller, and Fritz Lang—many of whom will be considered in the pages that follow.

As Donald Albrecht has noted, the ubiquity of the Art Deco mode on movie screens of the era helped to popularize contemporary design in America. As he states: "The adoption of architectural modernism by the popular arts had [a] notable effect. . . . It successfully promoted the modern style to the general public,

---

5. Joseph Urban worked on such films as *When Knighthood Was in Flower* (1922), *Little Old New York* (1923), *Under the Red Robe* (1923), *Yolanda* (1924), *Zander the Great* (1925), *The Man Who Came Back* (1931), and *East Lynne* (1931).

making it both more accessible and more palatable." And of all those arts, "No vehicle provided as effective and widespread an exposure of [modernism] . . . as the medium of the movies" (xii). Similarly, Warren Susman has observed how the "photograph, the radio, [and] the moving picture . . . created a special community of all Americans . . . unthinkable previously" (1984:160). In the 1920s and 1930s, that "community" was linked by its immersion in the Style Moderne as rendered by the movement's association with the movies.

Early film theorist Hugo Münsterberg once proclaimed that there should be a clear separation between the applied and the fine arts. As he wrote:

> We annihilate beauty when we link the artistic creation with practical interests and transform the spectator into a selfishly interested bystander. The scenic background of the play is not presented in order that we decide whether we want to spend our next vacation there. The interior decoration of the rooms is not exhibited as a display for a department store. *A good photoplay must be isolated and complete in itself like a beautiful melody. It is not an advertisement for the newest fashions.* (1970:361; emphasis added)

Given this view, we might assume that Münsterberg would have been displeased by the fate of the cinema in the 1920s and 1930s when there was an unprecedented correspondence between the movies, consumerism, and modern design.

THE ART DECO WOMAN

Woman is the mold into which the spirit of the age pours itself, and to those with any sense of history no detail of the resulting symbolic statue is without importance. —James Laver (1995:198)

Beyond the characteristics already delineated, Art Deco manifests a particular fascination with the figure of Woman. We were reminded of this in 2002 when a controversy erupted over two seminude Art Deco statues located in the U.S. Department of Justice. It was reported that the government had spent $8,000 to purchase curtains to shield the public's view of *Spirit of Justice* (a female figure) and *Majesty of Law* (a male one). This step was taken because recent attorneys general (including Edwin Meese and John Ashcroft) had apparently found it awkward to pose before the statues during press conferences (fig. 1.5). Evidently, Meese, for example, once stood uncomfortably in front of the naked *Spirit of Justice* while announcing the release of a report on pornography. While both male and female statues were now (in 2002) to be obscured, only one of them, in fact, actually revealed a dubious body part: *Spirit of Justice*, whose toga covered only one of her breasts (*Majesty of Law* was more discreet since his loins were hidden by a sculpted cloth). In all the press coverage of the incident, it was the *female* statue that received attention—an indication of the Art Deco Woman's continuing cultural power. *New York Times* columnist Maureen Dowd, for example, wondered whether Ashcroft's advance team was told to "remove naked lady statues" wherever he traveled, and (referencing the war on terrorism), she joked about the *Spirit of Justice* being clothed in a *burka*.[6] Curiously, the brouhaha in 2002 about the *Spirit of Justice* recalls another that took place in 1939 when the Golden Gate International Exposition opened in the Bay Area. Again, a female Art Deco sculpture—Ettore Cadorin's *Evening Star*—was a major icon of the fair. Apparently, when workmen at the site had to clean dirt off her naked form, the *San Francisco News-Call Bulletin* ran a photograph whose caption read: "Evening Star: She Gets a Bath." The following legend is written on the back of a clipping in the files of the San Francisco Public Library: "Workmen blushed as they were ordered to give baths to some of the nude female statues on Treasure Island . . . Here is Peter Petersen, Treasure Island workman, swabbing down the statue 'Evening Star' in the Court of the Moon."[7]

In truth, a discourse on sexual difference (either literal or metaphoric) informs the entire Art Deco aesthetic. According to McClinton, Deco can be divided into two broad stylistic schools that might be imagined along traditional gender lines. The "feminine" curvilinear mode favors such saccharine imagery as "rose[s], . . . garlands and baskets of flowers, fountains of water, doves, female deer and nudes" (10). Here belongs Frederick Carder's glass grille, with its spiraling background and its foreground depicting a doe (Duncan 1993:99). On the other hand, in the "masculine" geometric pole, "Curves gave way to angularity and motifs of design tended to be . . . dynamic" (McClinton:11). Eugène Printz's bookcase of 1927–28, with its low rectangular form segmented by vertical accents strips (Duncan:32), belongs here. Clearly, it is from the former strain that Art Deco's formulation of the Female derives.

---

6. See Dowd (2002); also see "Curtains for Semi-Nude Justice Statue" (BBC World News, January 29, 2002), cited on the BBC News Web site: www.news.bbc.co.uk/hi/english/world/americas/newsid_1788000/1788845.stm.

7. This caption was not published, evidently, but it appears on the back of the photograph stored in the library's archives. My thanks to Tim Wilson for this information, in his e-mail from the San Francisco History Center (3/26/02).

FIGURE 1.5

John Ashcroft and *Spirit of Justice.* (AP Wide World Photos)

Most certainly, Deco's fascination with Woman harks back to a similar gender fixation in Art Nouveau. There, however, the Female is envisioned quite differently, owing to several pervasive trends (fig. 1.6). One is the movement's fascination with Nature. In myriad pieces, natural and feminine imagery are eerily and seamlessly combined (as in the woman-dragonfly hybrid in a brooch by French designer René Lalique); and it is obvious that Art Nouveau sees Woman as more encumbered by brute physicality than rational Man (Greenhalgh 2000:82–83). Second, the movement was strongly influenced by the European symbolists (Gallagher:12) in both painting (e.g., Alphonse Mucha, Gustav Klimt, Henri de Toulouse-Lautrec,

and Franz von Stuck [for latter, see plate 4]) and literature (e.g., Wilde, Baudelaire, and Rimbaud). In this strain, Woman is often seen as a dangerous and degenerate figure whose favored incarnations are those of vampire and prostitute—a characterization promoted by the rise of psychoanalytic studies of perverse sexuality by Freud and Krafft-Ebing (Greenhalgh:82–85). Clearly, the anxieties expressed in both schools of Art Nouveau have historical markers: the Industrial Revolution, psychoanalysis, and women's suffrage. For Walter Benjamin, the corruption of the Art Nouveau female (or that of Jugendstil, as the movement was known in Germany and Austria), is tied to her opposition to motherhood. As he notes, "The depraved woman stays clear of fertility" (1999:556). Furthermore, she is marked by the coldness of modernity. As he comments, "The frigid woman embodies the ideal of beauty in Jugendstil" (559).[8]

While female representation in Art Deco has its roots in the ubiquitous woman of Art Nouveau, in the later movement Woman becomes more austere, high-tech, and neutral. For Weber, Deco's human forms (whether female or male) were often "abstracted to such a degree that they resembled . . . machines or robots" (11). This is apparent in a set of figural chrome Farberware candlesticks from the era (fig. 1.7). It is also evident in Fritz Lang's Deco extravaganza *Metropolis* (1926)—to be discussed in chapter 8—with its dichotomy of authentic and replicant Marias (see fig. 8.1). Hence, rather than be endowed with a sense of primal Nature, the Deco female is seen as more synthetic.

The female figure, whether conceived as realistic or abstract, appears in count-

8. Thanks to Petra Dierkes-Thron for bringing this to my attention.

less Deco objects. In fact, one of the medals for the Paris Exposition itself (designed by Pierre Turin in 1925) depicts a woman seated upon (what looks like) clouds and dangling a garland of flowers before her (fig. 1.8). Consider also the translucent works of glass crafted by René Lalique, with their sculpted maidens or etched nymphs. Ponder, as well, the bronze or glass bases for Deco lamps, candy dishes, and candlesticks — often shaped to the female form. Regard the metal ashtrays adorned with erect figures of women, or the knobs of glass powder jars, which were often shaped like female bodies or faces (fig. 1.9). Contemplate Lalique's car mascot, "Victoire" (1928), with its polished glass female head, hair outstretched in the wind (Duncan 1993:90). Reflect upon the graceful female figures that adorned glass vases by Marcel Groupy or Argy-Rousseau (Duncan:89, 94). Consider Alexandre Kelety's sinister bust from the late 1920s, *Modern Medusa*, fashioned of bronze and poised on a black marble base (Duncan:124).

But the craft most associated with the female figure was ornamental sculpture, items typically sold at jewelry stores. As McClinton notes: "Small sculpture figures were in demand as a decorative accessory in the house of the 1890s and they continued to be used into the twentieth-century. They were set on mantelpieces, on library shelves, on marble-topped girandoles or wall brackets" (185). Especially interesting were those made with chryselephantine. Such objects, produced largely in Paris and Berlin (Duncan:121), were fashioned from African ivory in combination with bronze, onyx, marble, gold, and exotic wood (Arwas 1975:5). They came into vogue as early as 1900, and their fabrication consolidated techniques of hand-carving and mass production (Arwas:7).

According to Victor Arwas, chryselephantine sculptures fell into four categories: *hieratic*, *naturalistic*, *erotic*, and *stylized*. "Hieratic" creations were "often . . . queens of the night, dancers wrapped in the metallic folds of rare and costly fabrics and encrusted with jewels at wrist and ankle, their movements frozen into strange theatrical attitudes" (Arwas 1975:7). In these works, the primary influence was Diaghilev's Ballets Russes, which was stranded in Paris as a result of World War I and the Russian Revolution. As Arwas notes: "Organised by Diaghilev to show off the most original Russian dancers, choreographers, composers and designers, [the ballet's] impact on art and decoration was enormous" (7). The second major source for hieratic Deco sculptures was the silent cinema: its costumes, hairstyles, and theatrical mannerisms (7). The "naturalistic" statuettes portrayed female athletes, nudes, and dancers. The "erotic" category (more linked to Jugendstil or Art Nouveau than the other modes) was tinged by an aura of perversity. Arwas speaks of

> kinky, highly sophisticated women dressed in leather trouser suits, insolently smoking cigarettes; swirling-skirted girls fighting the wine; girls in slips or gartered stockings holding whips; dancers doing a high kick; and haughty girls naked beneath their parted fur coats. They are the dream mistresses of sado-masochistic Berlin between the wars. (1975:9)

The "stylized" strain of sculpture was the most abstract, reflecting the influence of Cubism, Bauhaus, and the Arts and Crafts movement (see plate 2). As Arwas comments, here "features are simplified . . . and the treatment of clothing is increasingly geometric and decorative, without any attempt at realism" (9).

Clearly, it was not only the statuettes that were modern (with their polished onyx or marble ziggurat bases) but the look of the women represented in them. As Arwas remarks, these works generally depicted women who were "slender and boyish in shape, hair bobbed . . . . dressed in fashionably floppy pyjamas or as . . . Amazon[s]" (8). McClinton, who provides more detail on these sculptures, catalogs such types as

> cocottes [i.e., coquettes] with bobbed hair, dressed in trousers, long fitted jackets, cloche hats or hair in banderole and wearing exotic jewelry. An amusing bronze and ivory gamine, with high heels and clinging trousers, shirt neckerchief and peaked cap, poses with her hands in her pockets and smokes a cigarette. Dancing girls in tunic or bikini and tur-

FIGURE 1.7 (*Opposite, top*) The abstract female form as Farberware candleholder. (Author's collection. *Photo:* Joe Kapalewski, University of Pittsburgh)

FIGURE 1.8 (*Opposite, bottom*) Bronze Medal: Exposition Internationale des Arts Décoratifs et Industriels Modernes, Paris, 1925; designed by Pierre Turin. (The Mitchell Wolfson Jr. Collection, Wolfsonian-Florida International University, Miami Beach. *Photo:* Bruce White)

FIGURE 1.9 (*Above*) Glass powder jar with female head as knob. (Author's collection. *Photo:* Joe Kapalewski, University of Pittsburgh)

bans balance on one leg with outstretched arms. Others wear long-waisted dresses with bateau or V neckline, full circular skirts longer in the back and trimmed with several rows of ruffles, bowknots or ostrich feathers. All these figures stand on marble bases, circular, square, triangular or stepped. (193)

Winokur sees the modernity of the Art Deco female body as tied to earlier changes in corset and dress fashions spearheaded by the Parisian couturier Paul Poiret. Poiret converted the corset "from the S-shaping vehicle it had been to one that flattened the hips and buttocks, liberating the waist. Then he redesigned dresses in empire style, further constraining women within a tubular construction" (197). The effect was to "shear" the figure of woman "away from previously accreted meanings—mother, womanhood, domestic angel" (198). While, on the one hand, this modern woman signified liberation, on the other her slim, androgynous contour bore traces of radical constraint. As Winokur comments, Art Deco's female figure was a vision of woman "as apparently free but literally hobbled to prevent any menace" (196). Winokur's use of the term "menace" reminds us that, as conceived by men (who are, after all, the authors of Art Deco), Woman has often been viewed, on a cultural level, with a modicum of masculine fear. This is, certainly, another way of comprehending why her sexuality has to be romanticized or demonized (as in Art Nouveau) or abstracted or restrained (as in Art Deco). While such dread harks back to ancient times (as in tales of the Medusa, of the Sirens, of Circe, or of Eve), in the modern era (as we shall see), the figure of Woman takes on an added threat as she makes concrete gains in her social position.

Art Deco's female body was also one well-suited to consumerist manipulation—a hallmark of the movement's address. As Winokur notes:

The Poiret-inspired woman's body was compressed—"streamlined"—in order to sell things, reduced to zero in order to allow it to mean only what it sold. Breasts, for example, were reined in so that the feminine would not also mean the maternal. Streamlining the body, reducing its complexity, the absolute numbers of planes it contains, provided an analogy to the things sold: cars, trains, planes, etcetera. (199)

While the Art Deco Woman peddled products, her sculptural form was a product in and of itself. And while such objects constituted expensive acquisitions in the fin de siècle period, by the 1920s they were manufactured for the middle class, who purchased them as tasteful home furnishings or coveted gifts (Arwas 1975:11).

Hat's off to the young modern. She's done with ground thrills—they're all right for mother. She's through with crawling nose-to-tail-light—when the sky's free. She owns the snappiest, easiest handled air-roadster that ever took off in 80 yards of parental lawn, or taxied to a stop in 120. . . . Her Gypsy Moth is a two-place biplane, open cockpit, all-metal fuselage built for strength—with the slimmest silhouette that ever cut head-resistance to a minimum. —Advertisement for D. H. Gipsy Moth airplane (1930)

But what explains Art Deco's fixation on the figure of Woman or accounts for the brand of female it championed? Significantly, Deco's popularity coincided with the rise of the so-called New Woman in American society. In the chryselephantine coquettes "with bobbed hair . . . trousers, long fitted jackets [and] cloche hats," or in the gamines "wear[ing] long-waisted dresses with . . . V neckline[s] . . . bowknots or ostrich feathers," we clearly find references to the "flapper" (McClinton:193). Furthermore, in Arwas's categories of sculptural personae (ranging from the admirable athlete to the disturbing femme fatale), we see registered the ambivalence with which the New Woman was received.

Some historians have tied the emergence of the New Woman to the end of World War I, and to a rise in hedonism (for both females and males) that contrasted strongly with America's Puritanical past. Frederick Lewis Allen speaks of the "eat-drink-and-be-merry, for-tomorrow-we-die spirit," and the attendant "revolt of the younger generation" (1931:94). Walter Lippmann focuses specifically on the "revolution in . . . sexual morals" which some saw as linked to the changing status of women (1929:288). Echoing this position, V. F. Calverton writes that "one feature of this revolt that is seldom recognized is that its predominant emphasis is feminine" (1928:22).

Woman's appearance and demeanor were altered in this period, so as to highlight her independence and allure. As James Laver has noted:

A new type of woman had come into existence. The new erotic idea was androgyne: girls strove to look as much like boys as possible. . . . And, as if to give the crowning touch to their attempted boyishness, all young women cut off their hair. (1995:233)

Likewise, Allen mentions women's cigarette-smoking, wearing short skirts, and use of cosmetics (88–94).

For Sara M. Evans, the epoch was also marked by the growing number of working women, who "reshap[ed] the parameters of female experience" (1989:164). Women's economic autonomy led to a measure of personal freedom, with many of them living as "bachelor girls" (Evans:169). Robert L. Daniel notes that "the New Woman wanted to sample both marriage and a career. . . . Completing school, she secured a job and left home for an apartment of her own" (1987:23).

If upper-middle-class, a New Woman might also travel abroad. As Cushing Strout points out, "Despite the narrow limitations of the orthodox Grand Tour, Americans displayed a broa[d] zest in going to Europe" (1963:110). Regardless of their apparent sophistication, Americans were often viewed as "innocents abroad," who faced an "old" and "dark" world "evocative of guilt, [and] evil" (Strout:127). This was viewed as more alarming for the female tourist.

Central to the figuration of the New Woman was a cultural reversal of attitudes toward sexuality. Calverton cites advances in contraception, which "could remove [woman's] fear [of pregnancy], and shift the emphasis in [her] sex life from the procreational to the recreational" (121). The effect of such progress was twofold. First, constraints linking sex to marriage were loosened, since "the sexual element in life [could] be satisfied outside of marriage and without many of the impediments which the marital life enforce[d] upon the . . . woman" (Calverton:122). Second, the divorce rate rose (Allen:115), as many women left men (Calverton:75). As oblique evidence of changing views toward sexuality, a Modess Sanitary Pad advertisement in *Good Housekeeping* of October 1929 shows a young woman dragging an older woman toward a plane. The ad copy reads: "Don't be a Fraid-Cat Mother, There's No Danger." Another line of the ad refers to "Modernizing Mother," a phrase that applies not only to air travel but to new views of menstruation and female biology (269).

Contemporary morals began to sanction women's pursuit of erotic satisfaction, since "the 'sowing of wild oats' [was] no longer the particular prerogative of the man" (Calverton:91). The New Woman "met and dated males who were unknown to her family," a practice unthinkable in previous generations (Daniel:23). Women who "once had married for economic security, now . . . were to marry for love," an ethic which placed greater demands on the matrimonial bond (Banner 1974:117–18). In sum, public discourse "explored birth control, prostitution, divorce, and sexual morals on an unprecedented scale," making the term *Victorianism* a quaint "epithet" (Daniel:21).

The turmoil of the twenties revealed a certain artificiality in the cultural universe, a level of public theatricality. Allen calls the "wholesome," "old-fashioned lady" a "sham" (112); Lippmann questions whether society now displays "more promiscuity" or just "less hypocrisy" (286); Samuel D. Schmalhausen talks of the disintegration of the "props" of "civilized etiquette" (1929:367); Calverton considers modern marriage a "fiction" (69) and uses the same term to describe its outdated fantasy of a virginal wife: "Certain women have had to prostitute themselves in order that other women might remain respectable and that monogamous marriage continue as a flexible fiction" (169). Hence, the twenties liberated women from a degree of social posturing and performance.

Unfortunately, with the stock market crash of 1929 and the onset of the Depression, many societal gains for women were lost. Historian Lois Banner suggests that the " 'lady-like look' once again became the cynosure of the American woman" (197), and as evidence of this, Laver remarks on how hemlines were lowered and waistlines assumed their "proper" place: "It was as if fashion were trying to say: 'The party is over; the Bright Young Things are Dead' " (1995:240). Similarly, Daniel notes how the "alleged excesses of the flappers and the intrusion of women into the labor market provoked a reaction at the end of the twenties. Women's magazines . . . repeatedly reaffirmed traditional views of woman's role as wife and mother" (87).

It is in this period of great social change that Art Deco took hold in America, and the culture's conflicting views of women were inscribed in its various forms. If the ascent of the New Woman was curtailed by the Depression, so was the rise of Art Deco, which peaked in the mid-1930s. In addition, the style of Art Deco changed in this period. As Eva Weber notes:

> While the Paris-influenced, craft-oriented style of art deco furniture and household accessories of the 1920s tended to be directed toward a more exclusive clientele, and in design was more luxuriant and individualistic, such symbolic capitalism fell out of favor during the depression decade. In contrast, the household articles of the 1930s were created specifically for a mass audience, and their design was based on accessibility, ease of manufacture, and market appeal. During the 1930s, the streamlined style, the brainchild of the newly emergent industrial design movement, came to dominate the design of trains, cars, domestic appliances and household accessories. . . . These ideas sought both escape from and practical solutions to the grim realities of the depression. (20, 22)

ERTÉ AND ART DECO: WOMAN AS SILHOUETTE AND SEMIOLOGICAL SIGN

In order to achieve recognition artists have to go through a little mythological Purgatory: it must be possible to associate them with an object, a school, a fashion, a period, of which they can be called the precursors, the founders, the

witnesses, or the symbols. . . . Erté's Purgatory is Woman. . . . [T]o tell the truth [it is] as if he could never free himself from them (soul or accessory, obsession or convenience?), as if Woman signed each of his sketches more surely than his finely-hand-written name . . . Cherchez la Femme. She is found everywhere.
—Roland Barthes (1972:18)

As a final introductory comment on the Art Deco Woman, it is necessary to discuss one of the major authors of her figuration in the 1920s and 1930s, the French designer Erté (born Romain de Tirtoff). Through his fashion designs, artwork, and costume sketches, Erté revealed a fixation with the female form. Not only did Erté repeat endless variations of this image but, by circulating it, he helped to define the woman of the era. As Franco Maria Ricci notes: "Erté, in the 'twenties,' shaped the implicit form of the woman of [his] day" (1972:14). Erté's role in conceptualizing the period's vision of Woman was clearly tied to the influence he wielded as a major fashion illustrator. Starting with the January 15, 1915, issue of *Harper's Bazar* he created countless drawings on the magazine's cover, making him a publishing "myth" (Ricci:14). He first received a ten-year contract from *Harper's* in 1916, an arrangement that was renewed in 1926 for another decade (Erté 1972:142).

Erté's formulation of the modern female shared much with the Art Deco style. First, he saw Woman as a rather androgynous character. As Ricci comments, Erté's female was "born from the battles for emancipation" and seemed like "a woman disguised as a woman, really aspiring to the civilization created by man, wanting to become man" (14). Second, Erté's view of Woman did not evince Art Nouveau's tendency toward mystical symbolization. Rather, according to Barthes, Erté's Woman was not a "portrait of an idea" nor "an imagined creature," but a pure societal "convention" (22). Furthermore, Erté's notion of the female body was in line with Art Deco's sense of abstraction (versus physicality). Significantly, in many of the fashion publications of the era, one finds reference to the notion of the female "silhouette." For example, an article by Helen Koues in *Good Housekeeping* of February 1930 is entitled "Fashion: Paris Establishes the Silhouette." Similarly, a fashion layout (entitled "The Mode Becomes More Formal" in *Good Housekeeping* of April 1929) touts the designer Patou's "new princess silhouette" (77). This term clearly implies an aesthetic interest in the female *outline* rather than in her full corporeality. As Barthes notes: " The silhouette . . . is a strange object. . . . [I]t is the body which has explicitly become drawing, . . . [A]ll sexuality and its symbolical substitutes are absent; a silhouette . . . is never naked" (1972:24, 26). Again, this particular fascination with the female outline is apparent in many Art Deco objects—for example, "shadow" lamps in which a small metal female figure is backlit by a bulb behind a pane of glass (fig. 1.10). Here again, it is more the outline of the female sculpture that one apprehends, rather than its full figuration. Once more, the work of Erté invokes this celebration of the female outline: one of his illustrations (commissioned for the *Encyclopedia Brittanica* of 1929) is entitled "Silhouettes" (fig. 1.11) and shows four chronological versions of the female form (Spencer 1970:71).

Although, as a couturier, Erté focuses on the issue of female apparel (inextricably tied to her corporeal presence), Barthes sees the force of the body as muted in the designer's work. As he notes, it is "an illusion to believe that Fashion is obsessed with the body" (38). Furthermore, Barthes states that, with Erté, "it is not the female body that is clothed . . . it is the dress that is extended into body . . . for Erté's forms, properly unrealistic, are indifferent to what is underneath" (1972:26). Thus, the function of Erté's silhouettes are to "propose an object (a concept, a form)" rather than female carnality (26).

It is important to realize that Roland Barthes makes these comments about Erté in a specific context: a book of prints from the artist's alphabet series (1927–67)—images of letters fabricated almost entirely out of the female body (*Erté*, 72–74).[9] The fact that Erté creates a largely *female* alphabet signals that he envisions Woman not so much as an embodied, gendered being but as a *sign*, as part of a totalizing feminine (and Art Deco) *discourse*. As Barthes remarks:

> [The] alphabet . . . impregnates all of Erté's work with its meaning: behind every woman of his (Fashion sketches, designs for the theatre) we see a sort of spirit of the Letter looming, as if the alphabet were the natural, original and somehow domestic place of the female body and as if woman left it, to occupy the stage in the theatre or the Fashion drawing, only on temporary leave, after which she must resume her place in her native ABC. (1972:36)

FIGURE 1.10
The female silhouette as shadow lamp. (Author's collection. *Photo:* Joe Kapalewski, University of Pittsburgh)

---

9. There are a few letters in Erté's alphabet that contain images of men—either in conjunction with women (A or O), or alone (Q or W).

FIGURE 1.11

"Silhouettes" (1929) by Erté.

(Courtesy Sevenarts Limited)

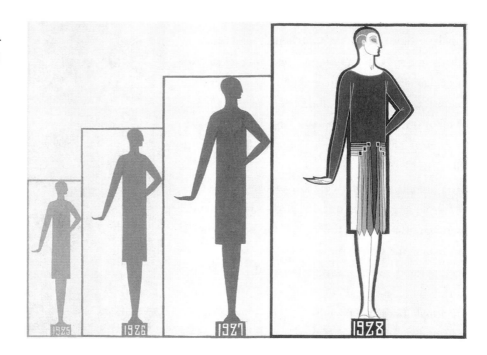

Interestingly, Barthes here associates Woman with language, a fact that flies in the face of conventional formulations of the symbolic.

An examination of the graphics for certain Erté "alphabet" letters allows us to consider particular points that Barthes asserts about the artist's conception of Woman. Earlier on, Barthes stated that Erté's conception of Woman was more "conventional" than it was "mystical" or 'symbolic." His statement seems a bit confusing when we consider Erté's design for the letter G (which is comprised of a woman whose fish-tail bottom curves to make the lower portion of that letter). While the notion of Woman as "mermaid" may initially seem symbolic, the fact that Erté locates it within his alphabet series would seem to signify that he sees it rather as a linguistic/cultural "convention"—rather than as an image that reflects some inherent aspect of Woman (as bestial or mysterious). Similarly, Erté's design for the letter D depicts a Diana figure with a bow, whose string is a slice of the moon (see plate 3). Certainly, this image draws upon a familiar myth of Woman from ancient times—but again its placement within a linguistic alphabet emphasizes its role within societal discourse. In some instances, however, Erté's alphabet characters do seem to retain a trace of Art Nouveau's femme fatale. The letter B is made out of a woman and a sinuous snake. While this image is a traditional one from the Bible (and, hence, again, a conventional formulation), it also has a sense of the perverse and "essentialist" link between Woman and Evil.

THE ART DECO STYLE

In writing on the work of Erté, Barthes seems to be distinguishing between the designer's fashion drawings and his alphabet—which are, in certain respects, quite different. This is the only way to make sense of Barthes's assertion that the artist refrains from using women's hair in his work. In Erté's fashion sketches, in keeping with the mode of the time, his women are generally pictured with short hairdos, a figuration that negates Art Nouveau's sense of tangled, flowing locks as a sign of female danger and decadence. As Barthes observes: "In Erté's gyneographies hair virtually does not exist. Most of his women—characteristically of the period—have short hair, bobbed à la *garçonne* [or in] a black skull-cap . . . a simple graphic underlining of the head" (30). Since hair is "Woman herself" and "her basic differentiation," this renders the female figure both an androgyne and an abstraction. Erté's minimalist conception of the female head is apparent in his drawing for the cover of a 1930 issue of *Harper's Bazaar*, which pictures a woman in a Cubist-patterned skullcap (Spencer:66). While in Erté's fashion work Woman's hair is *not* part of the idiom, in several frames of the alphabet series it *is*, and in this respect once more harks back to Art Nouveau. The letter C, for instance, is made up, in part, of curls of a woman's hair. This is also the case for the letter P.

For Barthes, not only does Erté's alphabet have semiological implications, it also contributes to the abstract conception of Art Deco's female form. As Barthes observes: "To construct this feminine sign, it is necessary to sacrifice something immense, which is the body" (1972:22). Ultimately, Barthes sees the linguistic aspects of Erté's conception of Woman as tied to the designer's notion of the silhouette, which is "an essentially graphic product: [that] makes of the human body a potential letter . . . [that] demands to be read" (38) In support of Barthes's sense that Erté is as concerned with his clothing designs for Woman as with her body, the two vertical lines that make up the letter N are composed of a dress dummy on the left and a female model on the right—and we have a sense that the two are precisely coequal. Counter to Barthes' formulation, however, one might point out that the bodies of the women in Erté's alphabet are often depicted nude (with full breasts); hence, they are marked by a touch of carnality. Nonetheless, Barthes' statement remains true when applied to Erté's fashion sketches.

While Erté borrows, for his Art Deco vocabulary, the curvilinear shape often associated with Art Nouveau, in his work this imprint has a different meaning. As Barthes comments, for Erté, "femininity is sinuous" in a cultural, not a natural sense (58). Thus, it is associated not with the brute nature of the Art Nouveau world, but with the ornate sense of "refined, civilized [and] socialized life" (58)—hence, Woman's traditional link to fashion, decoration, and the cult of beauty.

One aspect of Erté's alphabet on which Barthes fails to remark is its hesitant, homoerotic tendency, an aspect of the earlier Jugendstil that Benjamin references in his mention of the movement's spiritualized "lesbian love" (558). In at least two of Erté's letters, pairs of identical women are portrayed. In *H*, they are clothed in masks, headdresses, and skin-tight body suits and linked by a fur stole that surrounds them both; in the letter *V*, they are naked and depicted amidst flowers and their "tails" are entwined in a knot. This subtext of homoeroticism—a spinoff of Deco's endless proliferation of female bodies—will surface later in our discussion of fashion advertising (a discourse based on women looking at women) and in our discussion of the musical chorus line (in which dancing girls cavort with one another more frequently than they do with men).

In the spirit of Erté's semantic formulation, this book attempts to read the Art Deco female as a linguistic sign—for her aesthetic, historical, and cultural meanings. As in the case of Erté (and his interpreter, Barthes), such meanings will have been those assigned to Woman by Man—since it has been predominantly male artists, craftsmen, designers, and manufacturers who created the female form of the age.

In the next two chapters I will examine the transformation of the Art Deco style into a consumer culture aimed largely at women, by focusing on how the department store and women's magazines of the era addressed the female shopper and reader. In later chapters I will investigate the image of Woman in both the cinema and in motion picture theater design—to comprehend the semiological (or "somatographical") formulation of the Art Deco female (Barthes 1972:22).

2. COUNTER CULTURE

Art Deco, Consumerism, and the Department Store

ART DECO AND CONSUMERISM

In chapter 1, I focused on Art Deco largely as a stylistic mode—with its mixture of modernism, exoticism, and primitivism as well as its fascination with the female form. While I mentioned, by way of example, the movement's incarnation in various commercial artifacts (lamps, vases, statues), I did not highlight its status within American material culture. In this chapter and the next, I will do precisely that—interrogate the relationship between Art Deco and consumerism in America in the 1920s and 1930s. The focus of my attention will be on the *female shopper* of the era and on the connotations that the Style Moderne may have held for her. Though I will consider both middle- and upper-class individuals, the main discussion here will largely be on the urban woman since she was more associated with consumerism in the period than was her rural counterpart. Chapter 3 will then consider such fashion venues as the Sears catalogue, which reached women residing both in the city centers and in the heartland. Due to the economics of race in this period, mainstream American consumer discourse was aimed at the Caucasian woman. The black female only entered that rhetoric as a symbol of the "Primitive" or the "Exotic," rarely as the subject of its address.

I will treat the subject of female consumerism in some depth: first, because it has not received much attention in the literature on Art Deco;[1] and second,

Deco as revealed in America in the first third of the twentieth century was an art movement that was actually . . . an advertising strategy of the 1920s and 1930s. Art Deco romanticized and then sold soap, tires, and train tickets.

—Mark Winokur (1996:198)

---

1. The lone exception is a book published after this manuscript was essentially written: Anne Massey's *Hollywood Beyond the Screen: Design and Material Culture* (2000).

because it will have surprising relevance to our consideration of the cinema. As a primary source for this investigation, women's magazines of the era and, to a lesser extent, catalogues and decorating manuals proved indispensable. My emphasis on the female (versus the male) consumer should be no surprise, given that in this period the popular audience was often conceived as "feminine." As Andreas Huyssen has noted: "the notion which gained ground during the 19th century [is] that mass culture is somehow associated with woman while real, authentic culture remains the prerogative of men" (1986:47). Clearly, nothing could be more abject than consumer culture, with women seen as the primary "purchasing agents" of the American family (Marchand 1985:66). For Susan Stewart, however, the automatic association of women and shopping has deeper, more perverse and psycho-analytical resonances. As she notes: "The [stereotypical] conception of woman as consumer is no less fantastic or violent than its literalization in the *vagina dentata* myth" (1993:168).

It seems quite fitting that I should discuss a cutting-edge style like Art Deco in relation to consumerism since both concepts are associated with modernity. As Don Slater points out: "Consumer culture is in important respects *the* culture of the modern West—certainly central to the meaningful practice of everyday life in the modern world; and . . . bound up with central values, practices, and institutions which define Western modernity" (1997:8). For Slater, these tenets include "democracy," which burgeoned with the onset of a moneyed culture. Before the currency system, wealth was based on the possession of land and family heir-looms—acquisitions possible only for an aristocratic class that held its status by title or tradition. With the onset of colonialism and the increased circulation and exchange of exotic natural commodities (spices, coffee, tea, and minerals), indi-viduals outside the nobility could trade goods for currency. Once amassed, such funds could be used for the purchase of merchandise acquired beyond the circuit of lineage (Slater:22, 30). Industrialization is another development that Slater sees as having encouraged modern consumerism by facilitating the production of human-made goods. Such artifacts flooded the market and created a cornucopia of objects to be accumulated. In addition to proliferating possessions, industrial-ization also liberated objects from the aura of "uniqueness." No longer were cov-eted goods necessarily fashioned in an artisanal mode, with an emphasis on their "singularity" that assured their limited possession by the upper echelons. Now they were produced in identical bulk, a method that favored mass consumption. According to Slater, the modern concept of human individuality has been linked to the consumer's "right" to possess the objects he desires and to express himself through their acquisition. As Slater notes: "Consumer culture is about continuous self-creation through the accessibility of things" (10). Furthermore, consumerism is tied to the "freedom" to make personal decisions. As Slater remarks: "To be a consumer is to make choices: to decide what you want, [and] to consider how to spend your money to get it" (27). While some scholars have seen the modern subject's procurement of commodities as more indicative of greed than of creativity or liberty, Grant McCracken agrees with Slater that there are redeeming rhetorical aspects to consumerism. As he notes: "Consumer goods are bridges to . . . hopes and ideals. We use them to recover . . . displaced cultural meaning, to cultivate what is otherwise beyond our grasp" (1988:106).

Echoing McCracken, Tim Dant argues against conventional views of commodity "fetishism" that have circulated in consumer discourse. For Dant, the notion of the material object as "fetish" presumes that it has no "real" value—but only one that is somehow "misconceived" by its owner. While for Marx, the exchange value of the fetishized commodity is a displacement of its worth in terms of human labor, for Freud the fetish object is a phantasmagoric sexual substitute for the human being. Similarly, in a desacralized world, the religious fetish is merely a falsely endowed "magical" prop, with no real power to act upon the world. It is this sense of illusionary potency that theorists have also attached to consumer goods. For Dant, however, the perceived properties of objects are not simply fabricated but "more correctly 'rest' on things, giving them a role in material culture" (1999:55). There are six roles such objects can play. They can have a concrete "function" (e.g., a *moderne* toaster can toast bread); they can have a "signification" that relates to a social group (e.g., owning a Pierce Arrow can facilitate one's travel in elite circles); they can bear an element of "sexuality" (e.g., wearing designer clothing by Erté can make one more erotically attractive); they can deliver "knowledge" (e.g., a cruise on the *Ile de France* can teach one about foreign cultures); they can satisfy one's sense of "aesthetics" (e.g., regarding an elegant Tiffany ring on one's finger can fill one with sublime pleasure); and, finally, they can constitute vehicles of "meditation" (e.g., a family heirloom from the Art Deco era can link one back to past generations) (55–56).

Applying Dant's sense of the "functionality" of consumer objects to Art Deco, one can imagine that for some the style may have signified "modernity" and that their acquisition of its artifacts may have invested them with an aura of the New. Since consumerism, however, is also associated with the ever-changing "fashion system," an item's status as novelty can only be temporary, as it is replaced by the next vogue. Thus, as Slater notes: "Consumer culture lives in a perpetual year zero of newness." It "is about . . . the accessibility of things which are themselves presented as new, modish, faddish or fashionable, always improved and improving" (9–10).

For other consumers of the Art Deco mode, its artifacts may have carried the message of simplicity and sleekness—an antidote to the cluttered detritus of the past. For McCracken, the consumer's achievement of such an "ideal" is, however, always partial and fleeting. Because the consumer covets an entire "lifestyle," each acquisition is only synecdochial—a part of an unattainable whole (110, 114). This fact (among others) assures the continual resuscitation of consumer desire which is, by definition, insatiable. As McCracken observes: "What has been long sought is swiftly devalued and the individual moves on to another bridge, so that displaced meaning can remain displaced" (112). While, in most cultures, excessive acquisitiveness might be seen as "a social or moral pathology (sin, corruption, decadence)," in consumer culture "unlimited need . . . is widely taken to be not only normal for its denizens but essential for socioeconomic order and progress" (Slater:28–29).

Class tensions also contribute to the repetitive and endless nature of the modern consumer cycle. Among the meanings that certain objects hold for us is their connection to our economic superiors. As Slater comments, "One's desire for goods is a desire to emulate the consumption style of higher status groups" (153). While in earlier times people were only able to acquire prestigious merchandise through theft, inheritance, or marriage, in the contemporary era individuals can purchase such status symbols. Thus, modernity and consumerism bespeak a more fluid social world in which the fixity of cultural rank is somewhat offset by the liquidity and mobility of wealth. As I shall demonstrate, such class aspirations inflect the allure of Art Deco, which was often seen as a style associated with "puttin' on the Ritz."

As imagined by cultural theorists, the modern consumer has been seen as alternately "heroic" or "duped." According to Slater,

> The consumer was a hero to the extent that he was autonomous and self-determined, and that this autonomy depended on his rational capacities, on his ability . . . to know and define his own needs. . . . Yet we also have an image prevalent . . . of the consumer as a dupe or dope. This consumer—the mass, conformist consumer—is defined by his failure to live up to the standard of "maturity," of reason and autonomy. [The] consumer as dupe is a slave to desires rather than a rational calculator of them. (54–55)

For Slater, the degraded type of consumer has frequently been seen to be female—a prejudice that emerges from deep-seated cultural misogyny and from the fact that within modern domestic society, the female makes the majority of purchases.

Whether they conceived her as heroic or duped, American magazine editors and advertisers of the 1920s and 1930s attempted to attract the female shopper through an invocation of the Art Deco style. What was the nature of the address they formulated for her? What "ideals and hopes" did they try to harness in her? What fantasies of race and class did they seek to tap in her? How was her consumer desire forever renewed? What was the environment like in which she was hailed? How was she sold the Style Moderne mode as an appealing "design for living"?

"SELLING MRS. CONSUMER"

Women as customers were socialized to handle the consumption needs of their families . . . processing messages of advertisers and merchants in ways that made sense to them.   —Susan Porter Benson (1986:5)

The decade following World War I (until the Depression) saw an unequaled prosperity in America; thus, advertising markets radically expanded. Not only were myriad new products promoted, but advertisers embraced the concept of modernity, valuing the new against the old (Walker 2000:38). Like the advertisements they ran, many magazines championed novelty. An ad for a subscription to *Vanity Fair* that ran in *Vogue* of January 2, 1929, bore the following copy:

> MODERNISM is sweeping the intelligent world. You find it in music, in the arts, in literature. You can't just ignore it. Yet, what do you know about it? What do you think of it? . . . There is a way, an easy way, to know and enjoy the newest schools of modern thought and art . . . This forum is the magazine *Vanity Fair*. (14)

Along with the journals themselves, the products sold within them also advocated modernity and sought to associate the concept with the contemporary American woman. Thus, an advertisement for the Fisher car body in *Good Housekeeping* of March 1932 (obviously aimed at the female driver) reads:

> Turn the great book of Time to the page of our days and you will find as a major entry—"The Emancipation of Woman." Freed after untold centuries from the narrow restrictions of a purely domestic life, she has emerged [into] . . . a broader . . . existence. Entering this larger sphere her influence has acquired a greater scope. Commerce, science, arts . . . indeed every occupation . . . *feel the effect of her presence*. (125–26; emphasis added)

Clearly, a female "presence" was felt in the realm of women's magazine publishing, a field that was also marked by a hierarchy of class orientations. *Vanity*

Fair, Vogue, House and Garden, and *Harper's Bazaar*, for example, were intended for upper-middle-class and wealthy women. They assumed an "affluent, cosmopolitan reader" and advertised cutting-edge products (Walker:65). For middle-class women, there were the "big four" publications that ruled American domestic life: *Ladies' Home Journal, Good Housekeeping, McCall's*, and *Woman's Home Companion* (Walker:65). Though these journals hawked more conventional and moderate-priced goods, they, too, revealed the influence of the Style Moderne, which advertisers meant to associate with the domain of the upper crust (Marchand:140). As historian Nancy Walker notes: "If magazine editors assumed their readers to be middle class (whether defined by income, geography, occupation, community standing, or taste), the editors also assumed that these readers aspired to improve their class standing, largely by improving their material surroundings" (37). It is interesting, here, to observe that both the September 1928 and the July 1929 issues of *Good Housekeeping* (a mainstream publication) advertise *Harper's Bazar*, an upscale magazine (246 and 224, respectively). As Roland Marchand observes, there was no sense of "irony" at this time around depictions of the cultural elite. Rather, American consumers envisioned a mountable social ladder and "hungered for an authentic, certified, social aristocracy against which they might measure their own gains in status." Thus, advertisers had "no qualms about flaunting the image of an opulent, exclusive and clearly defined elite class before their audience," even in the Depression.

Obviously, implicit in the notion of a "woman's magazine" is the sense that certain subjects are of interest to females only. Most of these topics are assumed to be domestic in nature. *Good Housekeeping*, for example, first published in 1885, focused on "recipes, etiquette, household advice, [and] information features" (Endres and Lueck 1995:123). *Ladies' Home Journal*, premiering in 1883, was a "woman's survival manual with departments that offered practical advice on child rearing, useful household hints, [and] instructions for various crafts" (Endres and Lueck:173). *Woman's Home Companion*, first issued in 1873, offered "practical household advice, parenting guidance, and craft information" (Endres and Lueck:445). While many of these journals tracked progressive developments (with articles on suffrage, divorce, and child welfare), most supported traditional values. As Kathleen Endres and Therese Lueck state: "The editors never forgot that most of their readers were wives and mothers" (446).

While the majority of these magazines appealed to the broad concerns of the American woman (by concentrating on a spectrum of popular issues), some periodicals took a narrower perspective. *House and Garden*, which emerged in 1901, was originally an architectural digest but widened its purview to include the American domestic universe. Similarly, *House Beautiful*, which initially concentrated on interior décor, became a champion of contemporary versus Victorian design. As Endres and Lueck state, it "was in the forefront of the battle for 'modern' architecture in which 'form follows function' " (160). The readership for both *House Beautiful* and *House and Garden* was assumed to be largely female, since women were thought to be most involved with issues of home style.

Other women's journals were dedicated to *haute couture*, although even those included features on homemaking and décor. One of the most successful was *Harper's Bazar*, first published in 1867. Along with *Vogue*, it remained one of dominant American fashion publications for generations (Endres and Lueck:137). When it was purchased by the Hearst Corporation in 1913, it became directly identified with modernism. Thus, it "emerged as a colorful, sophisticated, large-size magazine with an aura of sophistication" (Endres and Lueck: 139). Another important fashion publication was *Pictorial Review*, which first appeared in 1899 as a venue for displaying dressmaking patterns. Along with highlighting couture, it manifested a liberal politics, with columns on such topics as women's rights. As its editor, Arthur T. Vance, wrote (albeit paternalistically) in 1910:

> We appeal to women who want to think and to act as well as to be enter-
> tained. It is a feminine age. Women are taking more and more part in affairs
> and our idea is this: that a magazine correctly to represent the women of
> this country must keep its readers in close touch with questions of public
> interest, and guide and direct this feminine activity in the most useful and
> practical channels. (Endres and Lueck:275–76)

These were the publications that the American middle- and upper-class Caucasian urban woman would have read in the 1920s and 1930s and through which she would have become acquainted with the modern mode. Beyond being instructed on this topic, however, she would also have been encouraged to desire contemporary artifacts that bore the Art Deco stamp and to purchase them for her person and her home. Not only was the Deco style useful to marketers in linking products with the notions of the chic and elite, its design aesthetic (including zigzag lines, diagonal motifs, abstract borders, asymmetrical layouts, fragmentation, montage-like juxtapositions) was helpful in selling products. According to Marchand, such tropes lent a certain simplicity to the advertising graphic, allowing illustrators to "direct the reader's eye more efficiently" (142). Furthermore, such Deco tropes lent an appealing sense of movement and expressivity to more static advertising copy (144–46).

"PALACES OF CONSUMPTION"

By the 1890s, the department store was the leading force in American retailing.
—Susan Porter Benson (31)

One of the primary vendors of modern wares was, of course, the metropolitan department store, and any discussion of the female consumer in the 1920s and 1930s must take account of its vast cultural influence. With its roots in the late nineteenth century, the department store was an established fixture of the merchandising world by the time of Art Deco's reign. The primary patron of the department store was the female shopper, who soon constituted some 80 percent of its customer base. Furthermore, on a social level the department store constructed an entirely new kind of public space for women (Benson:9, 76). A journalist of 1910 describes a typical (and gendered) shopping scene as follows:

> Buying and selling, serving and being served—women. On every floor, in every aisle, at every counter, women. . . . Behind most of the counters on all the floors, women. At every cashier's desk, at the wrappers' desks, running back and forth with parcels and change, short-skirted women. Filling the aisles, passing and repassing, a constantly arriving and departing throng of shoppers, women. Simply a moving, seeking, hurrying, mass of femininity, in the midst of which the occasional man shopper, man clerk, and man supervisor, looks lost and out of place. (Benson:76)

The department store was clearly a hierarchical business. While the lower-class woman was represented by the sales girl and the bargain-basement shopper, the institution's primary address was to the female patron of the middle or upper class. Especially important for this audience was the fact that the department store not only sold goods but appealed to women's desire for luxury and elegance. According to Benson, the goal of the American department store was to be a "palace of consumption" which "impress[ed] customers . . . through the design of store buildings and the provision of various services." This conception arose from client pressure: "Customers . . . were making an esthetic demand for 'beautiful and even artistic surroundings' in which to make their purchases." Not only were merchandise displays gorgeous and extravagant, but so were supplementary sites like the ladies rest rooms—outfitted with plush furniture, thick towels, complimentary stationery, and uniformed maids. Thus, in its atmosphere the department store sought to replicate the posh downtown men's club, providing an enticing milieu in which the female shopper might safely and respectably pass the day (Benson:81–85).

Without doubt, the department store made its mark through its promise of chic goods. As Benson notes: "Managers no longer simply tried to respond to their customers' demands and cater to their tastes; stores actively sought to influence the public's notion of what was stylish and appropriate." Therefore, they depended on aggressive sales techniques, far more than had old-fashioned neighborhood establishments: "Department stores stimulated patronage in various ways: they advertised in all available media and decorated their windows and departments with attractive merchandise, convincing customers to buy their wares on the basis of fashion" (Benson:101–102).

It should be apparent how this conception of the department store was amenable to the Art Deco style, and the close relationship between the two is evident in the pages of women's magazines of the 1920s and 1930s. First, there are the articles which describe the seminal 1925 Paris Exposition, making clear that many of the most noteworthy exhibits were sponsored by European department stores. Nellie Sanford reviews a 1926 show at the Metropolitan Museum of Art consisting of objects on loan from that famous exposition. She notes how some of the most beautiful displays were created by individuals associated with Parisian emporia: the Primavera decorators of Printemps and the Pomone group of Bon Marché (188).

Second, American decorating magazines routinely covered the opening of new or renovated American department stores, often reviewing their avant-garde architecture. Athena Robbins writes in a 1929 issue of *Good Furniture and Decoration* about the opening of Saks Fifth Avenue, Chicago. As she notes: "A fine new spirit of modernism is reflected by this new store, from the most fundamental elements of its design to the smallest details of its decoration." Evidently, its décor included such Deco hallmarks as black and frosted glass, chromium plate, and Japanese wallpaper. Revealing the ambivalence felt by Americans toward the Style Moderne, Robbins remarks that, while Saks's décor is "logical and orderly," it fortunately has "none of the feeling of mathematical precision which oftentimes causes a feeling of coldness and austerity detrimental to the appearances of a woman's shop." Finally, as though to emphasize the connection between design and consumption, she advises that "to really appreciate [Saks's] excellence one must actually see it at a time when it is crowded with many smartly dressed shoppers" (94). In a similar vein, in an article in *Harper's Bazaar* of June 1931, Margaret Glover reviews Hattie Carnegie's new store in Manhattan. A photograph depicts a very stark, avant-garde décor, with the caption: "A corner of Our Little Salon, a new modern room and an enchanting place in which to see your clothes."

But the most prevalent inscription of the department store into the pages of women's magazines was through advertising and photo spreads, much of which was placed in upscale publications and drew upon Art Deco design. Some ads promoted the department store itself. One for Saks Fifth Avenue's Sports Department, in an April 1926 issue of *Harper's Bazar*, offers a sketch of a woman posed on what appears to be a train—her scarf blowing in the wind (13). The accompanying text alerts us that Saks (an elite store) has "Ideal Costumes for the Modern Sportswoman." In the November 1928 issue of *Harper's Bazar*, there are several more examples. One comprises a two-page spread that promotes the Vingtième shops at New York City's pricey Bonwit Teller: "A series of little art salons on the third floor wherein are presented the loveliest of boudoir accessories, lamps and decorative gifts for the home" (4). These words are superimposed upon an almost Cubist drawing which blends images of a female figure, a woman's head, crystal goblets, and geometric shapes. On the opposite page are sketches of women in trendy dress, set against a pattern of abstract lines and shapes (5). Elsewhere in the magazine is an advertisement for ritzy Bergdorf Goodman of New York. Here a sketch reveals a room with a "modified modernist" décor in which well-heeled women are waiting. The ad copy reads: "In the Salle Moderne, sports clothes. Here, young things find whatever is . . . chic . . . for the country club . . . for motoring" (61). It is noteworthy how both the Bonwit and Bergdorf ads draw upon the cachet of French terminology: the *vingtième* shops, the *salle moderne*. While Bonwit's ad stresses the futuristic, Bergdorf's tries to walk a fine like between novelty and tradition.

Another upscale New York department store, Stewart, is advertised in several issues of *Harper's Bazaar* of 1929. In one from November, a sketch depicts Stewart's Deco-style building exterior, as well as a large female head and the outline of a car (all icons of modernity). The accompanying text notes how the "modern woman loves shopping in little . . . shops" and claims that Stewart's stresses "individuality" (49). Similarly, a Stewart ad in the December 1929 issue promotes the store's "gift floor." The ad is illustrated by a sketch of a modish showroom with recessed lighting, Deco chairs, patterned walls, and glass cases full of modern *objets d'art*. The text informs the reader that the gift floor was designed by architect Eugene Schoen and (to emphasize its exoticism) that Stewart's buyers have visited "little corners tucked away in the Old World, as well as famous bazaars, to make [its] collection the most complete in America" (43). Even the print font for the "Stewart" name (done in black lines against a white background) is an homage to Art Deco graphics. Finally, an ad for the Cuban department store El Encanto appears in *Vogue* of January 19, 1929—the month for wealthy people to head south. It depicts a Deco-influenced sketch of a Latin woman with a mantilla on her head, but touts the "old world atmosphere" of the establishment.

Other magazine advertisements invoke department stores by highlighting their various merchandising wings. One appearing in *House and Garden* of May 1929 for New York City's Macy's (a more middle-class establishment) promotes the store's china department by associating it with Paris and modernism.[2] Accompanying photographs of contemporary tableware, the ad copy reads: "Yearly the Salon des Artistes Decorateurs holds an important exhibition in Paris. In the 1928 showing, the work of Mlle. Suzanne Lalique was enthusiastically acclaimed."[3] Not surprisingly, her "splendid group of designs for modern china" are available to the reader at Macy's. Similarly, a September 1929 advertisement in *House and Garden* uses modernism to promote the decorating services of B. Altman and Company, another elite New York City department store. The ad is illustrated by a photograph of a dining room "on the floor of modern furniture." The accompanying text advises that if your plans require "the imaginative creations of leading modern designers . . . you will appreciate the immense resources that enable our decorators to employ the training and experience to your utmost advantage" (5).

Middle-American publications also invoked the department store but promoted more moderate-priced merchandisers like the Sears and Roebuck retail chain. One ad for Sears in *Good Housekeeping* of January 1930 depicts two women in fashionable dress—one wearing a chic fur-collared coat with a cloche hat. The products hawked in the ad, however, are more mundane than the women's couture: mattress covers, bedspreads, sheets, and towels. The *Sears Roebuck Catalogue* itself features the chain's home order service—instructing the reader (in an ad from fall 1925) not to "envy the well-dressed woman" but to order dress patterns for making stylish frocks herself (389). Again, this speaks to the more "practical" fashion orientation of middle-class publications.

---

2. Evidence that Macy's was a more middle-class store than Saks or B. Altman comes from the fact that its slogan was "Macy's attractions are its prices" (Hungerford 1922:97). Also, as Edward Hungerford notes, "While the house has not hesitated to install certain very lovely 'special' rooms *vide* the *salon* for the display of its imported frocks—the main thought in the construction of its present home in Herald Square was to build a retail market-place which would afford honest, efficient, comfortable marketing at the lowest possible prices. This meant that it would be inadvisable . . . to give the store the atmosphere of either a palace or a boudoir" (168–69).

3. Suzanne Lalique was the daughter of René Lalique and also a designer.

Many girls take their jobs seriously. . . . But there are countless others who use work as a stop gap. They are pinch-hitting until that some day when "he" will come along. He will probably come, too. Not today perhaps. Maybe tomorrow. But sooner or later. While one is waiting, one might as well get a job.
—Dorothy Stote (1935:77)

Among those who may have perused the pages of the Sears catalogue for their fashion ideas were the shop girls who tended counters at many of America's upscale department stores. For, while for the middle- or upper-class female of the 1920s and 1930s that commercial space was a consumer playland, for the working woman it was a site of labor.

Our Blushing Brides (1930), directed by Harry Beaumont, is a Depression-era film that depicts the lives of three young women employed by a fictional New York City department store, Jardine's. It is part of a trilogy produced by MGM about youthful females in the jazz age, the earlier movies being *Our Dancing Daughters* (directed by Harry Beaumont in 1928) and *Our Modern Maidens* (directed by Jack Conway in 1929). All star Joan Crawford (though in different roles).

Our Blushing Brides portrays the world of a trio of young employees of Jardine's. As Dorothy Stote's quote above indicates, all three (who share an apartment together) seem to be working as a temporary measure until they can find men to marry. Gerry Marsh (Joan Crawford) is a store "mannequin" who models the latest fashions for its upscale clients. She is realistic and down-to-earth about romantic matters and has a strong sense of morality and propriety. Connie Blair (Anita Page) works in the store's perfume department and is quite naive. When Davey Jardine (Raymond Hackett), a son of the store's owner, declares his love for her, she believes him and quits her job to be "kept" by him in a luxurious flat. An innocent, Connie trusts that he will one day marry her. When his engagement to a society debutante is announced in the newspaper, she commits suicide. "Franky" (Francine) Daniels (Dorothy Sebastian) works in the store's linen department and is a total cynic. When a prosperous-looking man named Martin Sanderson (John Miljan) stops in to purchase some blankets, she begins an affair with him, despite the fact that he is an obvious womanizer. As he tells her (with a sense of double entendre): "I always pay cash for what I want." Franky weds him and, for a while, lives a life of elegance and wealth. Eventually, however, the police come looking for Sanderson, who is revealed to be a practiced con-man. Meanwhile, Gerry has been romanced by Tony Jardine (Robert Montgomery), another son of the department store magnate. Tony has been attracted to her as she models clothes for an affluent Jardine customer. Gerry, however, has her feet on the ground and is suspicious of Tony's advances, assuming that any liaison with him will be devoid of a marital future. She, therefore, refuses his sexual overtures and their relationship flounders. After Connie's suicide, however, the two are reunited and Gerry realizes that Tony truly loves her. In the final scene of the film, we learn that they are engaged.

Many aspects of the film are in keeping with department store culture as documented by Frances R. Donovan (1929) in *The Saleslady*. While the women depicted in *Our Blushing Brides* are apartment dwellers who live in modest but acceptable surroundings, Donovan compares melodramatic with realistic portrayals of the saleslady's fate:

> The shop girl in fiction lives . . . in a little attic hall bedroom with soiled paper peeling from the wall, a hard bed in one corner, a washstand with its cracked bowl and pitcher in the other, and a geranium in a tomato can on the window sill. . . . There may be department-store girls who live in attic rooms nowadays, but I never met one nor heard of one. . . . Those who do not live at home have little apartments of their own where they live either alone or with another girl. (1929:176)

The self-reliance of the shop girls in the movie rings true with Donovan's description. As she notes, "The working-girl no longer depends upon heaven to protect her; she protects herself. She lives her own independent existence" (177). Clearly, this applies to her social life. As Donovan comments: "The girl in the city can be excused for a certain amount of unconventionality. The city makes no provision for introducing her to men. . . . [T]he modern business girl does not sit around and wait for introductions that never come her way. She finds her friends among men just as men find them among themselves and as women make the acquaintance of other women" (165–66). While in the movie each shop girl is exceedingly attractive (as is typical of female characters in Hollywood films), Donovan does not find this to be the case: "The girl who works in the department store today is no longer taken on as a decoration. She is, for the most part, selected by women and bossed by women—her sex appeal doesn't count" (189). While the film creates the impression that all shop girls are single women desperately seeking mates, Donovan emphasizes the number of married women employed in this fashion: "The department store is open not only to the spinster but also to the married woman. In fact, married women, like married men, have responsibilities that make them often greater assets to the store than the unattached" (189). While Donovan finds many professional salesladies to be neutral about marriage (since their job offers them financial security and a challenging and sociable lifestyle), she admits that romance occupies a great deal of the women's attention. On the store's gossip circuit, tales are related about salesladies who married "up" (like Gerry in *Our Blushing Brides*). As Donovan notes: "Most department-store girls are willing to marry a millionaire if he is otherwise agreeable but they don't expect to do so; they are too shrewd for that. The great majority of them, however, expect to marry and they do marry" (163). In fact, store newsletters (like Macy's *Sparks*) spread the word about engagements or weddings. Among the examples Donovan quotes is the following item from June 1926:

> We have a store romance in our Basement. The very intriguing Titian haired young lady in the Candy Department, Miss Gloria Schillingham, has good cause to smile sweetly at Mr. Tom McQueeney, former section manager in the China Department, since she has accepted his Fraternity Pin. They will be married this spring. (164)

Our Blushing Brides is also quite interesting in terms of the broader issues it raises concerning the status of Woman in the twenties. First, despite the alleged "modernity" of the film's subject matter (three young women alone in New York negotiating the perils of work and romance), its overall value system is quite traditional. The two women who squander their virginity on premarital affairs (one out of naïveté and the other out of skepticism) are punished: Connie dies and Franky is tainted by criminality. The one woman who "holds out" and successfully barters virginity for marriage is rewarded: Gerry gets her man and her fortune. Though the title of the film is vaguely ironic, Gerry ultimately incarnates an updated version of the "blushing bride." Thus, the characterization of Crawford's heroine is a long way from that associated with Greta Garbo (the subject of chapter 4), who embodies an Art Deco female of a more bold, maverick, and daring nature.

It is apparent from the film that department store culture of the era was firmly associated with the Art Deco mode. With sets supervised by Cedric Gibbons (who is discussed further in chapter 4), the mise-en-scène of the store is decidedly *moderne*. Its most elegant site is the fashion salon in which Gerry models clothes. The mannequins appear on a stage flanked by onyx black stairs and pose in front of a huge circular disk. When they appear in light-colored frocks, the disk rotates to its black side; when they appear in dark-toned outfits, it displays its white half. Thus, the women are silhouetted in the manner of a Deco graphic or shadow lamp. Triangular sconces grace the walls of the salon and a pedestal holding a decorative female figure adorns its floor. Interestingly, when Tony Jardine flirts with Gerry (who is modeling various contemporary outfits designed by MGM's Adrian), shots of him include the abstract female sculpture in the background.

As is clear from its narrative, *Our Blushing Brides* valorizes wealth as the standard to which all red-blooded Americans should aspire (this despite its Depression-era context). Much is made of the crush that a character named Joe Munsey (Edward Brophy) has on Gerry. But unlike Donovan's real women, who seem quite willing to consider their fellow laborers as mates, Gerry does not. Rather, because Munsey is a working "stiff" who drives a Ford and thinks a night on the town is a date at the movies, she does not give him the time of day. Clearly, she agrees with her roommates who have no interest in "some sap from the store." Instead, like them, she has her eyes firmly set on the upper-crust prize. Significantly, when one night she is alone in her flat, she plays a recording of "Puttin' on the Ritz."

Perhaps most noticeably, affluence in the film is entirely associated with the Style Moderne. When the women share an apartment together, their living space is fairly traditional—with its wooden buffet and silk lampshades. And when Gerry's two roommates move out and she is down on her luck, she takes an apartment in an old tenement where the furniture looks decidedly Victorian. But when Connie and Gerry become involved with the rich Jardine brothers, their environment is transformed—dominated by the modern mode. The flat that Davey Jardine sets up for Connie is done in a cutting-edge style ("Comme il faut," as she says). Near the front door is a modern cabinet with a ziggurat base and a striped inlaid top; triangular sconces hang on the wall; in a corner is a silver pedestal that holds a vase in which there are *faux* flowers with abstract "petals"; elsewhere stands a contemporary "tub" chair. The bedroom includes a bureau with patterned drawers, and an electric wall clock hangs over the bed. Connie greets Gerry in a fashionable outfit with a silver metallic bodice.

Similarly, Gerry's environment metamorphoses through her contact with Tony Jardine. At one point she is asked to participate in a fashion show hosted by a French couturier to be held at the Jardine mansion on Long Island (fig. 2.1). The setting for the event is the Jardine's *moderne* pool and garden. The background of the ersatz stage is made from elaborate white grillwork that is done in a scroll-like Deco fashion. Modernist towers also serve as part of the décor. In the center of the stage area there is a tiered fountain whose water spills down a series of ziggurat steps. The outfits worn by the women are influenced by Art Deco abstraction— with their brash stripes and geometric patterns. When Tony takes Gerry for a walk around the grounds, she stands on a balcony overlooking the mansion and a lake; suddenly she seems cast in a Maxfield Parrish illustration. But the most dramatic locale on the Jardine estate is Tony's tree house (a Bauhaus Treehaus, at that). It

FIGURE 2.1

Our Blushing Brides (1930): An Art Deco fashion show at the Jardine estate. (Courtesy British Film Institute)

has a stark semicircular window that runs from floor to ceiling and frames the outside greenery in a manner worthy of a Japanese print. The hideaway also has a sunken pit in which a modular sofa stands; elsewhere, the façade of a lacquer console is adorned by an abstract, geometric pattern.

Significantly, it is in this space that Gerry's engagement to Tony is later revealed to the audience. She wears a Deco pants outfit (now her own possession)—signifying her successful move from working girl to lady of the house. (In Depression-era America, married women were discouraged from remaining in the work force so as not to "deprive" men of jobs.) Clearly, the ultimate "consumer" goal of the savvy woman in the Art Deco age is to acquire a wealthy male who can assure her not only leisure but a lifetime supply of stylishly *moderne* accoutrements.

PLATE 1

"Nocturne" radio (model no. 1186, c. 1935); designed by Walter Dorwin Teague. (The Mitchell Wolfson Jr. Collection, Wolfsonian-Florida International University, Miami Beach. *Photo*: Bruce White)

PLATE 2

The Starfish Lady (bronze, ivory, onyx; c. 1925). Demetre Chiparus. (Gift of Stanley Siegel. Cooper-Hewitt National Design Museum, Smithsonian, New York City)

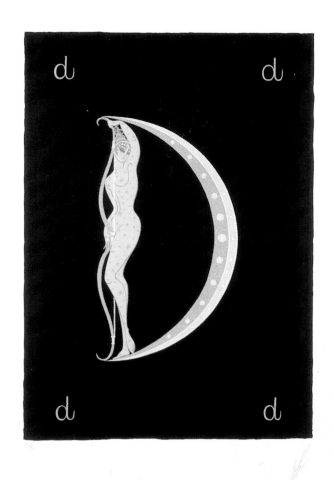

PLATE 3
Alphabet letter *D* by Erté. (Courtesy Sevenarts Limited)

PLATE 4
Franz von Stuck's painting *Die Suende* (*Sin*)
(after 1906). (Copyright (c) Frye Art Museum, Seattle)

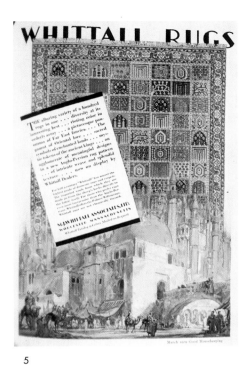

5

6

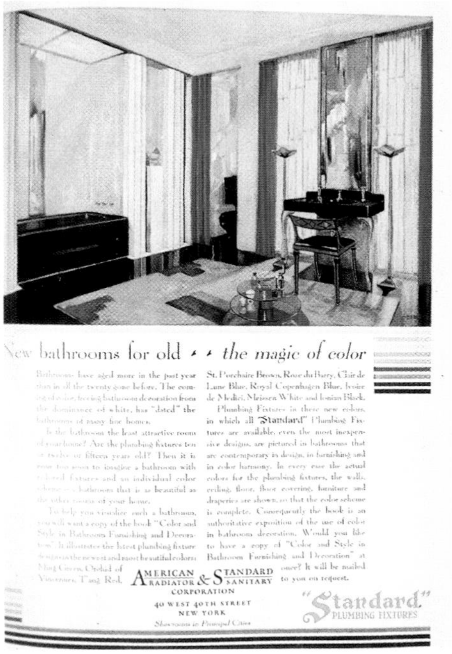

7

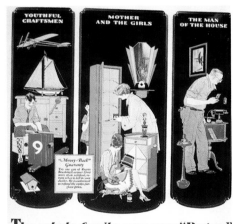

8

9

PLATE 5

Whittall Rugs advertisement (May 1929).

PLATE 6

Rayon advertisement (May 1929).

PLATE 7

American Standard Plumbing advertisement
(October 1929)

Plate 8

Rogers Tinted Lacquer advertisement (May 1929)

PLATE 9

Vollrath Ware advertisement (September 1929).

PLATE 10

Mural by Charles Stafford Duncan in the Ladies Smoking Room of the Oakland Paramount Theatre. (Courtesy Paramount Theatre of Arts)

PLATE 11

The glass "Fountain of Light" and metallic filigree curtain of foliage in the Grand Lobby of the Oakland Paramount Theatre. (Courtesy Paramount Theatre of Arts)

PLATE 12

The Paramount Theatre Auditorium's stage curtain, decorated with huge pyramidal leaves. (Courtesy Paramount Theatre of Arts)

PLATE 13

The "golden maidens"—a decorative motif on the railings and balustrades of the Paramount Theatre's Grand Lobby. (Courtesy Paramount Theatre of Arts)

3. DESIGN FOR LIVING

Marketing Art Deco to Women

Beyond selling women on the joys of department store shopping, Art Deco pack-
aging and advertising advanced a host of specific products for women which
ranged from those associated with her person (cosmetics, jewelry, and clothing) to
those tied to her home (housewares, appliances, and furniture.) Again, it was in the
pages of women's magazines and catalogues of the period (both before and after
the stock market crash) that this discourse of consumerism and material culture
was articulated. While, clearly, the most avant-garde and expensive objects sold
were aimed at the upper- and middle-class urban female shopper (and advertised
in such high-toned publications as *Vogue* and *Harper's Bazaar*), wide circulation
of the Sears catalogue made it possible for a broad range of American women to
acquire a degree of modishness. As Kenneth Yellis notes:

> Perusal of the Sears, Roebuck catalogues for the decade is very suggestive.
> . . . These catalogues were, presumably, important to women in areas and
> situations in which being strictly fashionable was not vital for their careers
> or social acceptance, such as women on farms or in towns out of the reach
> of the large urban department stores. But the styles in these catalogues . . .
> were no more than three months behind what was readily available in New
> York department stores. (1980:373)

Hence, a degree of egalitarianism reigned in the era's fashion system.

BEAUTY CULTURE

Keep young and beautiful, if you want to be loved. —Line from a song in
Roman Scandals (1933; directed by Frank Tuttle)

Given that Art Deco was linked in the public's mind with glamour and elegance,
it was attached to the marketing of myriad *beauty products*, ones often pitched to
the well-heeled female consumer. A *Harper's Bazar* ad from April 1926 sells
Houbigant perfume. The graphic is graced by a sketch of a woman dressed in a
flapper chemise, and states: "Today one does not tread a path of roses—that would
be passé indeed. Days—and nights—are fragrant now with subtle, intricate perfumes, cunningly devised to express the spirit of the smart modern world in a
dynamic age." A July 1927 issue of *Harper's Bazar* acclaims a scent called Bleu de
Chine by Isabey of Paris. Clearly, the perfume's name simultaneously invokes the
Gallic and the Oriental. Pictorially, the ad displays a contemporary sketch of a
female head—like those found on the façades of so many buildings of the period.
A Houbigant ad in *Harper's Bazar* of December 1928 promotes Au Matin, a bou-
quet that is "as *moderne* as the fragrance of a new day," and "has already achieved
a notable success in Paris." The bottle and its decorative case are embellished with
a stark geometric pattern that echoes the background against which they are posed.
The text of another Houbigant ad in *Harper's Bazar* of February 1929 has a Continental tone: "fragrance of flowers at dawn . . . finds *rendezvous* in a *parfum* and
poudre that are the achievement *moderne* of Houbigant and the notable *vogue* in
Paris" (emphasis added). An advertisement for Guerlain's Shalimar (from the
November 1929 issue of *House and Garden*) is illustrated by an abstract sketch
signed by Darcy, depicting a male hunter riding a heron; his figure is rendered in
the style of such Deco sculptures as that of Atlas in Rockefeller Center. The text
stresses the modernity of the scent: "The gay rebels who shook off the Victorian
yoke found their new daring incarnated in Jicky. The *elegantes* of today adore the
sophistication of Shalimar." An ad for another Guerlain scent, Liu, runs in
Harper's Bazaar of January 1930. In keeping with the perfume's Oriental name, the
ad depicts an abstract sketch of a Siamese cat—the very same figures that became
popular icons of the Deco style (as in Frankart bookends created by Arthur von
Frankenberg). Even the font of the word *Liu* is rendered in a geometric Deco
mode. Another Guerlain ad, again romantically illustrated by Darcy (and published in *Harper's Bazaar* of February 1931), portrays a woman enfolded in the
wings of an exotic bird. The ad copy foregrounds the female consumer: "She who
is exquisite forever seeks new elegance . . . " Finally, an ad for the Elizabeth Arden

fragrance, L'élan d'Elizabeth (in the February 1931 *Harper's Bazaar*), sports a highly modular graphic that exploits the perfume bottle's rectangular shape and stopper. Stressing Deco's associations with things French, the ad copy reads: " 'Tell me one English word that adequately defines *L'élan* please?' "

Ranking close to perfumes as "feminine" consumer products were *cosmetics*—often made by the selfsame companies. Articles in upscale women's magazines touted their importance for the contemporary woman. One in *Harper's Bazar* of July 1927 bears the subheading: "The Modern Mode Demands the Complement of a Harmonious Complexion" (Buchanan:58). In it, Lucile Buchanan calls "the art of facial grooming in America" one of "our modern problems" since, "the average woman to-day under the conditions of modern life . . . is liable to be lacking in color" (58). Merchandising companies also adopted a modernist aesthetic to advance cosmetic products. A January 1925 edition of *Harper's Bazar* carries an ad for Coty powder (translated, for effect, into French as Les poudres de Coty). It is illustrated by a frieze (in combined Art Nouveau and Deco styles) depicting two naked women. Likewise, a December 1928 issue of *Harper's Bazar* contains an ad for Helena Rubinstein which promotes several items reflective of the contemporary fascination with the Orient: Enchante Powder (which comes in a "Chinese Temple Box") and Mahatma Perfume. Other cosmetic containers display a geometric style: Valaze "Water Lily" powder, for example, is packaged in a hexagonal box with a triangular cover.

The pages of middle-class magazines also promulgate cosmetics. (In fact, during the Depression, Ponds sold itself as a democratitizing product that leveled differences between average women and the female Vanderbilts, Morgans, and Astors (Marchand:292–93). An ad in the April 1928 issue of *Good Housekeeping* peddles Armand Cold Cream Powder as a product for the "New Woman." As the copy reads: "For this era of woman's freedom and activity there is an ideal face powder. . . . It meets the different conditions of modern life to perfection" (191). Similarly, the March 1930 issue of *Woman's Home Companion* contains an ad for Ponds beauty products which bears a label designed in Art Deco font and adorned with a highly *moderne* sketch of a female face (53). Likewise, an abstract rendition of a woman's head is set against a modern background in an ad for Poudre de Fioret ("the creation of a famous French perfumer") that runs in *Good Housekeeping* of January 1927 (110). Moreover, an ad in the July 1929 issue of *Good Housekeeping* for Cutex perfumed liquid nail polish depicts a *moderne* sketch of a woman wearing Deco-style earrings, and the Cutex box and polish bottle are embellished with a triangle and sunray motif (171). Finally, certain cosmetic items in middle-class publications were sold through their association with the cinema. A photo of Clara Bow (an icon for the modern "flapper") adorns an ad for Lux Toilet Soap in *Good*

"Without smooth skin no girl can be really fascinating," *say* 39 *Hollywood Directors*

9 out of 10 screen stars use Lux Toilet Soap for smooth skin

NO MATTER where you see it—on the street, at dinner, on the screen—your heart beats a little faster in response to a faultlessly smooth skin, fresh and clear.

"The most important thing in making a girl lovely is an exquisite smooth skin," says Clarence Badger, director for Paramount—and sums up what leading movie directors have learned from their experience with the pictures. "Because beautiful skin charms so, it is a first essential in screen stardom," he continues. "Very, very smooth skin is the treasured possession of every screen star."

Especially in the popular close-up, must a screen star's skin be exquisitely perfect, if she is really to stir and to hold the hearts of her public. That is why 9 out of 10 screen stars depend on Lux Toilet Soap to keep their skin smooth and lovely.

Barry Bronson, Warner Brothers' popular star, says: "A star must have smooth skin. Everything shows in the close-up. And I find lovely Lux Toilet Soap wonderful for my skin!"

CLARA BOW, *fascinating Paramount star, in the bathroom which is one of the most luxurious built in Hollywood. She says:* "A beautifully smooth skin means even more to a star than to other women, and Lux Toilet Soap is a great help in keeping the skin in perfect condition."

Clara Bow

Of the 451 important actresses in Hollywood, including all stars, 442 keep their skin freshly smooth with Lux Toilet Soap. And all the great film studios have made this white, daintily fragrant soap the official soap in their dressing rooms.

These new incandescent "sun-spot" lights—film more highly sensitized than ever! A star's skin must show exquisitely smooth for the all-revealing close-up if she is to hold her public.

· Lux Toilet Soap

Luxury such as you have found only in French Soaps at 50¢ and $1.00 the cake . . . Now 10¢

FIGURE 3.1

Lux soap advertisement featuring Clara Bow (May 1929).

Housekeeping of May 1929 (fig. 3.1). The copy informs us that "9 out of 10 screen stars" use the product and that "39 Hollywood directors" have claimed that, without smooth skin, no girl can be "fascinating."

Aside from advertisements, articles in women's magazines also linked cosmetics to the Style Moderne. A December 1928 issue of *Harper's Bazar* contains a piece by Rebecca Stickney that reviews Lenthrick's "new modernistic salon" in New York City. Designed by Paul Chalfin, it contains such Deco touches as a color scheme of silver and blue, an abstract floor pattern, mirrored niches, and built-in furniture. Similarly, a column by Helena Leigh entitled "This Ageless Era," appearing in the March 1930 volume of *Harper's Bazaar*, shows a photograph of the new Helena Rubinstein salon with its Orientalist, pseudo–Middle Eastern arched entryway (70). The article also portrays another "modernistic room" (with blue glass tables) in the Salon of Kathleen Mary Quinlan (126). Finally, it informs the contemporary woman that Father Time has "become a frightfully outmoded old party in an age when grandmothers compete so successfully with their children's children" (70). Thus, obviously, Art Deco was associated with youth.

In addition to selling cosmetics, women's magazines advertised a variety of *accessories* for housing them, also done in the modern mode. A photo spread in *Harper's Bazar* of March 1929 is entitled "New and Decorative" and depicts a series of Deco-style accoutrements for makeup (e.g., powder and lipstick cases, compacts, etc.). In it, a Mauboussin powder case evinces an Oriental influence, with its "feathery design of Chinese character," and a compact by Chatillon is abstract in nature—made of "chic . . . black enamel . . . with green enamel corners and an ornament of marcasite." Similarly, an ad for Houbigant, in the May 1931 edition of *Harper's Bazaar*, depicts a "triple vanity" compact (of powder, rouge, and lipstick), whose exterior is decorated with "modernistic bands of color." Another Houbigant ad in *Harper's Bazaar* of May 1932 displays six compacts, all ornamented with the " 'Chevron' . . . A '*Motif Moderne.*' " Another ad for Houbigant in *Vogue* of June 8, 1929, touts "The Mode Moderne" and depicts a geometric powder case whose cover is a mass of angled lines. The ad copy calls it a "triumph of the mode moderne"

(141). Finally, an ad for Alfred Dunhill in the March 1928 edition of *Harper's Bazar* offers a profile view of a glamorous woman set against a black background—almost like a movie star portrait of the era. In the woman's hand, she holds a vanity—one, which we are told, is "slim, . . . trim and practical."

"MONITOR OF THE MODERN IN JEWELS"

Art Deco jewelry has always been in a class by itself. —Wendy Moonan (1997)

Along with perfume and cosmetics, *jewelry* was another consumer item associated with both Art Deco and Woman. Not surprisingly, it was aggressively marketed in the pages of magazines of the 1920s and 1930s—especially the upscale variety. A Mauboussin ad in *Harper's Bazar* of November 1928 bears the tag line "Monitor of the Modern in Jewels" and depicts some pieces done in geometric design. The ad copy emphasizes the French connection: "Originality . . . scintillating from every setting . . . dazzled a sophisticated America when it attended the exhibit of jewels which Mauboussin, the modern, brought with him from Paris." Another ad, in the same magazine (for J. E. Caldwell), links the Deco style to the Exotic. Accompanying the image of a piece of jewelry is a text which reads: "In the Oriental pearl necklace illustrated, charming contrast is added by carved emeralds of fine color—modern examples of a very ancient art which has survived for many centuries." Finally, an ad for Saks Fifth Avenue in *Vogue* of August 1, 1926, depicts Deco-inspired geometric bracelets with large links in oval, circular, and rectangular shapes.

Beyond advertisements, many illustrated articles touted jewelry's modernistic modes. One (in *Harper's Bazaar* of October 1930) is entitled "Precious Jewels Mark the Subtle Lines and Modern Note of Exquisitely Charming Femininity." Displaying jewelry rendered in Deco patterns, the ad's accompanying text emphasizes their geometrical conception: "A square-cut diamond is flanked on each side by baguettes, parallel and vertical" (100). Another article (entitled "Ornaments Strange and Exotic from Darkest Africa Influence Paris Jewelry") highlights the ties between Deco jewelry and "primitive" crafts. On one side of the page is a sketch of a bejeweled modern white woman; she is posed in front of a native black woman wearing tribal beads and earrings. On the other side is a sketch of another contemporary white woman; she stands before a South Asian female with a floral necklace. The accompanying text describes one of the modern jewelry pieces as a "slave collar of French Colonial inspiration"; another is listed as a "platinum necklace that bears the stamp of the French Colonial Exposition." A line of copy for the article boasts: "The French Overseas Colonies Lend Colourful Motifs to Modern Jewellery [*sic*] Design" (50–51). A third magazine spread (in *Harper's Bazar* of December 1928) is entitled "Blue and White" and depicts a bracelet, ring, and hatpin ensemble of geometrically arranged lapis, sapphires, diamonds, and blue lacquer. The text informs us that it is "designed for the woman who likes modern jewelry" (76).

More middle-class magazines and catalogues also extolled contemporary jewelry. According to Yellis, in fact, such accessories as costume jewelry (as well as hats, gloves, and handbags) were often used to extend and vary one's wardrobe so that "even the poorest women had it in their power to dress comfortably and attractively for an active life with minimal cost and care" (372). The *Sears Roebuck Catalogue* of 1927 displays three pages of Deco-influenced, moderately priced bracelets (733–34, 742). An article entitled "Jewels on Your Christmas List" in the December 1926 issue of *Woman's Home Companion* depicts photographs of Deco-inspired baubles for holiday gift-giving. A June 1930 issue of *Good Housekeeping* advertises Simmons Chains and Necklaces. The copy highlights a particular necklace and remarks that "this piece makes a really smart gift with its futuristic white gold-filled links and simulated crystals" (276). A photo spread in *Good Housekeeping* of December 1928 pictures cutting-edge, geometric-shaped necklaces, earrings, and bracelets. The copy hawks "Modernistic jewelry . . . of crystal-like squares and triangles" (72). Finally, in a "primitive" vein, an ad for Marcus and Company jewelers in *Vogue* of March 13, 1927, compares the modern jewelry wearer to the ancient one, through two abstract pictures of women—one sitting by a pyramid and another standing before a contemporary skyline. As I have noted, modern designers in the early 1920s were influenced by the discovery of Tutankhamen's tomb. "Suddenly, they were adapting Pharaonic motifs—Horus the falcon god, lotuses, scarabs and sphinxes—in their jewelry" (Moonan:E35).

FASHION SHOWS

The Pavilion d'élégance [at the Paris Exposition of 1925], decorated by Jeanne Lanvin, showed work of over 60 couturiers displayed on stylized models.
—Sara Bowman (1985:17)

News articles about *clothing* were also aimed at the female consumer of the era. While nowhere is there a fashion style identified specifically as "Art Deco" (as certain jewelry, decorative objects, or architecture were), there is a contemporary mode of dress that coexists with the broader Style Moderne.[1] As evidence of this, one advertisement (to be discussed later) calls an outfit pictured a "Modernist" gown.[2] Furthermore, the epigraph quoted above highlights the numerous couturiers who participated in the 1925 Paris Exposition. As Sara Bowman informs us, at the same time that the event was taking place, "newsreels were used to show the latest fashions in Paris to American cinema audiences" (72). Finally, many theorists have seen the emergence of clothing fads as the very hallmark of modernity itself. As Jean Baudrillard has noted: "Modernity is a code, and fashion its emblem" (1993:90).

While, certainly, the most cutting-edge and original couture was available only to upper-classes patrons, the development of a *prêt-à-porter* industry in the period meant that middle- and lower-class women no longer had to make their own clothes and could more readily enjoy a commodified sense of style. As a sign of this, the sale of yard goods and notions in this period took a sharp plunge (Yellis:378). The success of the ready-to-wear industry was also facilitated by the fact that American business was a master of mechanization, rationalization, and organization. Furthermore, the simplicity and sleekness of the modern look was hospitable to the mass production of garments devoid of intricate, old-fashioned frills. Thus, by the end of the 1920s a certain "democracy" reigned within the fashion system. As Stuart Chase remarked in 1929: "Only a connoisseur can distinguish Miss Astorbilt on Fifth Avenue from her father's stenographer or secretary" (quoted in Yellis:380).

A perusal of magazines and catalogues of the era reveals a variety of fashion trends that are consonant with the Style Moderne. High-end European clothing design was often tied to contemporary art. For example, a layout in *Vogue* of February 15, 1925, shows a sketch of a woman in an avant-garde dress patterned of triangles and zigzag lines. Its caption reads: "Modernist Art Applied to Painted Fabrics" (56). Similarly, a column entitled "Paris Paints Its Frocks in Cubist Patterns" discusses clothing design by referencing the 1925 exposition and displays dresses with bold geometric patterns. The article especially highlights the work of designer Madeleine Vionnet: "It is from . . . [modern] art that she borrows such details as the triangle embroideries, the little pleats grouped in waving rows or crossing one another in diagonal lines" (88).

We also find some fashion spreads that evince Art Deco's fascination with the

---

1. For this reason, in this chapter and others, I will often speak of "Deco-influenced" or "Deco-inspired" fashion or, alternately, of "moderne" or "avant-garde" fashion.

2. See the I. Miller ad in *Vogue* of June 1, 1926.

Exotic. One in the December 1926 issue of *Woman's Home Companion* (entitled "That Extra Touch") displays a dress embellished with designs of Native American arrows and feathers (91). In a 1927 *Harper's Bazar* piece entitled "Color Makes the New Clothes New," Marjorie Howard features a zebra-skin wrap by Max Fourrures, modeled by a woman posed against a white zigzag screen. The accompanying text reads: "It is entirely in the modern spirit, this use of exotic skins for evening wraps" (60). Beyond its rarity, most likely zebra pelt was favored for its chromatic and linear starkness. As Howard notes: "The ivory white and gleaming black of the zebra . . . produces an extraordinary effect" (60). In a similar vein, a *Harper's Bazar* fashion spread of May 1926 (with sketches by Erté) displays a female figure wearing earrings and beads which spell out the words *une femme étrange*; a caption reads: "An afternoon frock for the exotic woman . . . " (Erté 1926:112).

More specifically, the Oriental influence on clothing is also apparent in a column by Howard entitled "Paris Keeps on Shingling" (from *Harper's Bazar* of June 1926), which describes a white "pagoda" gown (of almost triangular shape), designed by Madeleine Vionnet. As the author remarks, it "definitely borrows an air from another world . . . but is, at the same time, extremely modern in feeling" (87). Likewise, a second fashion spread in *Harper's Bazar* of March 1925 (entitled "The Really Desirable Oriental Garments for Negligees Are the Fine Old Pieces of Antiquity") recommends using antique Asian garments (like boy's ceremonial coats) as nightgowns. The same Orientalist influence is present on the pages of more middle-class publications. The *Sears Roebuck Catalogue* of Winter 1930–31, for instance, promotes "stylish Japanese lounging garments" (348), and a Listerine ad in *Ladies Home Companion* of July 1929 depicts a woman in a bold Chinese-style robe feeding her bird.

Some fashion essays stress the use of metallic accents, clearly a nod to Deco's fascination with new industrial materials. In "A Folio of New Fabrics" (in *Harper's Bazar* of September 1927), the author speaks of "an intermingling of metal threads," and of the popularity of silver and gold "lamés." Similarly, an advertisement from *Good Housekeeping* of February 1929 touts rayon—a form of synthetic silk introduced in 1924.[3] The ad depicts a mannequin in lingerie sitting before a modern vanity, and the copy reads: "The magic of modern skill . . . in lovely underthings."

Other articles emphasize the geometric designs of fashionable accoutrements.

---

3. For entry on "Rayon," see *Encyclopedia Brittanica* (online version) at www.search.eb.com/eb/article?eu=64437.

A piece entitled "Accessories That Denote Discrimination" in *Harper's Bazar* of October 1928 presents photographs of a smoking ensemble which has a checker-board pattern that "gives a note of modernism to a three-piece set for the feminine smoker" and is done in "red and blue enamel with silver trimmings."

Fashion spreads also emphasize the androgyny of clothing—another trend in the Deco era. As we saw in chapter 1, this vogue was, in part, spurred on by women's growing role in the American workplace (and their demand for comfort-able frocks) as well as by their striving for civil rights equal to those of men. Inter-estingly, the trend affected not only day but night wear. A *Harper's Bazar* article of March 1925 ("The Little Revolution in Negligees") states that "the tendency toward masculinity in dress has made the strictly tailor made suit popular, has brought in the shingled head, the *garçonne* dress, the severely plain glove and shoe, and the one-piece bathing suit, but only in the realm of the negligee has it actually imposed masculine trousers." Significantly, a second article ("The Pajama-Negligee Has a Promising Future") in the same publication promotes pajama outfits made with fabrics designed by Austria's renowned and avant-garde Wiener Werkstätte artists.

Fashion articles and layouts in more middle-class journals also endorse the Style Moderne. One, for example, in *Good Housekeeping* of 1928 depicts two women posed in lounging outfits beside a Deco chair. The caption reads: "Many girls prefer pajamas and the Futurist model of broadcloth, above, emphasizes a print and plain combination, selecting a modernist print top and white trousers" ("Useful Christmas Suggestions..."). Another article by Helen Koues ("Fashion: Paris Establishes the Silhouette") in the February 1930 issue of *Good Housekeep-ing* displays a sketch of a modernly dressed woman posed on a flight of stairs. The essay reads: "Everywhere, all over America, women are asking the question: Will the new clothes remain? . . . Will the new silhouette last?"

As is evident from the titles of several articles already cited, numerous fashion essays in middle-class publications invoked *moderne* couture by reference to the two cities with which the movement was most identified: New York and Paris. Thus, a regular column appearing in *Good Housekeeping* throughout the 1920s is entitled "In the Smart New York Shops." Similarly, a fashion layout in the January 1927 issue of the publication says, "Paris Makes These Smart Clothes" (52); and a spread in the June 1930 issue shows the reader "Play Clothes from Paris," con-ceived by such modern designers as Schiapparelli and Patou.

In a similar vein, an American film romance of the period dramatizes the craze for Paris creations in the United States (this despite its Depression-era con-text). In *Fashions of 1934*, directed by William Dieterle (a European émigré),

Sherwood Nash (William Powell), an American con-man, concocts a scheme whereby he copies Paris fashions in New York and sells them to American women (as authentic) at a discount. When the European clothing arrives by ship, a delivery man on Nash's payroll brings the fashions to Nash's studio before transporting them to the shops of the French designers who have ordered them. At Nash's office, Miss Mason (Bette Davis), a young sketch artist, draws the clothing which seamstresses later copy. In one humorous scene, a wealthy New York matron who has bought a French designer dress at great expense interviews a woman for a maid's job in her house and finds, to her shock, that the applicant arrives in the very same outfit. Later on in the narrative, Nash decides to go to Paris to photograph the newest designs. Once there, we view a fashion show of chic clothing, set in the cutting-edge salon of French couturier Baroque (fig. 3.2). Interestingly, given what we have learned about the androgyny of Art Deco fashion, while Nash is in Paris, he learns the secret of the success of this designer. In order to create his daring new clothing line, Baroque copies and adapts the dress of men from the seventeenth through nineteenth centuries. Thus, in one of his fashion shows we see a revolving platform that is divided into sections. Over each is a scrim on which is painted a full-length picture of a man in some old-fashioned manner of dress. One by one, the scrims are lifted and behind each is a female model wearing a new Baroque design that plays off the arcane masculine costume. Another aspect of contemporary fashion that is mocked in the film is the era's rage for exotic ostrich feathers. As we recall, in chapter 1 Katharine Morrison McClinton described certain chryselephantine sculptures that depicted women in outfits "trimmed with several rows of ruffles, bowknots or ostrich feathers" (193). In *Fashions of 1934*, Nash promotes the use of such feathers in dress design because he has made a lucrative deal with an American ostrich breeder.

Beyond fashion columns, advertisements in women's magazines also promoted the Style Moderne in clothes and accessories. One for J. E. Mergott (in *Harper's Bazar* of February 1929) displays an abstract, collagist graphic featuring a triangular, metal handbag frame. Another for Worth (in *Vogue* of May 15, 1927) depicts a woman in a dress of abstract sunray patterning with a dramatic shawl. An ad for clothing by Jeanne Lanvin of Paris, in *Harper's Bazar* of October 1928, portrays a woman (in a taffeta gown with stark sunray decal), posed on ziggurat steps. Several ads for shoe companies (run in *Vogue*) are also modernist in style. One for Cammeyer (from April 13, 1929) depicts a quasi-Cubist sketch of a female nude accompanied by illustrations of footwear (22). Another for "Shoes by Saks Fifth Avenue" (in *Vogue* of March 2, 1929) portrays no shoes at all but only a highly

abstract circular sketch of a woman surrounded by shapes. Yet another ad for Saks Fifth Avenue shoes (in *Vogue* of March 15, 1927) portrays an illustration of a skyscraper (illuminated by Kleig lights) on which a man is posed holding a shoe. One ad for I. Miller (in *Vogue* of June 1, 1927) depicts a sun pattern on which shoes are poised on linear "rays" (14–15); the name of the company is done in *haute* Deco font. Another ad in the same magazine features I. Miller shoes posed on abstract tropical leaves (18). A final I. Miller ad in *Vogue* of June 1, 1926, depicts a shoe called "The Euclid," which is decorated in zigzag lines. The ad copy reads: "Geometric! One side different from the other! Whimsically adorned with diamonds, triangles, lightning zigzags in vivid, effect contrast! . . . for the fashionable Modernist gowns!" (8). Given that these ads for footwear are among the most elegant of the era, one might retrospectively harbor the suspicion that Art Deco merchandising had a virtual foot "fetish."

Middle-class magazines, too, promoted Deco-inspired dress, although the clothing was a bit more conservative in nature. Not surprisingly, many of the ads

FIGURE 3.2

Fashions of 1934: The salon of Baroque in Paris. (Courtesy British Film Institute)

and layouts again focused on the up-to-the-minute cities of Paris and New York. One ad for modern clothing in the *Sears Roebuck Catalogue* (Spring/Summer 1926) sports a sketch of the Eiffel Tower and claims that the fashions shown "originated in Paris" (24). Another for Whiting and Davis "modern metal and patent leather bags" (in the June 1931 issue of *Good Housekeeping*) has a tag line which reads: "Paris Says Women Will Spend Millions on Contrast." The copy continues: "News leaks out of Paris—another trend is fast gathering momentum—and presto it's all over America in print and pictures! Again Whiting and Davis is 'on time.' Once more the 'merchandise of the moment' is ready for you" (181). Another ad in the Spring/Summer 1926 edition of the *Sears Roebuck Catalogue* shows fashions "adapted from New York," and is illustrated with a skyscraper outline (3). And an ad depicting a photograph of a woman in a *moderne* fur-trimmed coat and cloche hat (in the Sears catalogue of 1927) assures readers that "New York's loveliest models have posed . . . in these newest coats" (59).

Fashion ads in middle-class publications are interesting for two other reasons: their practicality (as compared to elite journals) and their ties to the film industry. In shoe ads, for example, the pumps shown are heralded for their comfort. One for Martha Washington Footwear in the September 1928 issue of *Good Housekeeping* bears the tag line "Modern Manner Based on Comfort." Its copy states: "Now comes Style, tripping along in her gay, youthful way, declaring: Style in footwear begins with comfort" (235). Another for Drew Arch Rest (in the same issue of *Good Housekeeping*) depicts a sketch of a modern woman in fashionable cloche hat and fur stole reaching toward her feet. The tag line reads: "The Mode is measured by the Foot." The comfortable shoe displayed is described as "smart," "slender and suave in line . . . in the season's newest style" (289).

As for linking fashion and the film industry, ads for practical footwear assume the lead. A series for Foot Saver Shoes directly invokes the cinema. One is illustrated by a sketch depicting actors before a camera, ostensibly making *Lady Winde-mere's Fan* (1925). In it, a woman sports a turban-like hat and a *moderne* dress. The ad copy reads: "For the Movie actress who is constantly on her feet . . . comfort is imperative. Yet she must register grace . . . [and] poetry of motion. . . . Foot Saver Shoes ideally meet these exacting demands." Here, the reader is asked to identify with the chic movie actress as a stylish role model but is assured, at the same time, that she need not sacrifice comfort.

We might note that in addition to such print ads, fashion newsreels of the era linked stylishness with the cinema. In one such movie, *Fashion News* (produced by Fashion Features of New York and Hollywood in the 1920s), several actresses are shown modeling clothes in Technicolor glory.[4] Laura La Plante (1904–1996), for example, shows off a black-and-white felt chapeau. Raquel Torres (1908–1987) displays a matching hat and handbag adorned with felt floral appliqués. Finally, Ruth Elder (1902–1977) models several ensembles "pour le sport." In one segment, she emerges from an airplane as though she were the pilot. Clearly, fashion, modernity, and the cinema were seen to be related (and salable) commodities.

THE BODY POLITIC

It is not possible to conceive a garment without the body . . . the empty garment, without head and without limbs (a schizophrenic fantasy), is death, not the body's neutral absence, but the body decapitated, mutilated. — Roland Barthes (Bruzzi 1997:31; ellipses in original)

Beyond selling products to adorn the female form (cosmetics, clothing, and personal accessories), Art Deco sold the *modern female body* itself by using it as an ornamental icon in advertisement copy.

In some cases, as we have seen, it is the clothed female body that is displayed as part of a fashion layout or apparel advertisement. At other times, a woman is pictured solely as an ad's "protagonist," to sell some product unrelated to her person (e.g., a car, silverware, home appliances, etc.). In keeping with the modernity of advertising style and its associations to Art Deco and Expressionism, the bodies of women depicted are often somewhat distorted. Roland Marchand calls this style "grotesque moderne":

> It was the increasingly abstract portrayal of th[e] "high fashion" version of the American woman that advertising men effectively propagated. . . . Men were sometimes depicted in modernistic illustrations. But never did advertising artists distort and reshape men's bodies as they did when they transformed women into Art Deco figurines. (1985:181)

Primary among the elements of this metamorphosis was the elongation of a woman's neck, legs, and arms in advertising sketches. (Recall that earlier I discussed the fact that the flapper "look" moved attention away from the female torso to precisely these bodily locales.) Interestingly, the "grotesque moderne" body type connoted both trendiness and class, with illustrations of working- or lower-class

---

4. This film is distributed by Em Gee Film Library in 16mm under the title of *Technicolor Fashion Parade #1*. No specific date for it is given on the film or by the distributor.

women displaying a rounder, squatter form (Marchand:182). While there was a progressive valence to associations of the transformed female body with the flapper and the New Woman, there were also conservative implications to her advertising pose. For Marchand, her canted stance implied a certain dangerous imbalance, while her ability to blend into a modernist tableaux suggested her continual pliability. Finally, her status as graphic design versus human being tuned into notions of woman as mere decorative object (184–85).

Sometimes, advertising copy used the abstract female nude figure to sell products. A series of ads for the shoe department of Saks Fifth Avenue are among the most exquisite of these. One for the Biarritz shoe (in *Harper's Bazar* of April 1926) depicts two female nudes raising a leather pump into the air (like Atlas lifting the world). The ad copy (printed in an Art Deco font) is arranged to form a triangular shape (12). Another Saks shoe ad (in *Harper's Bazar* of July 1927) again depicts a female figure lifting a shoe, but contrasts it with a sculpture of a woman. The ad copy states: "There is a new spirit abroad . . . expressed by moderns in sculpture—and Saks-Fifth avenue in footwear." It deems the shoe's "slave-link ankle strap . . . decidedly modern!" (7). Finally, a Saks ad (in *Harper's Bazar* of June 1926) is for a shoe that is, significantly, called "the pagoda." It depicts three abstract female nudes: one holds the shoe and the others kneel and flank her on either side—like chorines in a Busby Berkeley production number. An ad for Delman Shoe Salon (in *Vogue* of November 1, 1926) portrays a female nude amidst bubbles and a seashell, holding a shoe in her hand.

A J. E. Caldwell ad from November 1928 (previously described) depicts a string of pearls draped over a bronze statue of a female nude. In a "curatorial" note, the copy identifies the piece as "The Star" by Harriet Whitney Frishmuth—as though to connect the jewelry to art. Another ad for the same company (in *Harper's Bazar* of December 1928) depicts a black silhouetted female nude, around which are shown a variety of Deco-influenced diamond pieces. Here, the bronze ("Joy of the Waters") is identified as created by Frishmuth.[5] Similarly, an ad for Stunzi silks displays a statue of a female nude alongside its Deco fabric pattern. In a 1928 photo spread previously discussed, fashion accessories are clustered around a sketch of a female figure that bears traces of both Greek and Egyptian styles ("Accessories . . . ," 110–11). An August 1927 issue of *Harper's Bazar* carries an ad for Houbigant fragrances illustrated by a sketch of a seminude abstract female figure in a Deco bathroom. An ad for Onyx Hosiery (in *Vogue* of October 1, 1926) is accompanied by a sketch of a nude female—supposedly Psyche. Numerous ads in *Vogue* for Saks Fifth Avenue (as in one from October 1, 1926) are illustrated only with an abstract

---

5. Frishmuth's work is discussed in Alastair Duncan's book *Art Deco* (1993:133).

drawing of the female body. An ad for Margot Landberg cosmetics (in *Vogue* of March 16, 1929) depicts a profile sketch of a nude woman kneeling by a pond smelling a lily pad which she holds in her hand. This is similar to a porcelain piece by Boyer crafted in 1927 (Arwas 1992:284). Finally, a column by Marjorie Howard concerning modern decoration is illustrated with a sketch of a bronze female nude statue located within a wall niche (Howard 1929).

Though the examples above demonstrate Art Deco's use of the female body (nude or clothed) in advertising copy, it may, at first, seem paradoxical, from a contemporary perspective, to link this icon to a female reader. For, from a traditional feminist viewpoint, we might have assumed that such quasi-sexualized images (most often designed by men) would have been addressed to a male audience. Certainly, however, the kinds of products that this female body sold (women's shoes, dresses, and jewelry) make apparent that its aim was to stimulate the consumer impulses of the woman shopper (presumed to be heterosexual in this era), who viewed the graphic image as a kind of "stand-in" rather than as an object of erotic desire.[6]

Aside from being used as an icon for ad or design copy, the modern female body was a site of real concern for women attempting to achieve the Deco ideal of a slim contour. In an article in the November 1928 issue of *Harper's Bazar*, Baron de Meyer (a famous fashion photographer) states that his recent trip to Europe reveals that there is "no hope of relaxation for women inclined to rotundity; that the comfortable curved lines were, as yet, not acceptable; that the pursuit after slenderness was as great as ever; that narrowness of the hip-line was even more accentuated than it was last season" (93). As though responding to his complaint, an ad for Bergdorf Goodman, in the same issue, touts the Juno Room, which provides "ready-to-wear [clothing] cut to the measures of the rounded Juno type of figure . . . not merely enlarged from those of the flat Diana type" (61).

INTERIOR DECORATING

If we are Moderns by taste and temperament, we are not likely to choose for our homes the furnishings of long dead eras. —Winnifred Fales (1936:170)

In addition to selling products for the female person, Art Deco marketed *merchandise for the home*, whose decoration was considered within the purview of

---

6. Clearly, a homosexual woman might react differently to the use of the female nude in advertising copy.

women. The mode favored in elite magazines was clearly *moderne* and aimed at the upper classes. Hence, *Vogue* of March 15, 1927, runs a piece entitled "Furniture in the Modern Manner" and states that "a new type of architecture is training the eye to appreciate furniture of modernistic simplicity" (84). Similarly, *Vogue* of May 11, 1929, carries an essay by Edith Morgan King entitled "Modernism?" in which she reports on her tour of leading decorative arts manufacturers in Europe and Scandinavia, claiming to have been a "convert" to modernism since the Paris Exposition of 1925 (104). Spaces and furnishings like those depicted in *Vogue* were, generally, out of the reach of middle-class Americans. Nonetheless, this mode of decoration was decidedly a "standard" to which average people might aspire. As evidence of this, an illustrated article by Helen Koues in *Good Housekeeping* of December 1929 is entitled "*Good Housekeeping* Studio Builds an Apartment in the Modern Feeling," and a photo spread in *Good Housekeeping* of September 1929 depicts how "The Studio Builds a Bedroom in the Modern Feeling." Likewise, a photo spread in the February 1935 issue of *Good Housekeeping* is entitled "Trends of the Day in Modern Decorating" and states that "the Modern style appeals to many, particularly to young people, because of its twentieth century tempo, [and] its simplicity" (69). Another article in *Good Housekeeping* of September 1935 (by Elizabeth Otey) is entitled "Modern Art Influences in Our Houses," in which she remarks: "The lines of the modern house are simple and good. The overornamented house of the [eighteen] eighties or the poorly imitated period house is no longer our ideal" (72). Finally, a two-page layout in *Good Housekeeping* of January 1929 touts "Modernistic Exhibitions in New York Shops" and depicts such high-styled objects as lamps, statuary, and furniture.

Also apparent in the pages of middle-class women's magazines was the era's interest in Oriental furnishings. An ad for Whittall Rugs in *Good Housekeeping* of March 1929 (see plate 5) depicts a colorful carpet adorned by an image of exotic mosques. The ad copy promises that the rug will present "a picturesque fantasy of Far East fabrics . . . the gamut of oriental lore" as well as "sacred symbols of enchanted lands" (n.p.). Likewise, a photo spread in *Woman's Home Companion* of July 1929 displays Japanese-style room screens decorated with paper appliqués (52), and an ad in *Good Housekeeping* of January 1927 peddles a Japanese-style rug from Mohawk. The latter ad is illustrated by a sketch of a Japanese woman posed beside a huge fan and urn (which invokes the theme of the rug pattern). The ad copy reads: "Among the pretty legends which cluster 'round the fan in Old Japan is that of the exchange of fans between . . . [a] beautiful princess of Nippon and her lover." Women's magazines of the era also featured pieces on major artists associated with the *moderne*/Oriental style. A spread in the April 1928 issue of *Harper's*

Bazar concerns the French craftsman Jean Dunand, known for lacquer work (on screens, furniture, and *objets d'art*) that "have all the best qualities" of Asian artifacts. As writer Gardner Teall notes, this mode of decoration is as " 'new' to-day as it was when the ancients employed it some seven thousand years ago" (114).

Particular domestic spaces of the contemporary house receive the greatest attention in advertisements and photo spreads, and are all associated with the female: *the bedroom, the bathroom, and the kitchen*. Even today, psychologists of home design acknowledge the gender-bias of interior decoration. As Joan Kron notes:

> You cannot decorate a room before you know its gender. The Western home may not be as rigidly divided into male and female space as the Moslem home where male guests must not get a glimpse of the women of the house, but we still make some sexual distinctions. Gender jurisdiction lives in our dens, garages, and basements which are still male territories, and in the kitchen, living room, and dining room which are still predominantly female territories—no matter how many women are bringing home the bacon these days and how many men are frying it. (1977:48)

The glamorous Deco bedroom of a chic home was also a *boudoir*—that is, a "private sitting . . . [or] dressing room" for its female occupant (Morris 1978:155). Because of this function (and of the era's emphasis on a woman "doing her toilette"), one of the most coveted furniture pieces was the so-called "vanity." An article in *Harper's Bazaar* of September 1932 is entitled "The Stitch That Saves Time," and advises women about beauty treatments that protect the skin (34). Across the page is a photograph of a woman (wearing androgynous white-and-black-trousered lounging pajamas), seated in front of a white modern, curvilinear dressing table with black trim. Poised on a modernistic backless circular white ottoman, she peers into a mirror. On the vanity counter are a variety of objects she will use for grooming, like those that were simultaneously promoted in advertisements within the magazine (35).

One ad in *Harper's Bazar* of November 1928 hawks Du Pont's innovative material Lucite, with a tag line which reads "New Accessories for the Modern Boudoir." The ad includes a sketch of a woman holding a Deco-style mirror, accompanied by the following text:

> Soft lights, rustling silks, lingering perfume . . . here in the boudoir, the modern spirit expresses itself in every intimate detail. And here lovely Lucite, keyed deftly to the modern mood, completes the harmony of color and design in dressing-table accessories of unusual charm.

FIGURE 3.3

Wallpaper Association of the
United States advertisement
(February 1929).

Similarly, an article entitled "For the Dressing Table of Today," in the March 1929 issue of *House and Garden*, displays a variety of mirrors and hair brushes adorned with Deco designs. Middle-class publications like *Good Housekeeping* also touted Lucite vanity pieces. A Lucite ad from December 1928 promotes Orientalist modern mirrors, with copy that reads: "In today's smart boudoir the new Lucite accessories . . . unmistakably belong" (178). Beyond furniture and objects themselves, other up-to-date design elements were touted for the boudoir. An ad for the Wallpaper Association, in *Good Housekeeping* of February 1929, claims that "wallpaper will modernize any home," and depicts a woman sitting at a modern vanity, beneath Deco light fixtures, in a room adorned with a diamond/linear-patterned wallpaper (fig. 3.3).

Beyond the boudoir, lavish master bedrooms, done in a *moderne* style, were featured in many upscale women's magazines. As Kron observes, though the bedroom is usually inhabited jointly in most homes, its gender is decidedly female: "That the husband is a guest in his wife's bedroom is obvious" (49). In Howell Cresswell's coverage of the 1925 Paris Exposition, he describes one opulent bedroom on display whose Deco roots are clear:

> The bed, the head of which is reflected in the mirror . . . is elevated in an alcove about the main floor and seems to have been placed on the inside of a silvery white shell. . . . The bed . . . with wave-like sides [is] entirely in harmony with the sea-shell idea of the suite. . . . A silvered railing separates the alcove from the main room and just under the railing is a low lounge. The dresser by the window and the low chest under the circular mirror, the chairs, tables and stools all follow a broad circular movement. (193–94)

In a January 1929 issue of *House and Garden*, its regular column on the "Modern House" features a "Lady's Bedroom." A sketch depicts a Deco-style room with a lacquered platform bed adorned by a checkerboard spread. On each side of the bed is a square nightstand and ottoman. The geometric theme reverberates in the doors of the wall cabinetry. In the article, we learn that this modern bedroom has "an air of seclusive comfort and luxurious intimacy" that contrasts with the "chill and forbidding atmosphere" of rooms of the past. This setting is especially appropriate for the "less robust and more highly strung personality which is representative of the 20th Century" (Bernhard 1929:68). More middle-class publications also featured up-to-date bedrooms in their articles on home design. The April 1928 issue of *Woman's Home Companion* runs a two-page photographic spread entitled "Modern Furniture Reflects the Changing Habits in Daily Living," which foregrounds a *haute moderne* bedroom.

If middle-class journals were to feature the latest innovative furniture, however, it was more often for the living room—a more public site in which to display modern purchases than the bedroom or boudoir. For example, in the monthly "Picture Section" of *Woman's Home Companion* of April 1928, a Deco room is exhibited (designed by Paul T. Frankl) with a skyscraper-style bookshelf, an abstract Orientalist screen, and a *moderne* chair. The text reads: "The moderns present new furniture for a modern age. Strongly influenced by Oriental design it is unaffectedly practical and restrained in form" (133). Contemporary accoutrements for the living room were also promoted. An ad for Kirsch Drapery in *Good Housekeeping* of January 1929 says: "The Modernistic spirit has been expressed and permanently accepted . . . in art . . . in architecture . . . in furniture . . . in dress . . . AND NOW Art Moderne at the Window" (207).

Not only were Deco furniture and belongings reviewed or featured in women's magazines, they were sold directly to the public through advertisements. One for Dynamique Creations in *Harper's Bazar* of October 1928 presents a vanity almost exactly like one discussed earlier. The ad text reads: "For the *modern* bedroom. Restraint . . . simplicity of line . . . nowhere does modernist furniture find its place more happily than in the bedroom" (159). Another (done in lush color) from *Good Housekeeping* of May 1929 promotes the new synthetic fabric rayon as a chic furnishing material (see plate 6). As the ad copy states: "The modern decorator chooses rayon fabrics."

In addition to having aesthetic implications, the use of modern furnishings was seen to have a sanguine impact on housework. In her book on interior decorating, Winnifred Fales states the following:

> One phase of the Modern Movement has not, I believe, been stressed as emphatically as it deserves. I refer to the actual saving of time and labor in the daily care of the home, consequent upon the elimination of superfluities, which means dust-catching details, as well as the number of objects in the room. Compare the smooth, unbroken surface of any piece of Contemporary furniture with the masses of carved and pierced ornament which covered the frames of corresponding articles in the period of Louis XIV. (1936:164)

Significantly, Fales bolsters her advocacy of modern furnishings to the female consumer with a "feminist" argument:

> There is no implication of laziness in the desire to minimize the number of hours consumed in mere mechanical routines. In these days of enlarged interests and responsibilities, when women are taking an active part in local and national politics, educational projects, club work, and philanthropy, to say nothing of the thousands engaged in business and the professions, it is essential that we conserve both time and energy by planning homes that require us to spend the fewest possible hours in waving a dustcloth and pushing a vacuum sweeper. Housekeeping carried to extremes becomes a disease . . . *Vive la Moderne!*" (1936:164–5)

The bathroom was another space identified with women, especially for its potential as a luxurious site in which to do one's *toilette*. A photo spread in the December 1, 1925, issue of *Vogue* depicts a *moderne* bathroom with the caption: "Striking Examples of Modernist Decoration in Paris" (72). An advertisement for the Mosaic Tile Company, in the September 1929 edition of *House and Garden*, pictures a stunning tiled bathroom, with a commode located in a curtained alcove and a tub set into a niche decorated with a cascade mosaic. An ad for Standard Sanitary Manufacturing Company, in the April 1930 issue of *Harper's Bazaar*, announces that "The Period of the Chippendale Bathtub is Drawing to a Close." Shown is a geometric tub beneath a modernist leaded glass window. Across the room is a sleek vanity; and, on the wall, a shelf holds a Deco lamp with a female figural base. An advertisement for Associated Tile Manufacturing Company in the August 1929 issue of *House and Garden* portrays a grand "octagonal bath-dressing room" designed by Frederick G. Frost. The space is declared an "architectural jewel," "one of the marvels of modern life" with its "springing arches," "cobweb [floor] pattern," and "octagonal tiled dressing table." A photo spread displaying the bathrooms of Mrs. Charles Payson emphasizes Deco's female iconography. A mural above the sunken tub of the master bath depicts a nymph with Eros. A "basin screen" concealing the sink's plumbing presents another female figure ("In the Manhasset Residence . . . " 114–15).

More mainstream magazines (for example, *Good Housekeeping*) also ran articles like "Renovating the Old Fashioned Bathroom." In this piece, the BEFORE picture shows a tub with claw feet, while the AFTER photo displays a *moderne* curvilinear tub with shelves built into the tub's tile wall. An ad in the December 1926 issue of *Woman's Home Companion* features Crane plumbing and heating equipment, and displays them within the context of a gorgeous modern bathroom with a geometrically designed floor. Another ad for Kohler in *Good Housekeeping* of June 1929 touts how their bathroom fixtures have been used in a museum display: "In the Metropolitan Museum of Art—Exhibition of a Modern Bath and Dressing Room" (fig. 3.4). Finally, an ad for American Standard plumbing in the October 1929 issue of *Good Housekeeping* is done in bold color and depicts a highly *moderne* bathroom with black tub and sink, a Chinese-red window curtain, and an abstract rug of green and tan (see plate 7).

The above description of a modern bathroom reminds us that along with favoring black, white, and silver, the Deco mode also promoted certain brash and exotic colors (like Tropical Green). Significantly, due to industrial advances in the printing trades, the years between 1924 and 1928 saw a huge increase in the number of color illustrations included in popular magazines (Marchand:122). This fact is apparent from certain advertisements of the period in which color is added to help invest the product sold with a sense of superior style. One for Valspar [Wood] Finishes in the May 1929 issue of *Good Housekeeping* displays a color palette (for floors, walls, trim, furniture, and accents)

and recommends bold tones for bathroom, kitchen, and sun parlor, while advising more muted ones for living and dining rooms. Similarly, a color ad for Rogers Tinted Lacquer in *Good Housekeeping* of May 1929 shows members of the family refinishing furniture. In the segment that depicts "Mother and the Girls," the women are shown painting a chest, vanity, and mirror frame in daring tones (see plate 8). Finally, an advertisement for Standard Plumbing Fixtures, in *House and Garden* of April 1929, promotes Orientalist porcelain fixtures of Ming Green or Ta'ng Red.

In some ads for the modern bathroom, hygiene rather than color or glamour is at issue. This connects to Art Deco's valorization of advanced technology. A September 1929 *House Beautiful* ad for Vitrolite (a wall and ceiling material) presents a tiled bathroom with a mirrored tub alcove, Deco wall sconces, and a palm tree mural. As a "new-day . . . structural material" with a "fire-glazed surface," Vitrolite is "impervious to liquids, moisture and odors." Vitrolite also has the benefit of sanitation: it "is utterly different from the porous, stain and odor absorbing materials

FIGURE 3.4

Kohler advertisement

(June 1929).

heretofore used in bathrooms." Similarly, an article in *Harper's Bazaar* of August 1931 reports on "Bathrooms [That] Glisten with Cleanliness." In more middle-class publications, cleanliness is also associated with the Deco-inspired lavatory. In two issues of *Good Housekeeping* (May 1933 and July 1933), Bon Ami cleansing powder is advertised with illustrations of modern bathrooms.

In a related manner, sterility is championed in advertisements pertaining to the kitchen—yet another room identified with women. In one ad for Williams Ice-O-Matic Refrigeration, in *House and Garden* of April 1929, we are told that "modern housewives demand a constant icy-cold" temperature since "they know bacteria are powerless in icy-cold" conditions. Likewise, in an ad for Monel Metals in *Good Housekeeping* of February 1929, we are told that not only is the substance (used for sinks and countertops) as "modern as tomorrow," but that it "always looks clean." The literature on kitchens also reflects Art Deco's fascination with the machine. A *Good Housekeeping* feature on the "Modern Housekeeper" (in the December 1928 issue) showcases several "up-to-date" cooking devices, including a contemporary-looking electric "sandwich toaster" (80). Similarly, an ad for General Electric/Hotpoint in *Good Housekeeping* of December 1934 profiles such kitchen machines as a "streamline design" electric iron and a "strikingly modern" Chromoplate electric percolator (151). As Fales states in her 1936 interior decorating manual: "Strongly as one may object to the term 'Machine Age,' when applied to modern architecture, there can be no doubt of its fitness when considering the kitchen." She continues: "Streamlining [is] now a commonplace in the design of trains and motor cars, and an accepted feature of kitchen equipment" (156).

More middle-brow magazines such as *Good Housekeeping* also hawked high-tech appliances for the kitchen, though, generally, a few years later than did elite publications. An article in *Good Housekeeping* of March 1935 entitled "Toast the Toaster" discusses "a pioneer among modern table appliances" and states that "the modern style appeals to . . . young people, because of its twentieth century tempo, its simplicity" (Taylor:85). Similarly, an ad for General Electric in the June 1934 issue of *Good Housekeeping* calls the latest refrigerator a "New Style Sensation." Fittingly (given the year), such stylish acquisitions would be practical in nature.

The final category of domestic locales associated with the Feminine is the children's room, which stylish women were urged to furnish in a Deco spirit. In an article in *House and Garden* of April 1929 entitled "Modernism Enters the Nursery," we are told that the "fanciful" quality of contemporary design is especially appropriate for babies. The walls of the room depicted are painted with a jungle animal motif, reminding us of Deco's interest in the Exotic and the Primitive. The same issue contains photo spreads for "A Modern Room for a Boy" and "A Modern Room for a Girl"—both done in Deco style.

Beyond being pressured to ornament her home in the Style Moderne, the woman of the 1920s and 1930s was urged to fill it with *contemporary objects*. A 1929 ad for Black Starr and Frost jewelers of New York City shows a sleek rectangular-shaped clock set with lozenge-like feet on a pedestal. The ad copy wonders what "modern goddess would not be enchanted with [it]?" An ad for International Silverplate from November of the same year touts "Silverware of Beauty and Distinction in the Tempo of the Times," and offers a highly geometric pattern. Yet another ad for trendy International Silverplate in *Good Housekeeping* of June 1929 sports the tag line: "Decorative Modern and in Keeping with Fine Traditions of Silversmithing" (fig. 3.5). An ad for Schumacher and Co. fabrics (in *House and Garden* of July 1929) promotes "A Superb Brocade with the Imperious Simplicity of *L'Art Moderne*," bragging that it has been created by French designer Paul Follot (1877–1941) and exhibited at the 1925 Paris Exposition. An ad for Cannon in *Harper's Bazaar* of February 1931 shows towels with a geometric border, deeming them "bold, blithe and original." A series of ads (in issues of *Harper's Bazar* from 1928 through 1929) promotes ceramic pieces by Roseville Pottery in the "Futura" series. One ad (from November 1928) states that they are "done in the modern manner . . . [and] exhibit the vogue of today and breathe the spirit of tomorrow." Another (from December 1928) proclaims: "What personality there is in these modernistic shapes!" An ad for Lovely Linen displays "The Modern Table Youth Inspired" and advocates purchasing cloths of brash "two-toned modernity." An ad for the Wallpaper Association of the United States (in *House and Garden* of September 1929) offers patterns in "Modern" and "Semi-Modern" modes and advocates "Daring papers—that go the whole way with the unfettered young modernist to make a background for furniture based on dynamic symmetry." An ad for Steinway and Sons (in *House & Garden* of February 1929) depicts a modern piano behind which is hung an abstract painting entitled "Le Sacre du Printemps" by Sergei Soudeikine. The ad copy mentions the controversy around Stravinsky's famous work (in collaboration with Diaghilev's Ballets Russes), noting that "its influence upon contemporary music has been widespread and profound." Clearly, Steinway wishes to associate the piano with modern art as well.

Interestingly, Steinway ran similar modernist ads in more middle-class publications like *Good Housekeeping* (for example, in the issue of December 1928). Likewise, other *moderne* home accessories were displayed in that publication: geometric clocks by Telechron (shown in an ad in *Good Housekeeping* of December 1933); simple serving pieces (shown in a photo spread in *Good Housekeeping* of Decem-

FIGURE 3.5
International Silverplate
advertisement (June 1929).

ber 1933); sleek candlesticks (shown in a photo spread in *Good Housekeeping* of November 1932); Mary Ann shell pans ("a note of Modernism in serving foods") shown in *Good Housekeeping* of March 1929 (fig. 3.6); and Roseville "Futura" pottery (shown in an ad in *Good Housekeeping* of December 1928). A color ad for Fostoria glassware in *Good Housekeeping* of October 1929 offers geometrically shaped Vaseline yellow, salmon, and light blue plates, cups and saucers, and proclaims: "Here is modern glassware in colors . . . shapes . . . patterns . . . pieces to delight every hostess." An ad for Rogers Brothers Silverplate table setting (in *Good Housekeeping* of June 1929) reads: "Time has done beautiful things to your table. Decked it with gay and modern glassware . . . changed the old 'china set' to a varied, colorful service . . . New style, new taste. . . . Now the VIANDE knife and fork. Totally new" (148). Another ad for Rogers Brothers Silverplate (done in color) in *Good Housekeeping* of September 1929 shows a modernist statue of a woman (wearing Deco-inspired clothes and jewelry) against an abstract background of new, streamlined tableware (102). The tag line calls the two a "perfect ensemble" and advises that women be as "vital" in their silverware as in their "personal wear." An ad in the September 1929 issue of *Good Housekeeping* displays Vollrath Ware enamel pots and pans in daring colors like gray and tangerine. They are "Modern and Correct," says the tag line (see plate 9). Finally, a photo layout in *Woman's Home Companion* of July 1929 exhibits table accessories that are "Modernistic in Color and Design," including a coffee serving set done in bold black and white triangles and diagonal lines (64).

Significantly, while most of the articles in women's magazines made the Art Deco home seem an elegant paradise, at least one characterized it as a site of stress. In "A Day in a Modern Apartment—How People Manage," published in *Harper's Bazar* in April 1928, Lucile Buchanan states: "No one who has not gone through it can imagine what a strain this Modern life is." She remarks that the contemporary bathtub must be "sneaked into by some perfectly stunning black and gold marble steps." As for the modern dressing table, she finds that its high-tech "knick-a-knacks" make it resemble a "glorified icebox." As for the up-to-date nursery, she mocks the fact that it is kept "extremely simple . . . just a few good futuristic rugs, a cactus plant or two, [and] some dynamic furniture" (110–11).

DIRECT ADDRESS

The Ford Tudor Sedan, for your own personal use.
— Ford Motor advertisement (1926)

That the majority of advertisements in women's magazines were aimed at the female shopper is accentuated by their use of direct address to the reader. One ad for the French Line's glamorous ocean liner *Ile de France* (in *Harper's Bazar* of March 1928) presents a sketch of a lady in a chic black sheath dress, entering the ship's avant-garde dining room. The text reads as follows:

> If you're modern, sophisticated, with a *"flair"* for clothes, a sympathy for the new, the smart in decoration . . . if you adore surprises in colour, line, conversation, or tinkling in a little glass . . . then you'll find your most inspiring background when you enter the hand-wrought iron doors by Subes of the Salon Mixte on the "Ile de France." Light ash and silvered bronze for the walls . . . ten tall windows, veiled by Rodier in white as frail as frost and curtained with the gayest flower-printed silk.

FIGURE 3.6
Mary Ann Shell Pans advertisement (March 1929).

Similarly, in an ad for *Harper's Bazaar* fashion services (in *Harper's Bazaar* of February 1932), a photograph of a Bauhaus-influenced room is accompanied by the text: "When you come to visit us, or to consult with us at *Harper's Bazaar*, this is where we shall meet you . . . in our Fashion Service Reception Room. It is a wise room, fashionably speaking." Likewise, an ad for Rogers Brothers Silverplate in *House and Garden* of October 1929 presents the new pattern of "Silhouette." In so doing, it addresses the female reader as a contemporary woman:

> Look at you, a modern. Look at all the lovely details that go to make you — a 1929 you. Paris has given [a] certain swirl and line to your hat. To your frock. Your jewels. Your footwear. Something crisp and clean . . . and right! Certain basic lines, lean lines, stream lines running sweetly through all of

them. That's modernism, in its newest, truest sense. And that's SILHOU-
ETTE . . . 1847 Rogers Bros.' new modern pattern [with the] same basic
lovely lines . . . For your dinner table and not for the woman who is ten years
behind you in thought. . . . Modern as this day and age, but ageless in style,
quality, and length of service. . . . The lines of SILHOUETTE are the sure,
basic lines of good taste, and good taste knows no calendar.

Middle-class publications also used direct address to lure the female consumer. A *Sears Roebuck Catalogue* of Fall 1929 sports an ad for chic fashions with the tag line: "Paris sends you this Dress" (117). Similarly, an ad for a fabric company aimed at the frugal female shopper states: "If you make your own clothes . . . Belding's Silks . . . are charmingly styled in the new manner" (277).

With the onset of the Depression, retail sales fell for the kind of trendy domestic and personal accoutrements identified with the opulent Deco style. By 1933, nearly half of America's banks had failed, manufacturing output had dropped by about 50 percent, and some 25 to 30 percent of the workforce (between 12 and 15 million individuals) was unemployed.[7] Hence, many American families had to engage in belt-tightening activities to "make do." As Susan Ware notes, even middle-class women engaged in small economies

> like buying day-old bread, warming several dishes in the oven at once to
> save gas, and relining coats with old blankets. Sheets were split down the
> middle and resewn to equalize wear; adult clothing was cut down to child
> size. . . . Such families still had food on their tables, but the meat was of a
> cheaper cut; the family went to fewer movies; if they had a car, they went
> on fewer Sunday drives; if they could not afford a large apartment, they
> moved to a smaller one. (1982:2)

Thus, with disposable income reduced, people continued to shop but spent less, and companies that sold consumer goods had fewer funds to devote to advertising on the pages of women's magazines. Endres and Lueck comment on this situation. In discussing *House and Garden*, they assert that while in 1930 the magazine was still "stuffed with advertising," such placements had fallen in comparison to those of 1929. Additionally, the magazine had problems sustaining its audience and cut subscription costs to attract more readers (Endres and Lueck 1995:150). As they continue: "Soon, advertising was off as well; 1932, 1933, and 1934 were difficult

---

7. See entry on "Great Depression" in the online version of the *Encyclopedia Brittanica* at www.search.eb.com.

years for the magazine. . . . The magazine did not recover from the depression until the late 1930s" (150). The Depression also brought "hard times" to another representative magazine, *Ladies Home Journal*. According to Endres and Lueck, "the *Journal* suffered from advertising cutbacks" (175). More significantly, the Depression era brought a change in the *Journal*'s leadership and perspective. With the editorial ascension of husband-and-wife team Bruce and Beatrice Gould in 1935, the *Journal* cemented its conservative perspective. Witness Beatrice Gould's vision of the American female:

> I believe it is a woman's job to be as truly womanly as possible. I mean to nourish her family, and to rest them, to guide them, and to encourage them. To be as pretty as possible, as helpful as possible, as loving as possible, so that if the whole rest of the world blacks out, each family has the center of warmth and comfort and cheer and tolerant good sense. (Endres and Lueck:175–76)

Thus, under the Goulds, the *Journal* campaigned for women to be "wives and mothers first" (176). Clearly, they did not privilege the "chic" woman as they once had, and "women were viewed as virtually the sole buyers of 'style goods' " (Marchand:131).

Thus, the economic slide of the 1930s had a chilling effect on the popularity of modernism—a mode identified with the energy of the Roaring Twenties and the post-World War I business boom. Nonetheless, as we have seen, the production and marketing of *moderne* goods continued. According to Marchand, "Even in 1933, most national advertisements offered no direct reflection of the existence of the depression" and, ironically, ad copy often "adorned the rich even more lavishly" than in the 1920s (288). Furthermore, through what Marchand deems the parable of the "Democracy of Goods," lower-class individuals were urged to buy products likely to be used by the upper crust (be it a bottle of Listerine, or a Hoover vacuum). On the other hand, ad-design became more "hardboiled" and cluttered, with sleek graphic aestheticism associated with the decadent twenties. Thus, in response to the Depression (and what retailers saw as "consumer constipation"), merchandisers did not give up; rather, they devised new advertising strategies (Marchand:300–301). An ad.in *Harper's Bazaar* of February 1931 for the magazine itself now urges female consumers to shop as an act of patriotism (not modishness) in an era of declining markets. Under the tag line of "A Quality Product Is Always a Sound Investment," the copy (formulated through direct address) reads:

Picture the effect of your individual purchase combined with those of like minded shoppers with a sensible perspective:

It means that thousands of unemployed can go back to work and that thousands of those now working full or part time can be assured of their jobs.

It means that factories, mines, railroads and stores can fill up their quotas of help with men who can again meet the eyes of wives and children without anxiety or evasiveness.

It means that groups of men step from the ranks of the unemployed to rekindle cold foundry fires, turn idle factory wheels, and resume their tasks of packing, shipping, selling and delivering.

It means that thousands of "white collar" workers, women as well as men, can be restored to their desks and counters and their self-respect.

A vast army of American workers to whom charity is abhorrent and idleness insupportable will eagerly set about restoring prosperity if you will help give them the opportunity.

Call it enlightened selfishness or call it a pleasant duty, but buy some quality product now . . . it's American . . . it's *noblesse oblige*.

Here the female shopper in Depression America is urged to indulge not in modern luxury (as "commodity fetishism" or profligate modishness) but in "enlightened selfishness," as consumerism meets citizenship and Art Deco drives democracy and recovery.

4. FILM MELODRAMA

Greta Garbo as Art Deco Icon

THE STAR AND THE STYLE

In chapters 2 and 3, I discussed the "selling" of Art Deco to the American female consumer and referenced the centrality of the department store in that commercial enterprise. Significantly, as a teenager living in Stockholm, a working-class girl named Greta Louisa Gustafson was employed by Bergstrom's—one of the city's major emporia (Paris 1995:23). When the establishment wanted a salesgirl to appear in *How Not to Dress* (1921)—a promotional film for their women's apparel line—they selected the beautiful Gustafson. She also was featured in the store's catalogue, modeling hats like those she sold in Bergstrom's millinery department. Years later, she recalled that among all her customers, she most "envied the actresses!" (Paris:24, 26).

Greta Louisa Gustafson, of course, eventually achieved the status of the women she so fancied—leaving Sweden in 1925 to become the film star Greta Garbo at MGM Studios in Hollywood. What is especially intriguing about the early years of her screen career is her continuing association with fashion—a factor that seems presaged in her early job as department store shop girl and mannequin. For, during the 1920s, Garbo would not only become a leading American actress but also a prominent on-screen symbol of the prevalent design style of the era—Art Deco. Her identification with this trend (and her constitution as one of its pivotal icons) is especially clear in those Garbo films set in the modern period, where her character is seen in contemporary context and garb.

In *The Torrent* (1926), Garbo's first American melodrama (directed by Monta Bell), she plays Leonora Moreno, a Spanish peasant girl with an extraordinary singing voice. As a young woman, she is spurned by Don Rafael Brull (Ricardo

The stuff [shown at the 1925 Paris Exhibition] was all made for exposition purposes and was not the normal output of commerce. It was extreme in its tendencies and not adaptable to the ordinary lives of our people. *Actresses* may temporarily take some of the stuff into their living quarters as a passing fad, but even they will soon replace it for another sensation.
—Arthur Wilcock (1925; emphasis added)

Cortez) because his betrothal would displease his overbearing mother, Doña Bernarda (Martha Mettox). Leonora leaves her village and travels to Paris, where she becomes "La Brunna"—a famous opera singer.

In early scenes of the film, when Garbo is playing a simple rural maid (fig. 4.1), her demeanor is reminiscent of that of Lillian Gish—subdued and Victorian.[1] But when Leonora appears in Paris, Garbo's bearing is totally transformed. Not only does Leonora become "La Brunna," but Greta Louisa Gustafson becomes Greta Garbo. Significantly, the structure of the film moves dramatically between these two characterizations. When Leonora bids farewell to her town, she sits on the back of a horse cart, a shawl draped over her head, Madonna-style. We are then told that "a curtain of gray years" intervened, and that "behind it, Leonora Moreno vanished" and "from it emerged a new star—La Brunna, the idol of Paris." We then see Leonora performing on an opera stage. Shortly thereafter, a title introduces us to "The Café Américain in Paris," a tony nightclub. La Brunna is shown in a stunning medium close-up, her hair slicked back, wearing a bold white-and-black striped fur collar (fig. 4.2). The café stage is done in a contemporary mode, with concentric arches and a tiered stairway. After watching the performance, Leonora approaches one of the players to offer him a tip. As she does so, we finally see the entirety of her dazzling outfit (designed by Kathleen Kay, Maude Marsh, and Max Ree): a metallic lamé full-length evening coat, completely trimmed and bordered with fur. Here, in Greta Garbo's first cinematic "glamour shot" (photographed by William Daniels, who would come to be known as her cameraman [Katz 2001:329]), she is adorned in chic fashion and inhabits a modernist space.[2] An Art Deco Diva is born.

---

1. Garbo later met Gish on the set of *The Wind* (1928), a film directed by her Swedish cohort Victor Sjöström.

2. Daniels was also later to work on the following Garbo films: *The Temptress* (1926), *Flesh and the Devil* (1927), *Love* (1927), *The Mysterious Lady* (1928), *A Woman of Affairs* (1928), *Wild Orchids* (1929), *The Kiss* (1929), *Anna Christie* (1930), *Romance* (1930), *Inspiration* (1931), *Susan Lennox* (1931), *Mata Hari* (1931), *The Painted Veil* (1934), *Anna Karenina* (1935), *Camille* (1937).

Throughout *The Torrent*, at heightened moments of the narrative, she returns to her Deco couture. After being reunited with Rafael in Madrid, the two plan to elope. But, again, Rafael is too cowardly to fulfill his promise. As Leonora futilely awaits him in her apartment, she wears a black-and-white geometrically patterned cape dress, with a stiff round ruffled collar. Thus, as she plays the "fool" to Rafael a second time, she looks like a Deco Pierrot or Harlequin (fig. 4.3). (Interestingly, a *Vogue* magazine layout of February 15, 1925 [entitled "Modernist Art Applied to Painted Fabrics"], depicts a fashion sketch of a woman with a short Garboesque haircut and wearing a dress with a similar pattern.)

But, clearly, it would not be interesting simply to enumerate the film scenes in which Garbo appears in Deco-inspired costume or perambulates through modernist sets. Rather, what I propose is to analyze the "semiological" role played by the Art Deco style in her films and the manner in which it "fashions" her screen image and star persona.

FIGURE 4.2
Garbo as "La Brunna" in *The Torrent*. (Courtesy Museum of Modern Art)

"AN ENTIRELY NEW FEMALE ANIMAL"

FIGURE 4.3 (*Opposite*) Garbo as a Deco Harlequin or Pierrot in *The Torrent*, with Richard Cortez. (Courtesy Museum of Modern Art)

The habit and the taste for freedom, adventure, and economic independence is becoming generated among millions of women who once merely trod the ancient beaten paths. —Havelock Ellis (1921:93)

In chapter 1, I discussed the association of the Art Deco style with the "New" or modern woman. There is no star of the late 1920s who so embodies this breed as Greta Garbo. In his biography of the actress, Barry Paris speaks of how Hollywood had trouble factoring her into its rigid dichotomy of mother versus whore. For she was "neither virgin, vamp, nor flapper, but an entirely new female animal" with "personality enough to make free love sympathetic" to a puritanical American public (Paris:117, 112). Realizing the uniqueness of her screen persona, Garbo wrote home to Sweden: "They don't have a type like me out here" (Paris:111).

Certainly, the publicity that circulated around Garbo highlighted her sophisticated persona. In a 1935 *Photoplay* article, Ruth Rankin fuels the anxieties of her married female readers in the wording of a caption she places below the star's photograph: "Maybe you are one of those wholesome-as-bread-and-butter women, and your husband does emotional cartwheels at the mention of the glamorous, languorous-eyed Garbo." Yet another *Photoplay* writer, Ruth Biery, in 1932 remarks that the "new type" of screen heroine Garbo represents "is an outgrowth of modernity"—the same trend that produced Art Deco (218). A caricature of Garbo done in the era by Nikolaus Wahl makes the actress's modernist figuration quite clear with its angular Futurist and Constructivist touches (Brokaw 1932:63).

In many ways, Garbo's independent female image also seems associated with her "foreignness," as though Americans could only tolerate such a risqué woman on-screen if she were not an "All-American Girl." Hence, the press of the period stresses Garbo's mysterious Europeanness, calling her "a Scandinavian blonde," a Stockholm "siren" (Palmborg 1930:36, 61) or "Venus" (West 1926:36). Another writer notes that Garbo's enigmatic aura attaches to her national status. As he remarks: "This much discussed mystery of Greta is no less than the mystery of . . . her own nation . . . Sweden . . . a country in which people relish silence and always go about swathed in dark shadows" (Cleve 1931:371). As evidence that Garbo fit into Hollywood's European "slot," as soon as Marlene Dietrich arrived on the scene, the two actresses began to be compared (Condon 1931).

The specter of the independent woman is apparent in numerous Garbo films of the period in which she plays a female who is unconventional on both the sexual and moral plane. In the words of Garbo's companion, Mercedes de Acosta, the actress played women who "lived gallantly and dangerously" (Paris:145). In *The Torrent*, Leonora abandons her sheltered rustic life to seek fame in a European metropolis. When we first encounter La Brunna in the Café Américain, other diners stare at her and remark that "she has had many affairs." Similarly, when Rafael flees to Madrid to elope with Leonora, a village elder chastises him for risking his honor "for a woman whose amours are the talk of all Europe."

Garbo enacts a similar character type in other movies of the era. In *Flesh and the Devil* (1927), she plays a seductress who ignites a feud between two lifelong friends. In *Love* (1927), a version of *Anna Karenina*, she plays a married Russian woman who has a sexual liaison with an officer. In *The Divine Woman* (1928), loosely based on the life of Sarah Bernhardt, she plays a country girl who is made a star by a womanizing impresario. In *The Mysterious Lady* (1928), she plays a Russian spy who, in the process of stealing secrets from Austria, double-crosses her lover. In *A Woman of Affairs* (1928), she plays a female whose scandalous sexual past destroys her marital future. In *Wild Orchids* (1929) she plays a wife who allows a flirtatious Javanese prince to court her. In *The Kiss* (1929), she plays a married woman whose dalliance with a younger man leads to her husband's murder. In *The Single Standard* (1929), she plays a footloose bachelorette who has an affair with an artist-adventurer, accompanying him to the South Seas. In *Mata Hari* (1931), she plays a spy whose erotic charm ruins both men and nations. Finally, in *The Painted Veil* (1934), she plays an iconoclastic young woman who reluctantly decides to marry and then quickly turns adulterous when she and her husband travel to China. In all these films, the "license" of Garbo's screen character is identified with an Art Deco aesthetic.

In some works, it is the strain of Deco Orientalism that takes precedence.[3] It is significant that when, in *Wild Orchids*, Lillie Sterling (Garbo) meets up with the roguish Prince de Gace (Nils Asther), she is accompanying her elderly husband John (Lewis Stone) on an ocean voyage to Java. When the prince romances Lillie on shipboard by moonlight, he compares her to Javanese women: "You are like the orchids of your country—you have the same cold enchantment . . . In Java the orchids grow wild—and their perfume fills the air." Later, when the ship docks, and she and her husband vacation at the prince's palace, she playfully dons a native costume (fig. 4.4), which he summarily rejects. Clearly, in the film and in American culture, Deco's championing of an Orientalist aesthetic (in fashion and domestic furnishings) is meant to infuse the staid Western world with the alleged carnality of the East. (As the prince tells Lillie earlier, "The East is a country of the

---

3. For work on Orientalism and cinema, please see Studlar and Bernstein (1997) and Hansen (1991).

353-81

senses—warm, mysterious—like the kiss of a lover.")
Though desirable, such sensuality can be suspect
when attached to a Western female.

Like Erich von Stroheim's *Foolish Wives* (1921),
Wild Orchids sees Lillie as somewhat justified in her
adulterous fantasies, given that her elderly asexual
husband completely ignores her and refuses to heed
her warnings about the lascivious prince. In a shipboard scene, for example, as she and John retire to
bed, she confesses that the prince has tried to kiss her.
John fails to hear her because he has fallen asleep. In
allowing a certain sympathy for Lillie's conflicted
desires, the film reflects cultural changes in contemporary attitudes toward female eroticism.

First, contraception relieved women of continual
fears of pregnancy. Second, Woman's quest for sexual
pleasure was acknowledged. As Samuel D. Schmalhausen noted in 1929: "The happy slogan of the
newer generation of feminists, honoring love as radi-
ant passion, is: orgasms for women" (380). Third, greater expectations were placed
on the conjugal bond. A newspaper article of 1919 states that "the rock on which
most marriages split is the failure of the husband to continue to be the lover"
("What Makes . . . "). Similarly, Havelock Ellis remarks in the early 1920s that it is
often a paramour "more than [a] husband that the modern woman needs"
(Ellis:101). This is, certainly, the situation confronting Lillie in *Wild Orchids*, as her
atrophied lust for life is awakened by the seductive Eastern prince. While, on one
level, the positive aspects of exoticism are identified with Art Deco, so are the negative. And, ultimately, the narrative validates the latter view by having Lillie
remain with her repressed Western husband at the film's end.

Similarly, in *The Painted Veil* (directed by Richard Bokeslawski), Garbo's character is an unhappily married woman who takes a lover when she and her husband
move to China. As she engages in adultery, she seems to "go native," a fact that is
registered in the progressive orientalization of her wardrobe. In one scene, for
example, she wears an outfit with a Mandarin-style collar and hat. In another, she
attends a Chinese festival dressed in a gown that (in a polymorphously perverse
fashion) seems inspired both by Chinese and Indian design (fig. 4.5).

Finally, *Mata Hari* (directed by George Fitzmaurice) is another Garbo film
that reflects an Orientalist Art Deco aesthetic. The historical namesake of the film

was Margaretha Gertruida Zelle, a Dutch dancer and spy who was in German service during World War I. The movie makes no attempt to foreground her European roots; instead, it offers us her adopted Middle Eastern persona. When we first see Mata Hari she is performing an exotic dance in a Parisian nightclub. As turbaned musicians play native instruments, and incense burns upon the stage, she enters wearing a long silky gown trimmed with sequins and layered with flowing scarves and shawls. On her head is poised a jeweled cap, topped with a multitiered spiked ornament. On her forehead rests a pendant that dangles from her headdress. Her face is framed by huge earrings. On the stage is a large Eastern statue to

FIGURE 4.7

Garbo in an Orientalist tunic

and pants outfit from *Mata

Hari*. (Courtesy Museum of

Modern Art)

FIGURE 4.8 (*Opposite*)

Mata Hari (Garbo) in the

apartment of Alexis (Roman

Novarro) beneath his reli-

gious icon. (Courtesy

Museum of Modern Art)

which she makes an offering. As she does so, she intones: "Shiva, I dance for you tonight" and mentions the "sacred temples in Java" (fig. 4.6). To emphasize the scene's exoticism, many shots are framed through the multiple arms of the statue. At one point, her routine becomes decidedly erotic, as she throws off her shawl (as though executing a striptease) and begins to undulate emphatically. Throughout the sequence, two men in the audience intently watch her perform—General Shubin (John Barrymore), an old lover, and Lieutenant Alexis Rosanoff (Ramon Novarro), a suitor-to-be. The latter gapes and gawks, entirely overtaken with desire for her. Not only is this the most extreme Orientalist moment in Garbo's career, it is also the campiest. Garbo is not especially graceful, and her attempts at Middle Eastern choreography are awkward. Though the film was a success, Paris notes that Garbo's "worst pictures often got the best receptions" (212). As a testament to the iconic status of the film, Andy Warhol immortalized Garbo's *Mata Hari* "look" in his silkscreen *Myths: The Star* (1981).

In later sequences of the film, while Mata Hari's garb remains exotic, it is somewhat toned down. After her dance performance, when she encounters General Shubin, she wears a less outrageous headdress as well as a relatively simple full-length, wrap-around lamé dress. Later that evening, as she mixes with guests at a casino, she wears a second jeweled cap with attached earrings, and a sequined tunic and pants outfit that fits her like snake skin (fig. 4.7). When Alexis accompanies her home, we glimpse her apartment, which is rendered in Middle Eastern style with arches, patterned doors, statuary, and heavy drapery.

In a later scene, Mata Hari wears another Deco costume—this time of a more contemporary kind. Her hair is hidden in a sequin-bordered skull cap. Jewels adorn the collar of her coat, the off-the-shoulder bodice of her dress, her belt, and the outfit's decorative appliqué. Significantly, it is in this Deco gown that Mata Hari comes to Alexis's quarters to seduce him and to coordinate the theft of his military secrets. In contrast to the Orientalist/*moderne* style of her own apartment, his rooms are arrayed with traditional paintings, including portraits of his ancestors. Most prized of these belongings is an icon of the Madonna, which hangs above a candle that Alexis has promised his mother would never be extinguished. When

Mata Hari rouses him, she orders him to turn off all the lights—even that of the shrine. "Put out that one too!" she commands (fig. 4.8).

As in *The Torrent*, this scene establishes an opposition between Garbo's character and her suitor's mother. Here, too, Alexis must disregard a maternal wish in order to be seduced. By emphasizing this antithesis, the films clearly conceive the modern woman as decidedly *non*maternal. This characterization is in keeping with Roland Marchand's notion that the tubular and angular shape of the "grotesque moderne" female (like Mata Hari) suggests "a rejection of the traditional motherly image" (1985:184).

Two other films of the period cast Garbo as a highly unconventional female. In *The Single Standard*, based on a novel by Adela Rogers St. John, she plays a free spirit named Arden Stuart. As the film opens, an insert reads: "For a number of generations men have done as they pleased—and women have done as men pleased." This statement makes ironic reference to the film's title and the fact that there is a *double* standard in morals and behavior. Arden is introduced to us at a fancy party set in a grand but traditional mansion. She is described by other guests as "a good sport," and the kind of female to whom "a man would never need to lie." After announcing herself "sick of cards and hypocrites," she leaves the gathering, declaring that she wants "life to be honest [and] exciting." She commands a chauffeur to drive her away at "70 miles per hour," and he obliges by taking her to a scenic spot. The two become amorous, though he cautions her against being seen with him. He asks, "What will people think?" and reminds her that, as a girl, she "can't get away with the things a man can." She responds disdainfully: "What difference whether girl or man? Both have the right to—life."

When Arden and the chauffeur return to the party, a scuffle ensues, as the mansion's owner fires the driver for overstepping his bounds. In a shocking development, the chauffeur drives off and crashes his car. An intertitle informs us abruptly that "the first chapter in Arden's life" had closed and that "months later she was still trying to understand it." Certainly, this is a very radical way for a film of 1929 to begin. Not only is the heroine immediately portrayed as promiscuous (before we have time to develop any sympathy for her), but her first lover is dropped entirely from the narrative and his fate is left hanging.

It is significant that, in the sequence which opens the "second chapter" of Arden's life, she resides in a Deco home—one adorned with pedestals and statues, geometrically patterned doors, modernist vanities, boudoir lamps, and platform beds (figs. 4.9 and 4.10). Furthermore, after leaving her apartment, she wanders into a gallery advertising (in Art Deco print) "Modern Art." It is there she meets the

FIGURE 4.9

Garbo in modernist lounging outfit in an Art Deco décor (*The Single Standard*, 1929). (Courtesy Museum of Modern Art)

artist-sailor Packy Cannon (Nils Asther)—a playboy-adventurer with whom she becomes enamored. In the film's portrayal of Packy, there are clear references to Paul Gauguin. One of Cannon's paintings portrays exotic native women, and he is about to set sail for the South Seas ("past pale dreaming islands—in eternal sunlight"). On a whim, Arden accompanies him on the voyage, and we see her on board wearing masculine attire. But after weeks of "strange lands . . . lonely seas . . . the fiery tropic sun," Packy asserts his independence as a maverick who refuses to be tied down.

Arden leaves and when she returns from her ocean sojourn, people snub her. When one of the town matriarchs decides to invite her to a party, another inquires: "You're not going to invite Arden Stuart after that disgraceful scandal?" Displaying a liberal spirit, the matriarch replies: "You'd be proud to entertain Packy Cannon, right? Well what's sauce for the gander is no longer apple-sauce for the goose." The soirée occurs in a rather traditional home, which shows clearly how the Deco aura is associated, *selectively*, with Arden. That evening she reencounters Tommy

FIGURE 4.10

The Single Standard: Production still with Mack
Brown in the foreground.
(Courtesy Museum of Mod-
ern Art)

Hewlett (Mack Brown), a former friend and suitor. He reveals his love for her, and
his wish to "take care of" her. Years pass and we find her married to Tommy and
now the mother of a young boy. Having failed as a wild Deco woman, she becomes
a conventional parent. As Barry Paris puts it, Garbo's character is a "girl who
demands sexual equality but settles for motherhood" (163). While Arden's home is
decorated in a neutral style, in one particular scene she wears a Deco-inspired
lamé coat dress—a signal that trouble lurks. When she learns that Packy has
docked in town, she agrees to meet him, and her passion is rekindled. At first, she
pledges to run away with him. But, on second thought, she declares: "One man
must always be first in my life . . . and he is—my son. My life belongs to others
now—not myself."

Several aspects of Arden's behavior are intriguing. Though she eventually
decides to stay with her family, it is fairly shocking that this wife and mother is
ready to abandon them. Even when she decides to stay home, her vow is to honor
her son, not her husband. From this, we surmise that, had not motherhood intervened, adultery would have been fine. Again, the polarity of the modern versus the
maternal woman seems central.

In the final segment of the film, we learn that Tommy perceives Arden's
renewed attraction to Packy but is unaware that she has, nonetheless, decided to
remain with her family. Being a noble man, he intends to set her free by staging a

hunting "accident" to release her from her marital bonds. As Arden realizes that Tommy's hunting trip is a morbid ruse, she is wearing a Deco outfit: a black and silver knit top, with zigzag design (fig. 4.11). Here, as things are most chaotic and unstable, she appears in *moderne* couture. Like so many American melodramas of the period, the film's denouement brings a conservative resolution. Tommy is saved as repression and responsibility triumph; the family unit is preserved.

Garbo's final silent film, and one of the last ever made in Hollywood (Paris:168), is *The Kiss*, directed by Jacques Feyder—a cinéaste who had worked in France with the school of "poetic realism." Here, she plays Irene Guarry, an independent French wife who has become romantically engaged with another man, André Dubail (Conrad Nagel). Like *The Single Standard*, the story opens with Irene meeting her lover. The setting of their tryst is, again, an art museum, which seems, self-reflexively, to highlight the film's high modernist décor. Interestingly, as Irene and André roam through the galleries, they pass paintings with Deco overtones: a Chinese print and a female nude. Though Irene and André temporarily terminate their affair out of a sense of propriety, another man immediately becomes enamored with Irene—Pierre Lassalle (Lew Ayres), the young son of her husband's friend. Though Irene is not truly interested in Pierre, she enjoys a flirtation with him, and promises him a photograph of herself to take back to college. One night, he appears at her home unannounced while her husband is out. When Pierre requests a farewell kiss, she obliges him. In the heat of passion, he oversteps his bounds and embraces her against her will (fig. 4.12). Her husband returns, unexpectedly, at this moment and witnesses the ambiguous scene. A fight ensues between Pierre and Monsieur Guarry and the latter is shot and killed. Since the homicide takes place offscreen, we do not know who has fired the deadly gun. When the police investigate the crime, Irene lies to them—pretending that she was alone that night and asleep when her husband was shot. A trial follows and André, a lawyer, defends her. When it is revealed that Monsieur Guarry was despondent over financial problems, his death is mistakenly ruled a suicide. After Irene is cleared of culpability in the case, she tells André the truth: that Pierre visited that night and that when her husband attacked

FIGURE 4.11

As Tommy (Mack Brown) feigns preparation for a hunting trip in *The Single Standard*, Arden (Garbo) wears a modernist sweater. (Courtesy Museum of Modern Art)

FIGURE 4.12

Pierre (Lew Ayres) attempts
to kiss Arden (Garbo) in *The
Kiss* (1929). (Courtesy
Museum of Modern Art)

the boy, she grabbed a gun and killed him. Despite her confession, she goes free, with André as her companion.

Many aspects of *The Kiss* are quite extraordinary, both on a narrative and a stylistic level. Again, the characterization of Irene is audacious: the opening scene shows her having an affair before we have even seen her with her husband. Furthermore, she feels no guilt or regret. It is her lover, not she, who decides they should no longer "defy convention." We comprehend, from the start, that Irene's husband is an insensitive bore, and we root for her liberation. Here, perhaps, we sense the influence on Feyder of the French impressionist film *The Smiling Madame Beudet* (1923), made by Germaine Dulac. But one illicit relationship does not suffice for Irene or for the drama. When her liaison with André is forestalled, another immediately ignites with Pierre. Again, she skirts the borders of indiscretion but, this time, her seductive games lead to death. At the end of the story (after telling the jury that she is "indifferent to public opinion"), she literally "gets away with murder" and is allowed to depart with her suitor. What, for Beudet, is only wishful thinking, becomes reality for the Smiling Madame Guarry. Even more brashly, a courtroom cleaning lady declares: "I don't blame her! Half us women would shoot our husbands—if we only had the nerve."

Beyond its plot, the narrative structure of the film is noteworthy for the manner in which it presents Irene's "testimony" about the facts of the crime. When the shooting first takes place, the camera remains behind the closed door of Monsieur Guarry's study, as the three central characters (he, Irene, and Pierre) battle it out. Hence, the spectator does not see what transpires. When the police later question Irene about the murder and she recounts her story, we see presumed "flashbacks,"supposedly from her perspective, to the night of the crime. Obviously, they are meant to illustrate her deposition.

When the police command her to tell them "exactly what happened," we see a flashback of Irene on the evening of the crime, reclining on a sofa, with a clock visible on a table nearby. From her positioning, we deduce that she can see it. The clock reads 9:25. When the police ask her, "What time was it exactly?"—we see a close-up of Irene (at the present moment) looking worried, responding: "Let me see." In her flashback of the clock, its hands spin wildly from 8:55 to 9:15 to 9:05—a trope that signifies she is deceiving the police by changing her story. We then return to an image of the murder night, as she crosses the living room and hesitates at the front door. An intertitle states: "I left the door open—no, I—," again revealing the slipperiness of her recollection. As the flashback continues, she walks into her bedroom and an intertitle states: "The windows were open, no I think they were—" At this point, the panes of glass magically go from open to closed (through a process of pixilation).

Clearly, through these inventive formal strategies, Feyder suggests that Irene is practicing deception, though at this point we do not know the facts of the situation. If we suspect she is lying, we assume it is to protect Pierre, and not herself. Whatever the case, these images violate the inherent "veracity" of screen imagery (even of a fictional kind) and instead communicate fraudulence. While many people point to Alfred Hitchcock's *Stage Fright* (1950) for pioneering this dramatic effect (of a visual lie), Feyder accomplishes a variation of it earlier on. When, after the trial, Irene recounts her tale to André, we finally see what really happened that night in the study: in the heat of the fight, Monsieur Guarry reaches for a blunt object. Afraid he might kill Pierre, Irene takes a gun from Guarry's desk drawer and shoots him. It is crucial that the instability of the text (its refusal to fulfill film's "promise" to "convince" us of the truth of its imagery) attaches, selectively, to the figure of Irene—a questionable New Woman. As in other Garbo vehicles of this period, the prime means for signaling her threatening modernity is through her association with an Art Deco aesthetic.

As in *The Single Standard*, some events in *The Kiss* take place in the home of someone other than the heroine. In an early sequence, Irene and her husband dine at the Lassalles—a staid country estate with all the trappings of tradition. The Lassalle abode is seen again in a later sequence, when Pierre returns home after his fateful encounter with Monsieur Guarry. The Lassalle residence contrasts starkly with that of Irene, which is decorated in high modernist mode. Hers is such a complex domestic space that, to comprehend its entirety, the spectator must "stitch" together diverse views offered over numerous sequences. Even then, it is not clear whether the final composite terrain is geographically coherent. In the Guarry living room and entryway are flights of stairs, done in zigzag style. A Deco-style female dancing figure stands on a console in one corner of the salon. The floors are made of some black polished material, a tone echoed in the archway to another room. Bold geometric patterns are found on a wall-hanging, a sofa, and some curvilinear chairs. Black sconces (resembling tiered triangles) adorn a wall. The top of a rectangular cabinet sports an exotic ceramic camel. When Pierre comes to visit, he enters through French doors decorated with stained-glass panels that might have been conceived by Frank Lloyd Wright. Monsieur Guarry's study has a geometrical desk with a triangular lamp. His bedroom walls are decorated with a linear ceiling border.

But it is Irene's boudoir that is most radically Deco—as though the more a room is associated with the female body, the more avant-garde its environment becomes. Irene's bed—whose base is done in black-striped lacquer—is set on a raised platform. At headboard level is a brash geometric design reminiscent of Native American iconography. A wall sconce echoes the same theme. A black abstract sculpture stands on a pedestal by Irene's bed, and the windowpanes of the room bear traces of an Arts and Crafts aesthetic. Some of the curved chairs are done in a fabric with a linear pattern. Some lamp shades reflect a geometric design, while others draw upon an African motif.

In one bedroom scene (after Irene and André have parted), the connection of woman and décor is made quite forcefully. An intertitle declares: "Weeks of loneliness—of social routine—of striving to forget." Then we get an extreme close-up of Irene's face as she adjusts her lipstick with her finger. As the camera pulls back over her shoulders, we realize that we are peering into the mirror of a luxurious Deco vanity with a mirrored base. On its surface are several modernist objects, and above those are V-shaped wall sconces. Irene herself wears a black and silver metallic off-the-shoulder dressing gown that lends a modernist touch to her body (fig. 4.13).

FIGURE 4.13

Garbo in *moderne* dress at an Art Deco vanity in *The Kiss*. (Courtesy Museum of Modern Art)

The sets for *The Kiss* (as well as for *The Torrent*) were designed under the auspices of Cedric Gibbons (1898–1960), the head of MGM's art department for some thirty-two years.[4] Under his contract with the studio, Gibbons was credited for all MGM films produced in the United States, although he played a prominent role in the creation of only some (Heisner 1990:341). The man who actually worked day-to-day on *The Kiss* was Richard Day (1896–1972), a designer who, during his long Hollywood career, worked not only at MGM but at Universal, Paramount, United Artists, 20th Century-Fox, and RKO.

While Gibbons did not work on all 1,500 projects for which he is credited, his broad aesthetic dictated the "look" of studio production—and it was one that was decidedly up-to-date. As MGM historian Gary Carey notes: "All [Gibbons's] designs were drawn in accordance with what he called his philosophy of the

---

4. Merrill Pye also worked on *The Torrent*.

uncluttered—they were clean, functional and often highly stylized, a look that was to cause a major revolution in movie decor" (Heisner:75). While some say that Gibbons attended the landmark Paris Exposition of 1925 (Heisner:78), others claim he did not (Wilson 1998:124). Regardless, the lessons of the show had a tremendous influence on him. Not only did his film work bear the stamp of modernity, but so did his own avant-garde residence, designed in 1930. As Beverly Heisner notes: "Art directors like Cedric Gibbons were credited, and correctly, with affecting public taste. *Theatre Arts Monthly* of October 1937 opined that Gibbons had introduced film audiences 'to the modernistic settings now so much in vogue' " (Heisner:39). Cedric Gibbons himself once said:

> In the past the designer of settings has built a notable background for the action of a story. Now he must go one step further; *he must design a dramatic background of corresponding value to the theme of the picture.* By that I mean a background that augments the drama transpiring before it. *The keynote of this is making the set act with the players* [emphasis added].[5]

Several things are thought-provoking about this statement. First, Gibbons imagines a set as "dramatic" as well as reflective of the narrative "theme." Second, he envisions the set as capable of "acting," in a manner commensurate with the players. Hence, if the set must act with the players, the players must act with the set—establishing an equivalence between them.

It is precisely this kind of "equity" that we sense in the dynamics of *The Kiss* and other Garbo films of the twenties and early thirties. The Art Deco sets do not merely provide an artistic backdrop for the actress, nor do they simply fulfill the need for screen realism. Rather, they bear great symbolic force: establishing parity between décor and heroine, marking both as avant-garde and perilous. In truth, modernism seems not only to affix to Garbo in these films but to *emanate from her*—to *constitute itself at the moment she commands narrative space.* In this regard, such sets fit the category that Charles Affron and Mirella Jona Affron deem "embellishment" in their schematization of filmic mise-en-scène: "Often opaque, the sets of these films call upon decor for the powerful images that serve either to organize the narrative or as analogies to aspects of the narrative. As a consequence, art direction in these films displays an elevated level of rhetoric, of style" (1995:38).

But an Art Deco aura attends not only to the architecture around Garbo but to her costumes. In *The Kiss* (as in *A Woman of Affairs, Love, Mata Hari, The Single Standard, Wild Orchids,* and *The Painted Veil*), her wardrobe was designed by

---

5. Cedric Gibbons, in telegram from New York dated March 9, 1929.

"Adrian" (1903–1959).[6] Adrian worked in Hollywood between 1925 and 1952 and was the chief costume designer for MGM. Earlier on, he had studied in Paris and was a great admirer of Erté's work. Like Gibbons's sets, Adrian's costumes were strongly associated with an Art Deco style. It is interesting that, as Hollywood's invocation of the Style Moderne grew stronger, America's influence on the fashion world began to supplant that of France. An article in *Photoplay* of April 1934 by William Gaines entitled "Hollywood Snubs Paris" is accompanied by the following display lines: "Movie capital is self-reliant as a style center. Designers no longer look to 'shabby' Paris for ideas." As Gaines notes: "The fact is evident that Hollywood now influences New York much more than Paris does" (Griffith 1971:192). "If the French capital wants to get back in the style swim [Gaines continues], it might do well to look over some . . . creations in the forthcoming Paramount productions" (Griffith:192). James Laver also credits broad changes in couture for minimizing the sway of France. As he notes: "A curious result of the new modes was that they notably diminished . . . the dominance of the great Paris fashion houses. The Frenchwoman does not naturally look like a boy; she did not fit into the new fashions as easily as her contemporaries in . . . the United States" (1995:236). Significantly, these statements reveal how the American fashion industry (historically subservient to the French), was attempting to assert the kind of hegemony long associated with the *U.S. film* industry which, by the 1920s and 1930s, had a strong foothold in France.

The most modern Adrian-designed outfit Garbo wears in *The Kiss* is the dressing gown she sports as she sits at her vanity after breaking up with André. But in other scenes she wears more tailored contemporary couture. When she and André have their tryst in the museum, she wears a simple form-fitting V-necked dress, accompanied by a fur stole. On her head is the requisite "cloche" hat that all but hides her hair. Such millinery (which favors a short coiffure) makes of the female face a simplified, abstract sculpture, and Garbo's stark bone structure is ideal for this fashion. A photograph made to promote *Mata Hari* clearly illustrates Garbo's "Deco" physiognomy (fig. 4.14). According to Michaela Krützen, her demeanor was highly constructed:

> Photos from 1927 show how Garbo altered her appearance during her first months in the United States to conform to an ideal of beauty which she did not naturally fulfill. Her hairline was evened out, her nose seems to be made narrower and her lips were sloped differently. . . . Garbo's previously dark and crooked teeth were capped. Garbo was thus brought into line with an existing ideal. (1992:69)

---

6. He was also known as Gilbert A. Adrian, but was born Adrian Adolph Greenberg.

How closely Garbo conformed to the coveted "look" of the era can further be seen from perusing women's magazines of the period. One sketch in *Harper's Bazar* of December 1928 hawks some modern jewelry designed with geometric patterns of lapis lazuli and enamel. The model's hat fits close to her head and the shape of her features are reminiscent of Garbo's ("Blue and White":76) A Lentheric Parfums ad in *House and Garden* of September 1929 depicts a sketch of a female head (as though without hair). Again, the abstract lines of the face are similar to those of Garbo as she appears in many photographic portraits.

In the scene in *The Kiss* in which Irene meets Pierre at a pet store, she wears an elegant black dress and cloche hat. The collar of the outfit is decorated with a black-and-white checked border that continues down the front of her dress. For an evening at the Lassalles, she wears a simple low-cut sheath with sequined straps, adorned by a jeweled clip. On the fateful night of her husband's murder, she wears a lounging dress whose modernity is registered in its multitoned geometric patches and in the asymmetry of its lapels. Significantly, when Irene stands trial for her crime and a court reporter draws the scene for the news, his sketches (seen in close-up) look more like fashion prints than like forensic documents.

For Adrian, Garbo's modernist costumes were not meant to be sensational for their own sake; rather, they were tied to the *theme of the film* and to the *actress's role within it*. As he notes: "If modern clothes are to be worn [in a movie], I must know at what point in the story each dress will be worn, and the type of personality the star will portray" (Watts 1938:55). Elsewhere, he remarks that all costumes were designed "to mirror some definite mood, to be as much a part of the play as the lines of the scenery" (57). Hence, when enacting a hazardously independent modern female, Adrian adorns Garbo in haute Deco couture.

While at heightened moments of her films (when she is most audacious and tempting), Garbo appears in full Deco regalia. At times when the drama requires that she "pay" for her self-determination and eroticism, her demeanor entirely alters. In *The Kiss*, after Irene has shot her husband and is interrogated by the police, her hair (which has, previously, been straight) is suddenly frizzy. This gives her face a softer, more Victorian, appearance—one appropriate for a long-suffering heroine.

When Irene is arrested for murder and awaits trial, she wears a simple black dress. When she takes the stand, she appears in another dark outfit, one with a flowing cape and a hat with a trailing veil (fig. 4.15). Significantly, when André visits her in prison, two nuns (in long black robes) accompany her into the room. In truth, as the narrative progresses and Irene confronts her crime, she herself seems to wear religious habits.

The same can be said of the closing of *Mata Hari*. When she is tried as a spy, she wears a plain black cape and skull cap. When she is taken to the firing squad (with hair as short as St. Joan's), she is dressed in black and escorted by nuns. In describing the simplicity of Adrian's costuming of Garbo, Michaela Krützen talks of the "monastic severity" of his outfits (84). Similarly, in describing Garbo's offscreen persona, Frank Condon notes that "a strong monastic veil surrounds [her]" (1932:31). The link here, between Garbo's screen heroines and holy "mothers," reminds us of the divide established elsewhere in her films between Art Deco Woman

FIGURE 4.15

St. Garbo: Irene on trial in *The Kiss*. (Courtesy Museum of Modern Art)

and maternal female. It is significant that only when the former is stripped of her sexual and modernist charisma can she be associated with any brand of "maternity."

A final instance of this "moral" transformation in costume occurs in *The Painted Veil*. When, for example, her character commits adultery in China, her wardrobe is one of Deco/Orientalalism. When her affair is discovered, however, and she must repent, she travels to a cholera-infested area of the country with her scientist husband. There she becomes a nurse and dons a nunlike white habit replete with hood (fig. 4.16).

OFFSCREEN SPACE

Beyond functioning within the drama, it is likely that both the Deco look of Garbo's costumes and the radical nature of the women she played attracted the female audience. And Garbo was specifically known for appealing almost equally to men and women. Leonard Hall (1930) makes this point in an issue of *Photoplay*, when he says: "Garbo and her work, in addition to being tremendous rousers of men, have more women adorers than any male star of the screen. Women flock to

FIGURE 4.16

Garbo in a monastic white
hood in *The Painted Veil*
(with Herbert Marshall).
(Courtesy Museum of Mod-
ern Art)

her pictures, to wonder, admire, gasp and copy. In every county of the country, slink and posture a score of incipient Garbos" (270). This view seems borne out by the statement of a young woman of the period who said: "I'll bet every girl wishes she was the Greta Garbo type. I tried to imitate her walk, she walks so easy as if she had springs on her feet" (Ware 1982:179).

With girls between eight and eighteen in the 1920s going to at least one film a week (Ware:179), movie culture had a great influence on fashion. As one girl of the period remarked about her fascination with Joan Crawford: "I watch every little detail of how she's dressed, and her make-up, and also her hair." In response to this, the clothing industry of the era often produced retail tie-ins that copied certain costumes from films. Jane Gaines (1989) writes about the commercial clothing lines that were linked to Garbo's appearance in *Queen Christina* (1933), directed by Rouben Mamoulian. As a writer stated in *Costume* magazine: "The movie stars of the 1930s were an immense influence on fashion all over the world. Whatever they wore on the screen and in real life was photographed and discussed in the countless fan and fashion magazines of that period—and an adoring public tried its best at imitation" ("Adrian—American Artist," 14). To help the female audience with its mimesis, certain companies (like Cinema Fashions and Studio Styles) began to produce retail tie-ins, sold at major American department stores such as Macy's (Eckert 1990:107).

Garbo's film costumes sometimes occasioned fashion uproars for the average American female consumer. One writer speaks of Adrian's role in creating the popularity of Garbo-style hats (a worthy fate for a woman who began as a millinery shop girl and model). As the writer notes:

> If Adrian's [Joan] Crawford designed clothes were widely copied by the merchants of Seventh Avenue, then Garbo's Adrian-designed hats gave the millinery industry a needed boost. The most spectacular one was what is referred to today in American millinery as "A Garbo"—Adrian's cloche hat that has become a classic from the film *A Woman of Affairs* [see fig. 4.17]. Widely copied here and abroad, Adrian was encouraged through letters and appeals from women of fashion to design other romantic and frivolous hats. He responded with the skull cap Garbo wore in *Mata Hari*, the pillbox in *As you Desire Me*, the Empress Eugenie Hat for *Romance*, and the turban for *The Painted Veil*. ("Adrian—American Artist," 15)

We are certainly reminded of the popularity of Adrian's trademark cloche when we peruse a two-page *Good Housekeeping* fashion spread of October 1929 entitled "Felt or Velvet for Winter Hats," which is replete with such habadasherie. Adrian himself comments on the star's effect on fashion: "Garbo," he says, "wears the unexpected. . . . It is out of the unexpected that style is born, and the influence comes" (Peak 1932:8). For his creation of Garbo's startling costumes, Adrian had to leap beyond the confines of present-day apparel in order to create something more radical. As he notes: "I get entirely away from current trends, for screen fashions must, of necessity, be designed so that they will be, dramatically, months ahead when they will be seen on the screen by the world at large" (Watts:55). In a similar vein, he also states:

> I never take any notice of prevailing modes when I create a costume for [Garbo]. . . . I do not want to create anything old-fashioned feeling. I want to create a style for Garbo which continues to be individual in spite of its styles. If something she wears is interesting to the great mass [of] people, it has its influence as a nucleus for style. We are conscious of that influence which is so striking at the time but after a while—we see that it is essentially a good line [which] if modified, can be used. (Peak:8)

It is perhaps this attitude that explains why Garbo appeared on screen in Deco-inspired attire long before the trend had assumed great force in the broader American fashion world.

What is ironic, of course, is that despite Garbo's screen influence on fashion, in her private life she bore no resemblance to the innovative, dashing females she played. Some writers of the time remarked on the spectacular transformation that was necessary to turn Greta Gustafson into Greta Garbo. As Mayme Ober Peak notes in *Ladies Home Journal* of 1932:

> Scarcely a day passes that some Cinderella-like transformation does not take place behind closed doors of studio wardrobe departments. The most recent metamorphosis of a screen personality is the case of Greta Garbo. When the Swedish star came to this country two years ago, she was a gauche, heavy, large-booted girl with long neck and ungainly manner of carrying her head. Today she is the most sensational, glamorous vampire on the screen: doubly interesting and significant when you contemplate that she has influenced styles as no other actress has done. (Peak:8)

Similarly, Adrian comments on his initial view of Garbo:

When I first saw Garbo, she looked at least ten years older than she does today. She was wearing narrow shoulders, [and] high Elizabethan collars. She was hiding her youth and her real self. . . . I created the broad shoulders for her which has become the silhouette of today. Broad shoulders give a smaller hip, great youth, independence, all of which are part of Garbo's character. (Peak:8)

Furthermore, in her offscreen life she had little patience for *haute couture*. As Leonard Hall writes in *Photoplay* of January 1930, Garbo

can dress as she darn pleases, and does. If she wants to wear twenty yards of opaque cheese cloth to a formal gathering, it's quite all right with us. In the greatest scene Garbo ever played . . . she wore a slouchy old tweed suit and a squashy felt hat. She never looked so mysterious [or] more alluring. (270)

Garbo herself confirms this disregard of fashion when she says: "I care nothing about clothes. . . . When I am off the set I don't want to have to think of clothes at all. . . . I like to live simply, dress simply" (Paris:267). Confirming this, Felix Cleve notes that "in . . . the little bit of life that belongs to [Garbo], she is a brave child who does not paint her lips, dye her hair, or use perfume. She lives ascetically and wears long skirts, dresses that come up to her neck, and low-heeled shoes. She almost always goes without a hat" (372). The latter fact is, of course, especially amusing since she caused a craze in millinery design. Finally, Virgilla Peterson Ross, remarks: "[Garbo] flaunts a high degree of neglect in matters of manner and clothing. She has seldom been seen in evening dress off the screen, and on the few occasions when she cannot avoid it, and is, at home, she kicks-away her high-heeled shoes in the middle of the evening and puts on bedroom slippers" (29).

   Also at issue in Garbo's personal raiment was the question of its "androgyny." Recall that, in writing about contemporary screen characters, critic Ruth Biery of *Photoplay* observes: "The new cinema heroine can take care of herself, . . . since she combines, with her mysterious allure, many of the hard-headed attributes and even some of the physical characteristics—the tall, narrow-hipped, broad-shouldered figure—of men" (218). Writing in *Photoplay*, Adrian (1935) touches obliquely on the gender ambiguity of Garbo's dress. As he notes: "Her wardrobe consists of tailored suits, various top coats of the sport variety, sweaters, slacks, berets, sport hats, stocking caps . . . and sport shoes. I don't think she has an evening gown and if she has I'm sure she has never worn it" (272). Invoking the issue more directly, Garbo's niece, Gray Reisfeld, denies any "transvestism" in her aunt's apparel: "She had a great interest in fashion, but it was her *own* fashion. . . . The pants, the walking suits, the lack of jewelry—all that contributed to what was thought of as 'masculine' but what was really just uniquely *her*" (Paris:268). Of course, the focus on Garbo's androgynous dress was undoubtedly fueled by rumors of her alleged lesbianism.

Not only did Garbo refuse to fit the model of star Hollywood fashion plate, she utterly failed to fill the bill as a glamorous socialite. Gossip about her penchant for solitude was legion. Frank Condon calls her a "shy, retiring, unsocial person" and speaks of her "remoteness and inaccessibility" (Condon 1932:31). Furthermore, Stark Young writes in 1932:

> The managerial publicity for Miss Garbo . . . has created unceasingly the theme of her solitude. She does not make a part of crowds; she has moments when she likes to be alone; she flees publicity; she likes to live privately. . . . At any rate, conceive of someone who stays in when he could go out, who could see people but thinks it a kind of communion, peace, rest or right to be alone sometimes! This has made Miss Garbo almost a national puzzle. (176)

Moreover, unlike the many actors who cultivated fan magazine coverage of their private lives (giving access to reporters and photographers), Garbo created an iron wall between her personal and professional existence. Her discomfort with the Hollywood scene was quite evident in the 1930s when she took extended breaks between shooting films. Mark Winokur sees her alienation from filmmaking as a recognition that she could never portray a maternal figure, a requisite role for the aging female star. As he notes: "Garbo cannot become a mother figure, so she must quit films altogether. We take her reclusiveness as the confirmation that her version of Deco will be erased" (1996:225). But her ambivalence to Hollywood culminated in her retirement after the release of *Two Faced Woman* in 1941, a box-office flop. *Costume* magazine notes how Adrian had been forced to simplify Garbo's attire for the film. The writer states:

> The advent of World War II eliminated the European market, a market that strongly supported the Garbo films. In order, therefore, to make up for this deficit (Garbo's films in America did not bring in their costs), MGM was faced with the necessity of producing a Garbo film which, to make a profit, would have to appeal exclusively to American audiences. The *humanizing process of changing Garbo from a lushly romantic, tragic figure into a modern American supermarket shopper* was strongly resisted by Adrian. [He, at first] . . . prepared a series of costumes befitting a star of her magnitude. However, the costumes were considered too glamorous, and Adrian was

ordered to design something more plebeian. Adrian realized that an era of movies had ended for him. He said, "When the glamour ends for Garbo, it also ends for me." ("Adrian—American Artist," 15; emphasis added)

Both Garbo and Adrian retired in 1942—as though the fate of the Art Deco film designer and star were conjoined. Thus, to add another level of irony to the situation, while Garbo personally eschewed the excessive glamour associated with Hollywood luminaries, such flair ultimately seemed requisite for her screen popularity. It was also essential to the craft of Adrian, who said, "I got out [of Hollywood] when I began to see the underneath of the gold plate" (Lane 1980:166).

But other factors may have contributed to Garbo's eventual fading from the American film screen. With the stock market crash of 1929 and the ensuing Depression, American society took a more conservative bent, with the city and modernity (those emblems of Art Deco) now associated with Wall Street and the nation's economic decline. One scene in *The Kiss* reverberates with this historic event. The reason why Monsieur Guarry is facing economic ruin and seeks a loan from Monsieur Lassalle is because of the world financial crisis. It is referred to directly in the film, when Lassalle takes the stand and refers to a "panic on the stock exchange." With *The Kiss* opening on November 15, 1929 (only seventeen days after the stock market crash), it marks an important cultural moment. For, with the coming of the Depression, not only Irene Guarry but the modern woman stood trial—figures whose "extravagance" was linked to the 1920s and a period of dramatic social and economic change. With a return to tradition in the 1930s, woman's position was strongly affected. Robert Daniel notes how the "alleged excesses of the flappers and the intrusion of women into the labor market provoked a [negative] reaction at the end of the twenties." As we have seen in chapter 3, women's magazines began to propagate an ethic of conventional family values (1987:87), calling for women to be "wives and mothers first" (Endres and Lueck:176). Dimmed was the call for women to be "stylish," "independent," or "contemporary"—the very elements associated with Greta Garbo's screen image.

Garbo and the screen characters she incarnated in the 1920s and 1930s were both compelling and troubling—like modernity itself. Throughout her film career there had been self-reflexive moments that sutured the actress's identity to those of the Art Deco women she embodied. We have already explored the parallels between Leonora and Greta (how "La Brunna" becomes a star at the moment that Garbo does). But this self-consciousness is evident in other texts. In *The Single Standard*, when Lillie Sterling is followed by a "masher" on the street, she brushes him off by stating: "I walk alone because I want to walk alone." Similarly, the boat on which she sails with Packy Cannon is called the *All Alone*. Such phrases reinforce Garbo's reputation for aloofness and independence—qualities which transgress the requirement for women to be cordial and social. In the character of Irene Guarry in *The Kiss*, we also find echoes of Garbo herself. The ostensible reason that Pierre Lassalle visits that fateful night is to obtain her photograph to take back with him to college. Before he arrives, she searches through her desk drawer and unearths a series of portrait prints that resemble an actor's professional 8 x 10 "glossies." Furthermore, when the murder scandal hits the media, it is a tabloid sensation (as though she were a star), and we see numerous headlines accompanied by snapshots of Irene. Pointedly, as though to register the public's discomfort with the Art Deco female, the film shows people using the newsprint to wrap their garbage.

But Garbo's disquieting status as Art Deco icon is telegraphed most clearly in a scene from *The Torrent*. When Leonora returns to her native village for a respite, Raphael surprises her with a visit. He comes to her forest cabin in the midst of a storm (the literal "torrent" of the title), and she lends him one of her Deco furs to wear for warmth. Though he is now engaged to another woman (one approved by his mother), he is again taken with Leonora's beauty and professes his undying love. She cynically tells him: "I believed in love once and love failed me." Flaunting her success as a diva and courtesan, she shows him a variety of expensive objects that she has acquired from admiring men. One gift is a modern sculpture of a female nude. He peruses it suspiciously, then casts his eyes, in a comparative fashion, upon her. Nodding to him, she replies: "Why not? A great sculptor made it. He admired my figure." Flashing an angry glance at her, Rafael retorts: "Everything they say about you is true!" He then hurls the piece down, outraged that she has posed for the bronze nude, an act that confirms his worst fears about her jaded morality. Stripped of masculinity himself (in transvestite drag no less, a "Venus in Furs"), he impotently storms out the door (still wearing her wrap). In this scene (where gender roles are perilously reversed, and Raphael wears emasculating modernist drag), the discarded Art Deco statue incarnates both Leonora and Garbo: a threatening effigy of the disconcerting Art Deco Woman. It lies there in its brazen bronze nudity—despised and feared for its dangerous vision of female sexuality.

But perhaps the coming of sound also affected Garbo's popularity, since the silent aesthetic seems most conducive to her screen allure—with its discourse of actors as pictorial elements formed of costume, posture, gesture, and stance. As William Troy of the *Nation* observed in 1934:

The suspicion increases that Garbo will never be so effective, either as performer or *symbol*, as she was in the old silent medium. Like . . . a number of others, she had built up for herself a style of acting which depended for its special forcefulness on economy rather than variety of means. She belonged, that is to say, to the pantomimic tradition of screen acting, the essence of whose quality consisted in the almost *hieroglyphic simplification* of actress and emotion. (112; emphasis added)

Clearly, the Art Deco style (as both visual design and semantic language) contributed enormously to the "hieroglyphic" and "symbolic" screen language that Garbo uttered—one that linked a vision of female modishness to a sense of dazzling menace. Finally, in Troy's word choice (his use of the terms *symbol* and *hieroglyphic*) in relation to Garbo, we are reminded of Erté's female alphabet and the sense that Woman (as "designed" by culture) is subject to a sociolinguistic formulation.

5. ART DECO & THE MOVIE MUSICAL

In chapter 4, I discussed how the Art Deco style permeated the film melodrama of the late 1920s and early 1930s and attached to its heroine, who was characterized as a dangerous modern female. Likewise, the movie musical of the era had strong ties to the Art Deco aesthetic. The genre's centrality to that mode springs from numerous factors. First, the musical (with its chorus line) had always depended on the female figure, which we have seen is a fixation of Art Deco iconography. In Ray Enright and Busby Berkeley's movie *Dames* (1934), for example, a showman (Dick Powell) asks his creditors: "What do you go for, go see the show for?" and answers: "Tell the truth; you go to see those beautiful dames." Second, many of the excessive fashions of the Deco era were first inspired by dance costuming—a crucial element of the musical film. Primary was the impact of Léon Bakst's designs for the Ballets Russes. Here, one recalls that in 1927 Marjorie Howard wrote in *Harper's Bazar* that the Paris fashion season resembled "a great ballet" whose *"leit motif"* was "clothes, clothes, clothes." The third reason that the musical favored Art Deco design is that one of the privileged subjects of its sculpture was the female dancer. Consider the titles of the following works by French artist Demetre Chiparus: *The High Kick, Genre Dancer, Egyptian Dancer, Russian Dancer, Pirouette,* and *Dancer* (Arwas 1975:17–23). That so many Chiparus works focused on choreography is no surprise, given that Paris in the 1920s was "inebriated with dance, in any and every form" (Shayo 1993:28). Beyond the Ballets Russes, there were a plethora of popular Parisian music hall venues, including the Folies Bergère (whose rue Richer façade bore an Art Deco frieze of an abstract dancer), the Moulin Rouge, the Olympia, the Alcazar, and the Alhambra (Shayo:30). Furthermore, some chryselephantine sculptures of the period were modeled on famous performers.

Some [chryselephantine statuettes] are right out of the Ballets Russes, others from a smoky Parisian nightclub.
—Victor Arwas (1975:8)

Chiparus's *Russian Dancer* portrays Nijinsky in Diaghilev's "Scheherazade" (Shayo:148); *The Dolly Sisters* pictures a celebrated vaudeville dance team (Shayo:167). Fourth, musical imagery (independent of dance) was sometimes a motif in Art Deco design. One mural of the period portrays a banjo, wood pipe, and saxophone (Hiller 1971:55); a statuette called *The Snake Charmer* shows a woman playing a horn (Arwas 1975:66); and a French glass sculpture depicts Pierrot strumming a banjo (McClinton 1986:135). Finally, the abstract, elegant sets of the musical film (shot in studios and liberated from the constraints of realistic décor) presented a mise-en-scène with maximum potential to draw upon the Art Deco aesthetic.

ELEGANT DECO

Almost every set and costume [of Astaire/Rogers films] fairly shouts "Art Deco."
—Ellen Spiegel (1973:22)

When one considers musical performers of the 1930s, two names that typically spring to mind are Fred Astaire and Ginger Rogers. Starting in 1933 (with *Flying Down to Rio*) and ending in 1939 (with *The Story of Vernon and Irene Castle*), the couple appeared together in a series of movies produced by RKO Pictures that soon became legendary works of the genre. Indicative of the stars' historical status, when Woody Allen made *The Purple Rose of Cairo* in 1985, a film set in Depression-era America, he depicts his heroine escaping her domestic and economic travails by going to the theater to watch Fred and Ginger dance to "Cheek to Cheek" in a lavish night club. Unlike some other musicals of the era (that featured the nondiegetic revue format or that favored the theatrically staged dance routine), the Astaire/Rogers cycle was known for its "integration" of narrative and production number. This stylistic unity followed from the fact that the films were essentially romantic comedies in which the love affair that blossomed between the leads was articulated through choreography. If, in the "screwball comedy," witty repartée functioned as a substitute for lovemaking, in the Astaire/Rogers musical that role fell to dance. When, in films like *Top Hat* (1935) or *Swing Time* (1936), which Arlene Croce feels "come closest to the level of the magnificent numbers they contain" (1972:56–57), Fred Astaire chooses to dance with Ginger Rogers, it is clear that he finds his soul mate as well as his artistic partner.

Both *Top Hat* (directed by Mark Sandrich) and *Swing Time* (directed by George Stevens) share certain production circumstances relevant to their conception as works of the Art Deco style. In both films, set design was supervised by Van Nest Polglase (1898–1968), who worked at RKO from 1932 to 1942. (In actuality, associate art director Carroll Clarke was responsible for the details of the mise-en-scène in each [Croce:77].) In both works, Miss Rogers's gowns were created by Bernard Newman. Finally, both films premiered at Radio City Music Hall (see fig. I.1)—that temple of Deco architecture: *Top Hat* on August 29, 1935, and *Swing Time* on August 27, 1936.

In both *Top Hat* and *Swing Time*, the characters played by Astaire and Rogers are rather middle-class individuals who manage to circulate almost entirely within the realm of the upper-crust, a social stratum associated with the glamorous Style Moderne. As Croce has noted: "In the class-conscious Thirties, it was possible to imagine characters who spent their lives in evening dress—to imagine them as faintly preposterous holdovers from the Twenties, slipping from their satin beds at twilight, dancing the night away and then stumbling, top-hatted and ermine-tangled, out of speakeasies at dawn" (56). In *Top Hat*, Astaire is Jerry Travers, an American dancer who is hosted at ritzy hotels in London and Venice by his wealthy producer-friend Horace Hardwick (Edward Everett Horton). Here, Rogers plays Dale Tremont, a young woman who also travels to Europe in high style as a model for the chic fashion designer Alberto Bedini (Erik Rhodes). Similarly, in *Swing Time*, Astaire plays a dancer and gambler named John ("Lucky") Garnett who, at the film's onset, is engaged to marry a wealthy young woman named Margaret (Betty Furness). Rogers, on the other hand, starts the film as a lowly dance instructor, Penny Carrol, whom Garnett meets and takes on tour with him to New York City to play the upscale Silver Sandal Café. Such plot devices allow Astaire's and Rogers's characters to inhabit classy Art Deco spaces and cavort in evening suits and formal gowns while still maintaining the middle-class roots that endear them to the mainstream American audience. In some of the films (like *Top Hat*), fashionable European locales and characters figure as part of the narrative, in line with Art Deco's association with Continental elegance. Though Rogers's characters ultimately choose Astaire's heroes as their mates, they frequently have European suitors as well (though these figures are often mercilessly caricatured). In keeping with Art Deco's Francophilia, in *Top Hat* Astaire sings to Rogers about "la belle romance . . . la perfectly swell romance."

In both films, an Art Deco sensibility informs the spaces in which the characters reside, work, and perform. In *Swing Time*, the Gordon Dance Studio where Penny is employed is rather modern and stripped bare, with a group of Deco female statuettes on a shelf on the wall. Similarly, Margaret's home (in which her aborted wedding to Lucky is to take place) is contemporary but understated in its design approach. The question of stylish dress is raised in the film through a comic debate over whether Lucky's wedding trousers should have cuffs or not, a controversy fueled by his perusal of fashion layouts in *Squire*, a men's magazine. The film's Art Deco promise, however, is not fully realized until Penny and Lucky arrive at the Silver Sandal Café where they are to perform. In their first dance number there, "Waltz in Swing Time," the nightclub looks quite modern and beautiful, with its glossy white floors and luxuriously tufted walls. As Penny and Lucky dance, their dark shadows are projected on the floor and move abstractly alongside them. Much, however, is made of the fact that the Silver Sandal is about to be redecorated so as to be the "finest spot in town." Thus, when Penny and Lucky give their next performance there, the set is transformed into an even more extravagant Art Deco construction.

A musical's "production numbers" are certainly its privileged moments for displaying design and architectural elements since, in such episodes, the ongoing narrative is interrupted to allow for the eruption of visual spectacle. While Van Nest Polglase gets credit as the art director of *Swing Time*, the sensational set for the Silver Sandal is specifically attributed to John Harkrider and pays homage to a real New York City haunt, the Silver Slipper, on West 48th Street (which was no longer in existence by the time the film was released [Croce:112]). Here, in the café's "renovated" form, the couple performs the routine "Never Gonna Dance," in which Lucky attempts to convince Penny to join him despite her anger at learning of his engagement to Margaret. As in most of the Astaire/Rogers movies, the number grows out of the film's drama. Rather than occurring on a formal stage, it takes place in a "diegetic" locale — here, a nightclub.

Many aspects of the sequence are striking in relation to Deco themes. First, its cabaret site is one of indulgence, glamour, and romance. Furthermore, the look of the club reflects Art Deco's simplicity. The space is geometrically organized and composed primarily of stark black and white forms. Its prominent, symmetrical, and meandering twin flights of stairs not only provide an engaging space for dance but echo Deco's interest in ziggurat and curvilinear structures. As Ellen Spiegel notes: "[In *Swing Time*,] round tables meet long vertical wall panels, curving double staircases have sharp-cornered steps, sinuous moldings end in angular corners, and straight lines, whether on walls, dresses, or furniture, clash with unexpected semicircles" (19). The tables in the Silver Sandal sport low-slung, globe-like modernist light fixtures, while the bandstand boasts an urban skyscraper motif. While column-like supports also give the set a traditional feel, the high-tech materials used in its formulation (glass or Bakelite floors, chrome accents) stress modernity.

Finally, the costumes in the production number are streamlined and elegant. While Astaire is dressed in a trim, black tuxedo, Rogers wears a soft, white, form-fitting gown—like one in Philippe's chryselephantine sculpture *The Swirling Dress* (Arwas 1975:49). Clearly, the actors' attire serves not only to render them chic but to display their dynamic, choreographed bodies. Interestingly, Rogers evidently tried at times to subvert the stark *moderne* simplicity of her dresses by adding "little bows and flashing jewels all over . . . just to make sure she'd be noticed by the camera" (Morley 1995:38).

The music that accompanies the Astaire/Rogers number is also important; for it belies a modernist sensibility. The Jerome Kern song "Never Gonna Dance" (which Lucky sings to Penny before they actually start their choreographed duet) is backed by a syncopated beat and draws upon the discourse of jazz and blues. These tonal roots resonate in the song's lyrics, which describe Astaire's heart as "a crazy drum—beating the weird tattoos of the St. Louis Blues." When the couple begins to move, however, the music abruptly recaps "The Way You Look Tonight"—a classical (and Oscar-winning) ballad with a far more conventional feel to it. In keeping with this, the couple finally performs a waltz to the strains of a (Johann) Strauss-like composition. The score for this number thus evinces a sense of modernist pastiche—like a Braque or Picasso collage.

While such production numbers (involving a heterosexual performance team) would seem to propose a certain equality between male and female dancers, in truth they reveal a hierarchal relation. As Sally Peters notes, in the landscape of ballroom dancing, "the female body is a prize actively sought by the male, who uses his power, his finesse, and especially his body as lure" (1991:151). This is precisely what happens in "Never Gonna Dance," where Lucky must literally "seduce" Penny into joining him on the dance floor. While, in the Art Deco film melodrama (exemplified by those featuring Greta Garbo), the heroine's association with modernity signals her status as risqué and dangerous, in the movie musical the Deco female is more malleable and manageable. While the characters Rogers plays are spunky and plucky—sophisticated and independent working women with their feet on the ground—they are not threatening, a fact that seems signaled by the prim and ubiquitous bows at Rogers's collars in so many of her screen outfits. At the beginning of *Swing Time*, Lucky pretends he can't dance and so solicits lessons from Penny. It is in this context that the production number "Pick Yourself Up" takes place, during which she instructs him to try again, despite his apparent clumsiness. When Lucky must reveal his terpsichorean skills to save her job, he immediately outdoes his "teacher" and gains control of the dance floor. Though Penny is morally liberated enough to go off with Lucky to advance her career (despite the fact that he is almost a complete stranger), as soon as their romance falters she runs into the arms of another suitor, the Hispanic bandleader, Ricardo Romero (Georges Metaxa). Clearly, she is not one of those aloof females (embodied by Greta Garbo) who choose to fashion a "single standard" of gender behavior. Furthermore, in both *Swing Time* and *Top Hat*, Astaire remains the prime mover of the story. The films begin with *his* narrative, in the course of which he encounters Rogers. Thus, despite the feistiness of her persona, the characters she plays belie a certain passivity in relation to Astaire's hero. Finally, there is a chasteness about the films that bespeaks the influence of the 1934 Production Code. This seems signaled in *Swing Time*'s musical number "A Fine Romance," which complains of a love affair "with no kisses." Citing an Art Deco maritime design legend in the song lyrics, Garnett laments that Carrol is "as hard to land as the *Ile de France*."

In many respects, *Top Hat* is more exorbitant than *Swing Time* in its appropriation of the Art Deco style and spirit. The very title of the film signals the world of glamour in which the narrative will take place: fancy clubs, hotels, riding stables, jet planes, and resorts. From the beginning to the end of the drama (despite the locale or the time of day), Astaire is barely ever glimpsed without the formal haberdashery that names the film. As he chants in the musical number "Top Hat, White Tie, and Tails": "I'm stepping out, my dear, to breath an atmosphere that simply reeks with class"—this despite the film's Depression-era setting.

Virtually every set in *Top Hat* (except that of the stuffy men's club) is cutting-edge *moderne*. Hardwick's hotel suite has white furniture that is curvilinear and low-slung. A white pedestal holds a porcelain female statuette with whom Astaire momentarily dances in the number "No Strings." A white Deco-influenced line drawing is painted on the walls of the suite, depicting a woman on horseback surrounded by graceful hounds. The inside door of the abode is decorated with an abstract (almost cartoon-like) version of a Roman man's head adorned by a wreath crown—evincing Deco's love of the "Ancient." On the inside door of the modern, chrome-appointed bathroom is a line drawing of a (pink?) flamingo. Dale Tremont's suite boasts an elegant, modern, curvilinear bed shielded by transparent curtains and set against a satin-tufted wall. Elsewhere is a recessed circular niche, outfitted with built-in shelves. The doors to the hotel elevators sport abstract pictures of male heads that seem of either Roman or Egyptian derivation. As a further bow to the Ancient/Exotic, a dark line drawing on a wall depicts silhouetted Siamese figures. Some doors in the hotel are emblazoned with abstract harp-like images, and some walls feature mandolins and flutes, all evidence of Art Deco's interest in musical motifs. Finally, the hotel lobby has a balcony whose railing is punctuated with porthole-like "windows," giving the space the look of a modern ocean liner.

When Astaire performs the number "Top Hat, White Tie, and Tails," which (uncharacteristically) is set upon a theatrical stage, he dances before an abstract background with a line drawing of the Eiffel Tower and some wispy clouds. At one point, the stage lights dim so that he appears to be only a black silhouette. But by far the most extravagant set in the film is that for the "Lido" resort in Venice. Here, rather than the geometric and minimalist modernity of the Silver Sandal Café (a space that favored black tones), we have an overwhelmingly white, multitiered, curvilinear set that bears simplified yet fanciful and rococo touches, ostensibly indicative of Italianate modernist sensibility. Highlighting its "kitsch" aspects, Arlene Croce notes that the set was accented with "candy-cane colors" and ended up looking like a "celestial powder room" (56). During the "Piccolino" production number, dancers (in folk dress) perform on a floor covered in red Bakelite, at the center of which is an abstract circular star design (Croce:76). As the women are spun away from their partners, they remain connected to them by ribbons, which, from a high-angle view, create a patterned motif. The nightclub in which Travers and Tremont eventually perform is more ornate than *Swing Time*'s Silver Sandal — but still contemporary in its mode of embellishment. When, at one moment, Dale Tremont steps out onto the balcony (which overlooks a park), she seems to have landed in a Maxfield Parrish canvas (like his *Daybreak* of 1922). Significantly, later in the film, when Hardwick gets a black eye, Travers tells him that it looks like a "Maxfield Parrish sunset." One other reference to modern art occurs in the narrative. When Bedini, in broken English, reads a telegram to Dale that he continually peppers with the word "stop," she says that it sounds like it was written by Gertrude Stein.

When Mark Sandrich first decided to set the film in Venice, he imagined some location shooting; but he quickly realized that the politics of filming in Fascist Italy would not be popular with American audiences. Instead, RKO decided that the film should be shot entirely in the studio. As Croce describes it:

> Two adjoining sound stages were flung open, a winding canal was built across both of them, and this was spanned by two staircase bridges at one end and a flat bridge at the other. . . . The set was the Lido seen as one huge gleaming fairground, with dance floors, balconies, and restaurants on terraces. It was built to the second story. . . . The water was died black. (76)

The topic of Deco fashion is directly raised in *Top Hat* by the fact that Tremont is traveling with Bedini, an Italian designer (another nod to the impor-

FIGURE 5.1

FIGURE 5.1

Fred Astaire and Ginger

Rogers dance at a ritzy club

on the Venice canals in *Top

Hat* (1935). (Courtesy British

Film Institute)

tance of European couture in the Art Deco era). The film, however, must "save" Dale from the taint of immorality (of being a "kept" woman), by making sure that we understand that her relationship with Bedini is purely a business arrangement. This fact is further emphasized when the film comically invokes his homosexuality. At one point, he tries to convince Dale to marry him because he is "rich and pretty." At another, when Travers breaks into his room to look for Dale, Bedini complains to the management that there is a man in his bed. At yet another moment, Bedini proclaims: "I am no man, I am Bedini!" In addition to indicating that Bedini is no threat to the romance of Tremont and Travers, the mockery of the designer's probable sexual orientation also tends to highlight the fact that women's fashions are often created by men who have no sexual interest in women.

Dale's costumes in the film include a Chinese-influenced lounging outfit— once more indicative of the era's Orientalism. In the "Cheek to Cheek" dance

ART DECO AND THE MOVIE MUSICAL

number, she appears in a stunning (and much-discussed) white gown elaborately decorated with gracefully flowing ostrich feathers at both the hemline and bodice (fig. 5.1). As we recall, in William Dieterle's *Fashions of 1934,* the American con-man, Sherwood Nash (William Powell), planned on making a killing by touting ostrich feathers as the be-all and the end-all of the design season.

EXOTIC DECO

Astaire felt a close affinity for jazz and the blues. And many of his . . . films found Astaire dancing in admiring counterpoint with black dancers or incorporating their motifs into his own work.
—Stephen Harvey (1975:68)

As Arlene Croce has noted, Polglase's "Big White Set"—so evident in *Top Hat* and *Swing Time*—became a "fixed architectural institution" that appeared "in one form or another in nearly every Astaire-Rogers film" (25). But mise-en-scène was not the only thing "white" in the Astaire/Rogers musicals—so was the race of its typical cast. The upscale world in which Astaire and Rogers circulated was quintessentially one of pure Anglo-Saxon Protestantism. Occasionally, the films yield a degrading "bit part" to a black actor. In *Swing Time,* Ricardo Romero has a black man-servant. In *Top Hat,* however, Horace Hardwick is tended by Bates (Eric Blore), a white British valet.

As mentioned earlier, there was, however, a certain jazz influence to the music scored in the Astaire/Rogers films, as there was to most American popular music of the time—especially that authored by Jewish Tin Pan Alley composers like Irving Berlin (e.g., for *Top Hat*), George Gershwin (e.g., for *Shall We Dance?* [1937]), or Jerome Kern (e.g., for *Swing Time*). (See Gabbard [1996] and Rogin [1996].) In fact, the very first sound musical film—*The Jazz Singer* (1927), with a score by Irving Berlin, James V. Monaco, and Louis Silvers— featured Al Jolson as a cantor's son who wished to be a ragtime performer. In *Swing Time,* this subterranean jazz influence erupts in the "Bojangles of Harlem" number in which Astaire dances a "homage" to the heralded black performer Bill Robinson, famous for his appearances in such films as *Dixiana* (1930), *Harlem Is Heaven* (1932), *The Little Colonel* (1935), and *The Littlest Rebel* (1935). In terms of its stylistic (versus ideological) conception, the "Bojangles" routine is one of the most avant-garde numbers in *Swing Time.* After a chorus line of women in "cake walk" outfits execute some dance steps, we see a geometric linear background. Two panels separate (to the beat of African-sounding drums) and a huge, grotesque (and racist) synthetic head of a black man appears on the stage adorned by a canted derby hat and large lips. The hat is removed and the head transmutes into the soles of two shoes attached to absurdly long legs, at the top of which sits Fred Astaire in Jolsonian blackface. His dummy legs are then pulled away, and he begins to dance a Robinson-like tap routine against a linear white-and-black background. As he moves, he tap-dances on a floor decorated with geometric shapes. At a certain point in the number, a faux "shadow" of Astaire appears behind him (really a silhouetted process shot). At first the two icons dance in unison—one in the foreground and one in the background—but then they follow different steps and go "out of synch." By the end of the number, Astaire has three identical black shadows dancing behind him. This scene is not only a special effects *tour de force* but a symbolic revelation of a major "shadow" influence on the Art Deco style— the music and dance of American blacks. As Katharine Morrison McClinton notes, in the 1920s "everything Negro came into fashion"—jazz music as well as dances including the black bottom, the Charleston, and the turkey trot (9). For this reason, many works of chryselephantine sculpture in the era "reflect the interest in . . . nightclubs and dance crazes of the new Jazz Age" (Duncan 1988a:122). Similarly, certain porcelain figures depict jazz musicians playing various instruments (112).

African sources were also numerous in the Art Deco era. This is not surprising given that important exhibitions like the Paris Exposition Coloniale of 1931 were launched in Europe during the period (McClinton:9; Raulet 1985:41). In cataloging such themes, one thinks of the work of black American artist Sargent Johnson, who fashioned ceramic and metal sculptures as well as mural bas-reliefs. One of his terra-cotta busts from 1933 is entitled *Negro Woman* and shows the traces of an African mask. As Eva Weber notes:

> With these heads, which he also made in copper, Sargent Johnson drew on African primitive art as an appropriate antecedent to express the growing pride of Afro-Americans in their ethnic origins. . . . Johnson's heads were elegantly idealized; they depicted not individuals but noble types representative of the dignity and rich heritage of the black race. (1985:113)

Aaron Douglas, Charles Alston, Archibald Motley, Richmond Barthe, and Augusta Savage were other artists of the Harlem Renaissance who sought African undercurrents in their work (Weber:113). Such references were also apparent in major literary works of the modernist era—for example, in *Women in Love* by D. H.

Lawrence (1920). In one passage, Rupert Birkin recalls a "primitive" statue that he has seen at a friend's apartment:

> He remembered the African fetishes he had seen at Halliday's so often. There came back to him one, a statuette about two feet high, a tall, slim, elegant figure, from West Africa, in dark wood, glossy and suave. It was a woman, with hair dressed high, like a melon-shaped dome. . . . Her body was long and elegant, her face was crushed tiny like a beetle's, she had rows of round heavy collars, like a column of quoits, on her neck. He remembered her astonishing cultured elegance, her diminished, beetle face, the astounding long elegant body, on short, ugly legs, with such protuberant buttocks, so weighty and unexpected below her slim long loins. She knew what he himself did not know. She had thousands of years of purely sensual, purely unspiritual knowledge behind her. (256)

Clearly, in Birkin's fascination with an African sculpture, we see the modern era's attraction to allegedly "primitive" motifs. On the one hand, Birkin's thoughts belie a racist/colonialist sense of the African as "elemental" (as nearer to beetle than human). On the other, his musings bespeak an essentialist awe for the African as closer to Nature, as representing a life force that Lawrence felt Western, industrialized society had regrettably lost or perverted. It seems no accident that, in the passage quoted from *Women in Love*, Birkin recalls a statuette of an African *woman* (or that American artist Sargent Johnson privileges the female face in his mask). For, as is typical of modernism, Woman's body is an ever-present and highly charged site.

Within the canon of the musical, the actress who most captured society's joint passion for things "African" and female was the American performer Josephine Baker (1906–1975). Raised in Missouri and initiating her theatrical career in Harlem, she achieved fame in Paris as a dancer in the French music hall. As Sylvie Raulet notes: "In 1925, Josephine Baker, in the *Revue Nègre* drew fashionable Paris to the Théâtre des Champs-Elysées, where she fascinated the audience with her jerky rhythms and revived the success of the Ballets Russes" (41). As evidence of the Parisian attraction to anything having to do with American black culture, recall that in Garbo's film *The Torrent*, when La Brunna spends an evening at a Paris nightclub watching a variety act, she views a group of showgirls doing a Josephine Baker-type routine. Furthermore, when La Brunna moves toward the stage to give a male singer a tip, he is a black man dressed in overalls, with a banjo in hand, who sings a Stephen Foster-like song about "going home."

After performing in Parisian revues, Baker starred in several films, among them *Princess Tam-Tam* (1935), directed by Edmond T. Gréville. Although this is a French film, it will be considered here because of Baker's status as a Euro-*American* icon of the Art Deco era. The movie centers on Max de Mirecourt (Albert Préjean), a famous French novelist, who is both tired of his wife, Lucie, and of the Parisian high society set with whom she associates. He is also feeling uninspired as a writer. When he and his spouse bicker, he decides to escape to North Africa, both to punish Lucie and to stimulate his creativity. The locale for his trip is clearly overdetermined (as the historic site of French colonialist imperialism). As a companion for his journey, Max takes along his sidekick Coton (Robert Arnoux).

Soon after arriving in Tunisia (picturesquely rendered in on-site location shooting), Max encounters a native woman, Alwina (Josephine Baker), who lives on the streets, surviving by her wits and stealing food. One European traveler calls her a Bedouin. Alwina is portrayed as comically mischievous and is seen romping with the village youth as well as playing with monkeys and sheep. Depicted as an innocent yet almost "feral" being, she is attractive to Max because of her imagined naïveté and carefree uninhibitedness—traits completely opposite to the Parisian upper-crust from which Max emerges. He affectionately calls Alwina an "animal" and, when he observes her playing with children, tells Coton, "That's nature." Coton, on the other hand, deems her a "savage."

Unbeknownst to Alwina, Max decides to write a novel about her, finding his Muse at last. As he tells Coton: "First, [we'll] polish and educate her, then study her reactions." His book will be a love story, "an interracial novel" that will strike the public as very "contemporary." When Alwina accepts Max's invitation to stay at his villa, several "humorous" scenes ensue in which Alwina attempts to learn European ways: though she is given a soft bed, she chooses to sleep on the hard floor. While Max is in Africa, Lucie begins carrying on with a rich and flirtatious maharajah (Jean Galland) who lives in Paris. When Max gets wind of this, he decides to make Lucie jealous by returning to Paris with Alwina, whom he will pass off as an African princess. In preparation for their trip to Europe, Max and Coton train Alwina for high society: she is outfitted in stylish clothes, manicured, given dance and piano lessons, and taught to walk in high-heels. On the day they are to leave, she emerges in an Art Deco-influenced ensemble: a tailored white dress draped with a geometrically striped black-and-white cape; on her head she sports a matching hat that seems a modified "fez."

When Max and the "Princess of Parador" arrive in Paris, they cause a stir; one member of the elite starts a rumor that she is a "cannibal." When she accompanies Max at the opera, Alwina cuts quite a figure, wearing a *moderne* form-fitting evening dress adorned by a silver sash; a sequined scarf is draped over her head (Muslim-style), and huge, dangling, rhinestone earrings frame her face. Watching her carefully is Lucie, who is accompanied by her own exotic date—the maharaja. Princess Parador is soon the talk of the town, and an ensuing montage chronicles her newfound fame: we see modernist portraits of her hanging in galleries, as well as abstract caricatures of her like those which are done of famous theatrical figures (including Josephine Baker herself).

Despite Alwina's triumph, she is unhappy, and one night while Max is away she goes out with Dar (Georges Péclet), Max's fez-wearing Tunisian servant, who has joined him in Paris. The two go to a café-bar in which black musicians perform for an interracial crowd.[1] Inspired by the band, Alwina begins to sing "Under the African Sky" (apparently a standard French melody rather than being a "native" song). When she finishes singing, she suddenly gets up and starts dancing in a loose, contemporary fashion—shimmying, high-kicking, and tapping. Apparently "slumming it," some members of the high society set—including a friend of Lucie (Viviane Romance)—arrive at the bar and see her. The next day, Lucie's friend calls her and reveals that the princess was seen doing a "savage" dance at a sailor's joint the night before. Lucie decides to trick the princess into betraying her true low nature in order to humiliate Max. First, Lucie makes sure that Max and the princess are invited to a fancy reception at the maharajah's house. Then, when the event takes place, she instructs her woman friend to ply the princess with liquor. As the maharajah's guests watch a lavishly presented musical revue, Lucie's friend carries out the plan.

The first number is a modernist visual spectacle in which women perform in polka-dot outfits (using both white on black and the reverse). It begins with a rotary graphic reminiscent of one from Marcel Duchamp's *Anemic Cinema* (1925). Later in the number, the women appear in black-and-white outfits that seem more Art Deco "constructions" than clothes—with wiry, tubular sleeves and hats that resemble "Slinky" toys.

At a certain point, a black, bare-chested musician loudly beats a drum to announce the next routine. As Alwina sits in the audience sipping yet another drink, the percussive sounds of the music in conjunction with the alcohol begin to affect her and, almost unconsciously, she starts to sway back and forth, succumbing to the number's tempo and allure. Lucie's friend dares and taunts her, asking: "How can you resist that music? . . . Dance, come on, dance!" Alwina then leaps

---

1. Actually, the one "black" woman who is seen in the bar seems to be a white actress with cork on her face.

onstage and begins to gyrate—tossing her shoes off and stripping off her clothes until she is down to almost "native" dress. While the music, costume, and décor of the routine have a Latin feel (and we see gauchos and band members playing maracas), the camera privileges the black drummer—lending the sequence an African aura. To make the segment's polymorphous nationality more chaotic, the turbaned maharajah watches from the sidelines while another South Indian man periodically chimes a gong onstage. While the number's ethnicity is wildly diverse, it is unified by Oriental and "primitive" themes. The routine comes to a frenzied crescendo with Alwina dancing at a feverish pace—undulating frantically, rubbing her belly, and jumping up and down with legs spread wide apart. The sequence's assertive montage (of the black drummer's face, of musicians' hands on their instruments), and its use of extreme, almost blurred, close-ups of Alwina's visage, also afford it a quasi-experimental style. Throughout the performance, reaction shots of the white (and primarily male) European audience members show them alternately staring in amazement at the stage and protectively shielding their eyes—simultaneously horrified and intrigued by the princess's primal, erotic dance.

When Alwina realizes she has simply been a ploy in Max's marital love spat, she is upset and responds obediently when the maharajah tells her that she must return to Africa. At this point the narrative shocks us with an unexpected twist. We cut to Max and Coton, who are, inexplicably, still in Tunisia. Max is recounting the end of his novel which, we realize, has constituted the story line of the film. Thus, the drama of Alwina's arrival in Paris has been apocryphal—only an imagined plot for Max's fiction. To make sure we understand this, Alwina—still dressed in native costume and eating a coconut—enters the room as Max and Coton talk. In a later scene we find her wed to Dar, with a baby in her arms. The couple resides in the villa that Max and Coton once inhabited. There are now goats in the living room, and one of them eats a book Max has left there entitled *Civilization*.

By conjoining in one scenario the story of fashionable Paris of the 1930s and that of "primitive" Africa, *Princess Tam-Tam* marries two major Art Deco themes. These opposing tendencies are directly registered in the film's major production numbers—the first in the modernist performance of the chorines (simultaneously reminiscent of Ziegfeld or Berkeley girls) and the second in the lusty presentation by Josephine Baker. But of course Baker herself contained these very contradictions—on the one hand constituting an idol of the progressive Jazz Age and, on the other, gaining fame by incarnating Western stereotypes of the earthy, unbridled Negress. Indeed, a scene in the film seems to comment on Art

Deco's appropriation of things African. When Alwina first arrives in Paris and is shown her new apartment, her eyes fix on certain objects in the décor: artificial flowers in a vase, fake birds in a cage, and glass fish figurines on a table. She says to Max: "There are so many imitations here." In a sense, the same could be said of Art Deco itself, which in its modernist global embrace copied so many ethnic forms.

While Baker presents a bold and memorable female figure in the musical's narrative, her power is nonetheless diminished by her association with Nature, children, and animals. Furthermore (though hardly least), the film's "surprise ending" functions to contain the most alarming aspects of the drama—notably, its interracial romance and the colonizer's attraction to the colonized (Princess Parador as Princess Paramour).

FLAMBOYANT DECO

The importance of the cinema in art was it gave designers and decorators a chance to *let themselves go, untrammeled by the limitations imposed by bourgeois purses and bourgeois domestic tasks*. In them we see Art Deco in its fully-realized form.
—Bevis Hiller (1971:47; emphasis added)

While *Top Hat*, *Swing Time*, and *Princess Tam-Tam* all follow the form of the "integrated" musical—with dance numbers "realistically" sutured into the narrative, numbers choreographed by Busby Berkeley propose a different model. Although the dramas in which they transpire assume that their musical routines are performed on a conventional theater stage, the numbers themselves create such an "impossible geography" that they can only exist within a synthetic cinematic universe. Hence, Berkeley's dances resonate with extreme abstraction and mark a complete break with diegetic logic and space. It is precisely this quality that lends them their interest. Liberated from narrative logic, Berkeley's production numbers become autonomous designs.

While elsewhere I have interpreted Berkeley's routines for their symbolic discourse around the figure of Woman (Fischer 1989:134–48), here I want to read them for their articulation of the codes of Art Deco. For, clearly, the unearthly space in which his numbers evolve allows him to unleash his extravagant Art Deco imagination—"untrammeled" by the restrictions of narrative or spatial coherence. For this reason, it is possible to discuss Berkeley's numbers in relative isolation from the films in which they are situated, since only infrequently do they have much to do with the drama.[2] Hence, while Astaire/Rogers musicals place Art Deco elegance in ostensibly real settings (which contrast with Depression-era deprivation), Berkeley's films cast glamour as pure Fantasy.

Given the modernism of Berkeley's dance numbers, it is curious that the music which accompanies them is often highly traditional and at odds with the tone of the costuming and set design. "The Shadow Waltz" (from *Gold Diggers of 1933*) proceeds in conventional three- quarter time and is sung by a choir of angelic soprano female voices. A traditional waltz rhythm and vocalization informs "The Words Are in My Heart" from *Gold Diggers of 1935*. Finally, "By a Waterfall" (from *Footlight Parade* [1933]) reminds one of a Jeanette MacDonald/Nelson Eddy operatic piece, with its refrain: "By a waterfall, I'm calling you-ou-ou-ou . . . "[3] Likewise, the sensibility of the "framing stories" with which Berkeley opens his musical routines is often quasi-Victorian. But the visual aspects of his production numbers are highly contemporary and bear the stamp of an Art Deco aesthetic. While Berkeley was the choreographer-director of his musical numbers, but not the art director of his films, he had tremendous input into the design of the sets, given that his dance routines were inextricably tied to his conception of a complex architectural space.

In examining his production numbers, one must first consider their mise-en-scène—often an abstract version of Polglase's "Big White Set." In "The Shadow Waltz" (designed by Anton Grot) showgirls appear on a huge white curvilinear staircase structure that rests on a jet-black floor (probably of glass or Bakelite). Similarly, in "The Words Are in My Heart" (another Grot extravaganza), the camera registers a seemingly endless row of women playing streamlined white pianos on an onyx floor. Tiered steps (spreading out like fan blades) lead to a high, geometrically decorated window in the background. In "Dames" (from the 1934 movie of the same title), designed by Robert Haas and Willy Pogany, showgirls sit at Deco vanities or soak in modern tubs adorned with neon-trimmed mirrors. In "By a Waterfall," bathers cavort in and around a pool subsumed within an elaborately ornate Deco architectural site conceived by Grot (fig. 5.2). At the end of the number, they form a human pyramid that draws upon the "frozen fountain motif" so popular in Deco ornamentation (fig. 5.3). This iconography was used in several

---

2. In other work on Berkeley (Fischer 1989:134–38), I have, however, shown how the plot of *Dames* (1934) mocks the Hollywood Production Code and has direct relevance to certain production numbers which are slyly based on such "perversions" as voyeurism and fetishism.

3. All three songs mentioned were written by Al Dubin and Harry Warren.

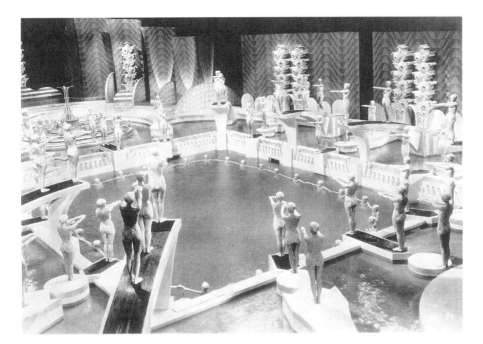

sites at the 1925 Paris Exposition, notably atop the Porte d'Honneur and in René
Lalique's crystal fountain (Raulet:52). Thus, Richard Striner deems the frozen
fountain motif "a worldwide symbol" of the Style Moderne (1994:23). It was repro-
duced in numerous consumer items or *objets d'art* of the period—including a diamond tiara by Mauboussin (Raulet:128).

Other moments of "By a Waterfall" invoke Art Deco graphics. In one shot, two
bathers are shown profiled in a mirror-image close-up and posed in the foreground
of the frame at opposite ends of a black-and-white arch. The composition is insistently pictorial and reminiscent of Art Deco layouts. Contributing to the shot's
graphic force is Berkeley's use of a void black background which throws the foreground into sharp relief and creates a silhouette effect on the female body. At
another moment, the camera reveals bathers swimming under water, and the
imagery sparks associations to Deco female figures sculpted or etched in glass.
Here one thinks of works like René Lalique's *Suzanne* (1932)—an opalescent
molded figurine (Duncan 1988b:106)—or of Vicke Lindstrand's 1937 vase for
Orrefors (a Swedish glass company), etched with a nude female torso (Duncan
1988b:111).

Beyond their look, Berkeley's sets function as elaborate stage machines, evok-
ing Deco's industrial imperative. In "The Words Are in My Heart," pianos turn
on a rack of tiered steps. In "Dames," the dancers are transported on a moving
stage that resembles a Möbius strip. At the end of "By a Waterfall," the bathers

FIGURE 5.3

Art Deco's "frozen fountain motif" as musical number in *Footlight Parade.* (Courtesy Museum of Modern Art)

are posed on a complex four-tiered rotating fountain. In truth, the entire faux tropical set that Berkeley uses in this latter number perfectly merges Art Deco's fascination with the Primitive/Exotic, with its love of high technology. As Berkeley states:

> I designed my set and consulted with the art directors, the engineers, the carpenters, the electricians and told them what I wanted. The . . . pool covered almost an entire sound stage. The pool measured eighty feet by forty, and while the number was being shot we pumped twenty thousand gallons

of water a minute over the falls into the pool. I had them build me plate-glass corridors underneath the pool so I could light and shoot from the bottom. People were constantly visiting the set to see if what they had heard was true. What with all the water pumps, the hydraulic lifts, and the dozens of workmen, someone said the set looked [like] the engine room of an ocean liner. (Quoted in Thomas and Terry 1973:70–71)

Berkeley also utilizes the camera as a high-tech tool. In "By a Waterfall," it goes below the water; in "The Words Are in My Heart," it travels under the floor; and in "Dames" it twirls through a mirrored chamber.

Berkeley's Deco vision is also extended through costuming. "The Shadow Waltz" begins with a framing story in which Ruby Keeler appears in a flouncy, form-fitting white dress decorated with an abstract sequined motif. When the production number starts, myriad women appear wearing geometric, modern-day versions of the "hoop skirt," which create complex spirals as they move. Significantly, Phillipe Devriez's bronze figure *Dancer* depicts a woman with similar attire (Hiller:89). Likewise, with exotic ostrich feathers all the rage in the Art Deco era, one may notice that the number "Spin a Little Web of Dreams" from *Fashions of 1934* makes use of the accessory both for costuming and as a prop in the choreography.

One of the major tropes for which Berkeley is famously known is the extreme high-angle shot (from the studio ceiling) of dancers below—arranged and choreographed so that their bodies create an overall and ever-changing graphic design. Such a moment occurs in "By a Waterfall" when the bathers form concentric rotating circles or join shoulders to create a snake-like line. A similar sequence takes place in "The Shadow Waltz" when a high-angle shot of individual dancers holding illuminated violins reveals a larger, totalizing violin pattern. Perhaps Berkeley's signature compositions are those which transpire in "Dames" or "By a Waterfall." In these, an aerial shot displays a star-like or circular pattern of women whose choreographed movements shift to create a kaleidoscopic effect. Certainly, these images might be read to dehumanize women—to make of them "biotic tile[s] in an abstract mosaic" (Fischer 1989:138). But it is also true that the geometric forms the females assume relate to the lexicon of Art Deco. Significantly, when, in "Dames," the bodies of showgirls "morph" into a black-and-white animated pattern, the arrangement mimics the modernist border of their towels.

But there are other issues at play in Berkeley's numbers that relate to Art Deco iconography. First, there is simply the obsessive *presence* of women in his numbers—far beyond the requirements of the musical chorus line. Rarely, in fact, do we ever see men—except for the framing stories (e.g., Dick Powell in the introductions to "Dames," "The Words Are in My Heart," "The Shadow Waltz," and "By a Waterfall"), or in a topical piece like "Remember My Forgotten Man" (from *Gold Diggers of 1933*), which concerns the World War I veteran. In the rare case where a production number is set in a nightclub (a locale typical for the Astaire/Rogers musicals but less common in those of Berkeley), the cast is "coed," as is the case in the famous "Lullaby of Broadway" routine from *Gold Diggers of 1935*. More typical are numbers like "The Words Are in My Heart," in which hordes of women play pianos, or "By a Waterfall" in which bevies of girls frolic in a pool. While, on one level, Berkeley's feminine fixation can be read in terms of the director's penchant for voyeurism and fetishism—on another level, it reflects the hyperbolic visibility of the female in Art Deco rhetoric.

Most particularly, it is in the Berkeley production numbers that we feel the incarnation of Deco sculpture, which focused unrelentingly on the figure of the female dancer. For example, there is a bronze piece by Chiparus entitled *The Girls*, in which the women look precisely like a musical chorus line (Duncan 1988b:28). Yet another of his works portrays a female with top hat and cane (Duncan 1988a:122). By the time of the Berkeley production numbers, however, the lines of influence are somewhat complicated. While initially it was the stage and screen that inspired the sculpture, later it may have been the sculpture that influenced the screen. Thus, when in "The Words Are in My Heart" the showgirls grab the edges of their dresses and spread the garments' accordion folds, we are reminded of the prevalence of outstretched fabric in such sculptures as Chiparus's *The Sunburst Dress* and *The Long Skirt* (Arwas 1975:17, 20, 21, 22, 27).

Alternately, the seminude swimmers of "By a Waterfall" are reminiscent of the "naturalistic" strain of Deco statuary that portrayed female athletes. For example, I own a small bronze Deco ashtray that features the figure of a woman in a diving pose (precisely like a chorine in the Berkeley number) (fig. 5.4). Furthermore, the metallic look of the bathers' caps and hair in "By a Waterfall" invokes a sense of sculptural material. When Berkeley's swimmers appear in nymph-like mode, they also resemble the "mythic" strain of Deco statuary, which favored maritime characters like the Lorelei. Here one thinks of Waylande Gregory's white, glazed figurine *Persephone* (Duncan 1986:110), of René Lalique's *Sirene* (McClinton:134), or of Armand Martial's bronze statue *Leda and the Swan* (Duncan 1988b:122). Finally, when (in the production number "We're in the Money" from *Gold Diggers of 1933*) a row of showgirls lines up behind Ginger Rogers and makes her appear to have multiple arms, we are reminded of the Exotic theme in Deco imagery, as apparent in such sculptures as *Odeon Dancer, Dancer with Fan Headdress, Dancer with Turban,* or *Fan Dancer* (Arwas 1975:25, 33, 44, 46).

Experiments with illumination were central to Art Deco interior design. As Winnifred Fales remarked in her 1936 decorating manual:

> In rooms with modern furnishings, glass panels masking either white or colored lights are frequently inserted in the walls or ceiling, simply as decoration. . . . Mantelpieces may be made entirely of diffusing glass, and lighted from within; or the mantel shelf alone may be of this substance, bathing in a faintly mysterious glow the objects arranged upon it. Columns, pilasters, and door and window casings of illuminated glass are also seen. (210)

Aside from general room illumination, lighting was also used to provide highlights for artworks within the décor. As Fales notes:

> Illuminated wall niches are one of the earliest and most interesting developments. The niche is lined with panels of diffusing glass, back of which electric bulbs are installed. When lighted, the sculptured figure, vase, or small collection of bibelots enshrined in the niche is thrown into delicate relief and given an ethereal beauty by the soft illumination of its background. (209)

Lamps were also important Deco objects that employed the female form. Most noteworthy were the Frankart boudoir pieces produced in the late 1920s: "small table fixture[s] created by Arthur von Frankenberg, [which] used nudes to hold up illuminated cylinders or globes" (Striner:65). (See fig. 1.2.) As Richard Striner notes: "Through such fixtures the spirit of the 1925 Paris Exposition was diffused to the point of pervasiveness in the years between the world wars. Here was exotica—or perhaps just a dose of escapist whimsy—for everyman and everywoman" (65). Similar to these lamps were those in which a metal figure was placed before a sheet of glass lit from behind with a concealed bulb. When the lamp was on, the female figure was illuminated in silhouette—emphasizing her corporeal outline (a trope that Erté would have appreciated). (See fig. 1.10.) As McClinton observes:

One of the most interesting lighting developments of the Art Deco period was the illuminated plaque or figure. These popular decorative lighting pieces may have first been introduced by Lalique to display his glass to the best effect. Whatever prompted their making the idea caught on, and illuminated plaques and glass figures with concealed light globes were made by all manufacturers of decorative glass (96).

Berkeley's production numbers echo various types of Deco lamps and illumination strategies. In "The Shadow Waltz" (whose title even touches upon the issue of lighting) dancers carry neon-lit violins (with trailing cords) that make the women seem virtually "plugged in." In *Going Through the Roof* (1998), a documentary on Berkeley, former dancer Dorothy Coonan Wellman recalls that when she and the other chorines appeared in that number, they got an electric shock each time their bows hit their metal helmets. When, in "By a Waterfall," the set's lights are dimmed and the pool lights turned on, the bathers alternately appear in dramatic black silhouette against a background of white or seem illuminated themselves. Finally, in the "Pettin' in the Park" routine from *Gold Diggers of 1933*, as women undress behind backlit screens, their evocatively suggestive contours are projected onto the screens' surfaces. When such lighting effects occur within a film, they are obviously highly theatrical. But such drama was sought as well in the home environment, where Deco style was profoundly influenced by stage lighting (Weber:19–20). Winifred Fales warns that such devices must be used with "restraint" in the home. However, "like the automobile, they doubtless will lapse from sensationalism into commonplaceness upon longer acquaintance" (210).

Berkeley's production numbers recycle yet another important Art Deco icon. Frequently, popular objects of the period contained the image of women holding or throwing giant beach balls or enormous bubbles or the like. This image appears on a set of Anchor Hocking glassware of the era as well as in such sculptures as A. Godard's *The Bubble Dancer* (Arwas 1975:50) or F. Preiss's *Balancing* and *The Beach Ball* (Arwas:90–91). Sometimes the globe emblem that the female figure carries represents the moon, as in *Aurore Onu*, a French bronze and alabaster piece from 1925 (Duncan 1988b:32). This type of image clearly predates Art Deco and is found, for instance, in a famous Maxfield Parrish illustration of 1904 entitled *Air Castles*, in which a young boy is pictured against a bubble-filled sky. Transposed to Art Deco, this kitschy globular imagery appears in several Berkeley production numbers. In "Pettin' in the Park," we find a group of women outdoors in wintertime. As snow falls, they are seen with giant white spheres (presumably huge snowballs), which they hold above their heads. In a high-angle shot, Berkeley transforms the group into an arresting abstract black-and-white pattern. In "Dames," the showgirls carry large black spheres as they magically soar up to the ceiling-mounted camera.

What makes Berkeley's contribution to the Art Deco musical even more interesting is his use of the iconography of music itself within the décor of the production number. We have already seen reference to this imagery in *Top Hat*, in which the walls of a Venetian hotel are decorated with pictures of harps, mandolins, and flutes. Such imagery was prevalent in Deco movie theater design as well. In the Oakland (California) Paramount, for example, built in 1931 (to be discussed in chapter 7), there are images of accordions, tambourines, banjos, and clarinets etched into the glass panels of entry doors. And on the walls of the theater's Women's Smoking Room is a mural of a female Muse holding a lyre (see plate 10). Finally, in the building's corridors are bas-reliefs of Artemis blowing a horn (see fig. 7.2). In Berkeley's use of neon violins in "The Shadow Waltz" and rotating pianos in "The Words Are in My Heart," we find the impulse to take traditional musical imagery and update it with a high-tech modernist flourish.

Aside from the iconographic parallels between the Art Deco mode and the mise-en-scène of Berkeley's musical productions, certain important ideological issues are also at play. First is the question of race. As we have seen, one strain of the Art Deco style appropriated and celebrated influences from Africa and American black culture. Both subjects arise in a Berkeley number entitled "Keep Young and Beautiful" from *Roman Scandals* (1933). That film tells the story of a man (played by Eddie Cantor) living in an American rural community called Rome during the Depression era. When he is kicked out of town by a rich man, he imagines himself as a slave in ancient, imperial Rome, and the movie depicts his fantasy. At one point in his dream, he escapes his masters and hides out in a woman's beauty salon. Concealing his body under a sheet, he is given a mud facial by the beautician, which he then manages to spread all over his body to camouflage his true identity. After the process, he emerges as a black-faced Eddie Cantor, with wide eyes and white lips (a familiar trope from Cantor's vaudeville days). He pretends to be a famous Ethiopian beauty specialist (even though he speaks in a preposterous black-inflected dialect of the Old South that of course today would be considered racist). As he moves through the ancient salon, he encounters hordes of blonde beauties (Ancient Rome according to 1930s Hollywood) whom he advises on how to "keep young and beautiful" in order to be loved by men. As he performs the number, we view white women in various postures (looking at themselves in mirrors, taking steam baths, etc.) while they are attended to by black females playing Ethiopian slaves. Thus we see black hands massaging white women's backs or combing blonde hair. In one image, we see a line of shapely white legs being patted by black hands; at the end of the shot, the black women's faces peer through the white women's limbs. Finally, as the white women begin to dance, they are rotated onto a huge tiered geometric "Big White Set" by revolving black and white panels which then pose them against a black background. When the women step down, the panels revolve again to reveal their white sides, this time with the black slave dancers posed against the white background—creating a "silhouette effect" by skin color (instead of light and shadow). The routine continues to alternate performers by race in a manner that gives a prejudiced racial thrust to Art Deco's fascination with "black and white." Ultimately, Cantor dives into a pool, which dissolves his blackface makeup, and the number ends. Clearly, here (in one of the rare Busby Berkeley routines involving black chorines), the role of the black American female is far different from that assumed by Josephine Baker in her performances. These black women (though stunning) are not presented as bold, but rather as slaves to the demands of white women's beauty culture. Though the black chorines themselves bear none of Baker's provocative sexuality, their tending to white women's bodies lends the sequence some of the homoerotic valence with which Art Deco iconography was sometimes imbued (like the chorus girls who share double beds in *Dames*).

But, to be truthful, white women in the film's production numbers do not fare much better themselves. In the routine described above, the song lyrics propose how women's lives should be dedicated to making themselves attractive to men. As Cantor intones: "Take care of all those charms and you'll always be in someone's arms; Keep young and beautiful if you want to be loved." The chorines obviously agree and sing such rhymes as: "Each wrinkle in your skin—rub it out and rub a dimple in." Or: "Be sure and get your man; wrap your body in a coat of tan"—a line that demonstrates white beauty culture's love/hate relationship with skin tones approximating those of the black chorines. In an earlier number (which proceeds from the song "No More Love"), white seminude slave girls (in floor-length blonde wigs) are captured and placed in bondage: held in chains with their arms pinned to a white pillar—their eyes raised toward heaven in meek subjugation. As the column rotates (with the women helplessly tied to it), other Caucasian slave girls in black costumes undulate wildly on the tiered white set as a man with a whip stands ominously center stage. A dance "drama" unfolds in which one of the slave girls is sold to a lascivious man and must perform a belly-dance for him. This would not be the last time that women appeared in sadomasochistic bondage in Berkeley production numbers. In "Spin a Little Web of Dreams" from *Fashions of 1934*, Berkeley has his chorines "trapped" as the shaft of harps.

In many of Berkeley's musical numbers, therefore, the relative passivity that we find in the stance of Ginger Rogers is taken to perverse extremes. Beyond embodying a series of retrograde female stereotypes (sexual object, slave, kewpie doll, bimbo), women in Berkeley's production routines become parts of a static, inanimate Art Deco design—mechanistic elements of a modernist construct.

EPILOGUE: "A TABLEAU OF JEWELS"

As noted earlier, Woman in the 1930s film musical seems to bear a special relation to Art Deco's chryselephantine sculptures—icons of feminine stasis. In part this is due to the fact that many such statuettes were indeed inspired by dance, dancers, and dance fashion. While such figures were also affected by both the theater and cinema, they eventually came to influence their own "sources," resulting in a two-directional interplay between Deco and cinematic aesthetics. Thus, the film musical's chorus girl can be seen as a type of animate chryselephantine sculpture. We may here be reminded of the legend of Pygmalion—the Greek king of Cyprus who fell in love with a female statue, then begged Aphrodite to bring her to life. In a sense, the directors of the thirties musicals (and especially Busby Berkeley) were cinematic Pygmalions—activating Deco's fixed sculptural visions of the female form.

The relation between the chorine and the Art Deco sculpture is made clear in a number from an early film musical based on the vaudeville format—*The Hollywood Revue of 1929*. Devoid of any narrative, the film presents a series of staged variety acts, each introduced by Jack Benny—routines that comprise comic skits, songs, dramatic readings, and musical numbers. Among the latter is the "Tableau of Jewels," a sequence with sets attributed to Cedric Gibbons and Richard Day, and costumes to Erté (fig. 5.5). When the curtain opens, we see a two-tiered structure sinuously outlined in luminous white pearls reminiscent of wrought-iron grill work (a popular Deco material). As the set rotates against a black background, we view stationary, posed women in diverse white costumes (thus making their bodies form a reverse silhouette). Each is placed in a kind of illuminated niche, another common Deco architectural detail. The chorines all resemble delicate chryselephantine sculptures, especially of the exotic variety. One woman, for example, sports Turkish harem pants and an Arab headdress. Despite the kinetic background music, the women do not move. Neither do they parade down the stairs like the famous Ziegfeld Girls. Instead, they are displayed in a tableau that is fixed and eternal—like immobile figurines on a shelf.

FIGURE 5.5

The chorus as chryselephantine sculpture in Erté's "Tableau of Jewels" in *Hollywood Revue of 1929*. (Courtesy Museum of Modern Art)

This sculptural motif is also evident in the silent film *Our Dancing Daughters* (1928), which marries the musical to the melodrama. The film opens by displaying an ornamental bronze Deco statue of a woman doing the Charleston. Next we see a pair of evening slippers on the floor which, through a dissolve, become magically "filled" by a woman's feet. Thereafter, we see a woman's legs dancing in front of a three-paneled mirror, and later, a full shot of the same subject. The next image presents an extreme long-shot of the woman (played by Joan Crawford) in her bedroom, a lush and upscale Deco interior (fig. 5.6). A few shots later, the woman stands before glass shelves—replete with Art Deco bric-a-brac—built into a window. On the top tier, prominently displayed, is a female statue captured in a Charleston dance pose (fig. 5.7). Thus, the opening sequence of *Our Dancing Daughters* (a movie that could serve as the heralded anthem of the New Woman in the Art Deco era) traces the precise progression delineated here in this chapter—from Deco décor to film set, from sculptured statuary to female screen character, from modernist mode to musical genre.

FIGURES 5.6
The well-dressed flapper (Joan Crawford) in her *moderne* bedroom in *Our Dancing Daughters* (1928). (Courtesy Museum of Modern Art)

FIGURE 5.7
Our Dancing Daughters: An Art Deco dressing room replete with *moderne* cosmetics, bric-a-brac, and a sculpture of a dancing woman. (Courtesy Museum of Modern Art)

6. STRANGERS IN PARADISE

South Seas Films of the Art Deco Era

As I have shown, various strains of the Art Deco style focused on the Exotic, the Ancient, and the Primitive—themes that were often intertwined in creative works of the period. While much of the Art Deco aesthetic highlighted a vision of the Future, these branches of the movement romanticized the Past. In chapter 1, I mentioned Deco's fascination with Africa, as well as with the Far and Middle East as represented in the decorative arts. Thus, in such works as Georges Fouquet's pendant of 1925 (fashioned from jade, onyx, and diamond to resemble an ancient Chinese mask), artists combined contemporary tropes from the Style Moderne with more traditional motifs (Arwas 1992:124).

Like other artifacts of the 1920s and 1930s, Hollywood movies also evinced a fascination with the Exotic. However, rather than formulating modernist works from traditional motifs, these films (entirely conventional in their style) invoked exoticism as pure *content*. Films like *Trader Horn* (1931), *King Kong* (1933), and the Tarzan series were set in Africa or on mysterious lost islands and told tales of Westerners' encounters with the jungle wilds. Movies like *The Painted Veil* took place in China and chronicled the transformation of white people under the influence of Oriental "carnality." Finally, works like *Cleopatra* (1934) were situated in the Middle East, cashing in on the era's fixation with Egyptology.

Here, I will concentrate on another region invested with symbolic meaning during the Art Deco era—the *South Seas*—a realm which also came to be represented in the movies. Most often, it was conceived as a tropical wonderland, largely untouched by modern civilization—clearly, a popular fantasy in Depression-era America. Most travel books of the time represent it in precisely this fashion. Frederick O'Brien's *Mystic Isles of the South Seas* (1921), which records the author's

Cinema could launch the viewer into the future with science fiction, and . . . into the timeless past.

—Fatimah Tobing Rony (1996:130)

journey to Tahiti and Mooréa, compares the locale to Thomas More's Utopia and calls it an "Eden with no serpent or hurtful apple" (20). Though the natives are conceived as "semi-savages" (305), they are also "magnificent" beings, marked by "beauty and natural grace" (231). While the men are handsome and virile (with a "mien of natural majesty"), the women are voluptuous in costumes that "conceal nothing" (228, 128). Sexually aggressive creatures, these maidens make "the first advances in friendship openly" (233). Though impressive, the natives have some flaws: they are indolent, naive, and lacking in morals. As O'Brien notes, "Only religion, [and] . . . taboos, held them in any restraint" (360). Nonetheless, the South Seas islands are a land of "joy," an unmitigated "paradise" (271, 330).

Similarly, James Norman Hall and Charles Bernhard Nordhoff, writing in *Faery Lands of the South Seas* (also published in 1921), speak of a domain of "primitive loveliness" (6) that seems to exist in "the realm of the imagination" (9). The authors see the indigenous people as simple, childish, humorous, and "permanently happy" (69, 274, 29). While the writers downplay the sexual abandon of the women, they regard them as visionary "mystics" (71, 73). Among the other South Seas travel diaries published in the 1920s are *Tahiti Days* (1920) by Hector Macquarrie, *Cruise of the Dreamship* (1921) by Ralph Stock, *Tahiti* (1922) by George Calderon, *Attols of the Sun* (1922) by Frederick O'Brien, *Summer Isles of Eden* (1923) by Frank Burnett, *Green Islands in Glittering Seas* (1925) by W. Lavallin Puxley, *South Sea Settlers* (1927) by J. R. Grey and B. B. Grey, and *Mid-Pacific* (1928) by James Norman Hall.

That interest in the topic persisted into the next decade is clear from a travel diary published in 1930: Gifford Pinchot's *To the South Seas*. Here, the author stresses the overwhelming beauty of the Marquesas Islands: "They bring irresistibly to mind the most theatrical efforts of the least restrained scene painters. They are beautiful with vividness, extravagance, and unexpectedness in form and in color" (345). Again, Pinchot finds the natives agreeable (despite their distressing penchant for human sacrifice): "They are simple, kindly, honest and most hospitable" (349). Other South Seas travelogues were published in the same period, including Alva Carothers's *Stevenson's Isles of Paradise: A True Story of Adventures in the Samoan South Sea Islands* (1931). While many works stress the idyllic aspects of South Seas life, some take account of the manner in which it has been compromised by exploration, colonization, technology, and trade. Writing of the Marquesas in 1919, Frederick O'Brien comments on how the history of the area is one "of evil wrought by a civilization, of curses heaped on a strange, simple people by men who sought to exploit them or to mold them to another pattern, who destroyed their customs and their happiness and left them to die, apathetic, wretched, hardly knowing their own miserable plight" (24–25). Clearly, paradise has also been lost.

While the books discussed are works of popular literature (appealing to a general interest in remote lands), one academic work of the era also had a profound effect on public consciousness: Margaret Mead's *Coming of Age in Samoa* (1928). Significantly, it was reviewed in such nonscholarly venues as the *Boston Transcript*, the *New York Herald Tribune*, the *Nation*, the *New Republic*, the *New York Times*, and *Outlook*.[1] Mead traveled to the South Seas (following in the footsteps of her mentor Franz Boas) in order to study adolescent culture (especially that of girls). The region was selected according to the belief that anthropologists must choose "quite simple peoples . . . whose society has never attained the complexity of our own" (Mead:7). Among the issues she studied were modes of heterosexual union. Aside from marital liaisons, she found the existence of considerable premarital promiscuity and postmarital adultery. This did not obtain for one type of female, the so-called *taupo*—the daughter of the chief.[2] Her virginity was fervently guarded so that she might marry the ruler of a nearby village. (The only young man who might attempt to subvert this system would be a youth from another encampment who could gain prestige by eloping with the sacred virgin of a neighboring enclave.) While in later years Mead's research came under attack (especially from Derek Freeman), in the 1920s and 1930s it held great sway and helped to promulgate the notion of the South Seas as a sensual land of innocent but "easy virtue." As evidence of the volume's broad circulation and appeal, G. A. Dorsey in the *New York Herald Tribune* recommends it "to every one interested in education or in the psychology of sex." Likewise, W. R. Brooks of *Outlook* states that the book will be "attractive to any reader who does not object to the handling of natural facts with ungloved hands." Furthermore, Mead herself published many articles derived from her research in popular magazines. One in *Scribner's Magazine* of November 1931 warns readers of romanticizing exotic cultures by taking a "tourist" perspective—imagining, for example, that South Seas society provides more individuality than that of the United States. And in a series of articles in *Parents' Magazine*, she uses her anthropological study to comment on American child-rearing practices. In an essay of September 1929, for example, she makes clear that the kind of *angst* that Westerners associate with the period of adolescence does not obtain in the Samoan world. In another

---

1. Citations for these publications are given in Marion A. Knight, Mertice M. James, and Matilda L. Berg, eds., *The Book Review Digest: Books of 1928*, 524; and *Books of 1929*, 640.

2. Mead spells the term "taupo," but in F. W. Murnau's *Tabu* (1931), in collaboration with Robert Flaherty, it is spelled "taupou."

article of September 1930, she discusses the manner in which the Manus people of the Admiralty Islands teach their children to swim and be comfortable in the water. Finally, in an essay published in March 1932, she contrasts the American manner of segregating children by age group with customs of the Manus people. By 1935, *American Magazine* deemed her one of "America's Interesting People."

In adopting the era's rather idyllic stance toward the South Seas region, the Art Deco style was contradictory and problematic. How could a cutting-edge movement justify its retrograde and nostalgic fixation on a "primitive" past? Perhaps it was a negative reaction to the Depression? Such a paradox, however, was not entirely new to modernism, witness the case of painter Paul Gauguin who (like the travelers cited above) fled civilization in 1891 for a life in Tahiti. Certainly, the publication of *Noa Noa*, his South Seas diary, brought awareness of his voyage to the public; an English translation of the book appeared in 1920 and was reviewed in the *Boston Transcript*, the *New York Call* and the *New York Times*. With major exhibits of the artist's work at the Boston Museum of Fine Arts in 1927, the Museum of Modern Art in 1929, the Baltimore Museum of Fine Arts and the San Francisco Museum of Fine Arts in 1936 (including such paintings as *Tropical Vegetation Martinique* [1887], *Ea Haere Ia Oe Go!* [1893], *Where Do We Come From? What Are We? Where Are We?* [1897], and *Contes Barbares* [*Barbaric Tales*, 1902]), it is apparent that Gauguin's style was influential during the Art Deco era (Clement 1991:263–65).

But the museum and the world of publishing were not the only realms where the era's fascination with the Tropics (or the Tropical) surfaced. It also showed itself in modernist design artifacts of the period available to the well-heeled, forward-thinking consumer. A lacquered Cabinet by Gaston Pirou (1931) depicts a wild animal in a rain forest (Arwas 1992:71), while a fire screen by Edgar Brandt (1925) represents a tropical waterfall (Arwas:91). A lacquer table (made in 1914 by Eileen Gray) takes the shape of a lotus flower, while a standing lamp by Brandt incarnates a cobra (Arwas:75, 87). Lacquer cabinet doors designed by Süe et Mare (c. 1920) present an underwater scene that includes a sea turtle. Alternately, a bookbinding created by François Louis Schmied in 1930 displays exotic flowers (Arwas:85, 233). A glass vase crafted by Schneider in 1925 is embossed with water lily pads, while a porcelain statuette sculpted by Boyer in 1927 displays a nude tropical maiden (Arwas:260, 284). Finally, Jean Dunand's lacquer relief sculpture for the Deco ocean liner *Normandie* portrays native men hunting.[3]

---

3. This lacquer relief sculpture from the *Normandie* is on one side of doors from the ship that are in the collection of the Carnegie Museum of Art in Pittsburgh. The other side contains "The Chariot of Aurora," also by Dunand.

Beyond such expensive modernist decorative objects, routine advertising of the period also revealed a fixation with the Tropical/Exotic, using it for provocative content or as backdrop. For example, an ad from *Vogue* of 1927 for Schumacher fabrics highlights the "Martinique" pattern—described as an "exotic chintz, filled with the life and color of the Tropics." Another ad in *Good Housekeeping* of January 1928 promotes towels by Cannon, featured at the Royal Hawaiian Hotel in Honolulu, located on "the most enchanted island of the Pacific" where "the climate is perfect, the sands are honestly coral, [and] the ocean truly turquoise." Finally, *Good Housekeeping* of October 1929 touts New Mix toothpaste in a black-and-white graphic with tangerine accents (fig. 6.1). It depicts a South Seas beauty with coral flowers in her hair eating an orange-tinted coconut. The caption beneath her reads: "Science sat at her feet (and you can't blame Science). By observing the glorious white teeth of the South Sea Island Beauties, Science learned that if a tooth paste is to keep teeth stainlessly white, its whitener must be fresh!"

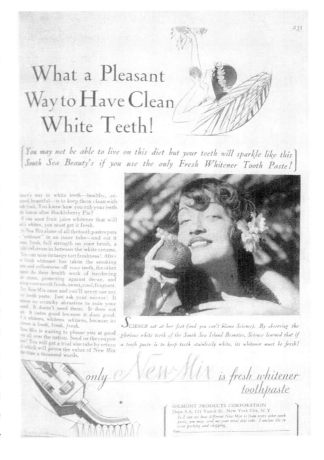

FIGURES 6.1

New Mix Toothpaste advertisement (October 1929).

Finally, a fascination with the Tropical/Exotic can be seen in certain public works of the era, like the Golden Gate International Exposition of 1939, which was built in a modernist, Art Deco mode. Billing itself as "A Pageant of the Pacific," it created "a stucco South Seas fantasy that combined the modernism of Art Deco with the jungle daydreams of Depression Hollywood" (Zim, Lerner, and Rolfes 1988:27). Among the constructions to adorn the fair were huge Elephant Towers reputedly modeled on those in Angkor Wat.

Clearly, the Western fascination with the Tropical/Exotic (be it expressed in literature, painting, the decorative arts, or architecture) restaged the oppressive power relations of imperialism—appropriating the iconography (and, often, the actual products) of Third World economies as a prop for privileged Euro-American lives. As Mark Winokur notes, it "aestheticized colonialism" and brought home "a tourist's view of the world" (1996:202). On the other hand, the era's fixation on the region also expressed a certain guilt about the First World's legacy there, and an attempt to find "redemption for the West" (Tobing:131). Whatever the stance, the arrogation of the Tropical/Exotic said more about its appropriators than its appropriatees. As Marianna Torgovnick has noted, "the primitive can be—has been, will be—whatever Euro-Americans want it to be" (1990:9).

Not surprisingly, the Deco era's enchantment with the Tropical/Exotic influenced cinematic narratives, especially those of the romance and adventure genres. Significantly, it entered the movies primarily as setting or content—not as an aspect of modernist style. Like films situated in Africa, those located in the South Seas provided the spectator with a magical view of an unfamiliar terrain that both heightened the story's drama and offered the spectator a vicarious "travelogue" as well as an escape from current economic travails. In this chapter I will consider six such movies (silent and sound) that represent diverse modes of production. Two, *Moana* (1926), made by Robert Flaherty, and *Tabu* (1931), by Flaherty and F. W. Murnau, utilize elements of the documentary genre;[4] another, *White Shadows in the South Seas* (1928), directed by W. S. Van Dyke for MGM, blends ethnography with fiction. *Venus of the South Seas* (1924), directed by James R. Sullivan, is an independent drama of the silent era, while *Hula* (1927), made by Victor Fleming, is a Paramount studio production. Finally, *Bird of Paradise* (1932), directed by King Vidor, is a sound feature produced by RKO Pictures.

Unlike the period's melodramas and musicals, most of these films do *not* incorporate elements of the Art Deco aesthetic (which is logical, given that they are set in "primitive" societies while the Style Moderne is identified with urban contemporaneity). Rather, the films plumb one of the movement's major background themes—a fascination with the Primitive/Exotic. Alternately, in the next chapter, I will have the opportunity to explore, concretely, the South Seas motif in Art Deco design when I discuss Oakland California's Paramount Theatre, a 1930s "picture palace."

GONE NATIVE

The news that Murnau and Flaherty were quitting Hollywood to make their own films in faraway places created quite a stir in the film capital.
—David Flaherty (1959:15)

Tabu is made at an interesting point in the careers of both Murnau and Flaherty. The former came to the United States from Germany in 1926 as one of the famed

---

4. As will be discussed, *Moana* and *Tabu* are not "pure" documentaries (though no such entity exists) but have many staged and scripted elements.

European "art" directors who were meant to lend a touch of class to the American studio system. After having won great critical acclaim on the Continent for *Nosferatu* (1922) and *The Last Laugh* (1924), Murnau was hired by Fox Studios where his first production was one of the masterpieces of world cinema, *Sunrise* (1927). He followed that triumph with *The Four Devils* (1928) and *City Girl* (originally called *Our Daily Bread* [1929]). After two years' reign as the "German Genius," Murnau tired of the Hollywood atmosphere. He bought himself a yacht, which he named the *Bali*, and (like Packy Cannon in *The Single Standard*) decided to travel to distant and alien lands, to "go back to nature" (Eisner 1964:282).

Primitive locales had always been of interest to documentary filmmaker Robert Flaherty—who had made the pioneering *Nanook of the North* in 1922 (about Eskimos in the Hudson Bay). He then journeyed to the South Pacific to direct *Moana* (1926) in British Samoa. Later, he collaborated with W. S. Van Dyke on *White Shadows in the South Seas*, but Flaherty left before the film was completed (Katz 2001:462). While Murnau was in Hollywood making *City Girl*, Flaherty was also associated with Fox Studios, working in Arizona on the development of a film about the Pueblo Indians. The two men met through Flaherty's brother David, who was in Hollywood while Robert was in the Southwest. Murnau sought David's advice on his yachting plans for the South Seas, while revealing to David that Fox was about to cancel his brother's Native American project. In the wake of this news, Robert Flaherty and Murnau began to consider collaborating on a film about the South Pacific (Eisner:215).

With this enterprise in mind, David Flaherty and Murnau traveled to Tucson, where with Robert they discussed the idea of shooting a film about a Polynesian pearl fishermen. As it happens, the subject of pearl diving is ubiquitous in the South Seas documentary, romance, and adventure films, and this is so for many reasons. First, it is an ancient practice, yet one that has been exploited by twentieth-century Westerners for the modern jewel trade. Second, pearls have long been one of the major exports of French Polynesia. Finally, pearl fishing is an extremely dangerous line of work since divers (who often work without mechanical aids) sometimes seek depths as great as 100 feet in order to find their treasures.[5] Hence, the topic has a great deal of inherent drama.

Murnau was enthusiastic about the project, and he and Robert Flaherty signed a contract with Colorart, a small independent film company. David Flaherty and

---

5. This information is from the *World Almanac Knowledge Source* (online version). Entries consulted: "Diving" and "French Polynesia."

Murnau sailed from California to the South Seas on the *Bali* in April 1929. Robert later took a steamer, but reached Tahiti first and began to set up shop (Eisner:215). Murnau and David Flaherty took their time getting there, making many stops along the way, giving the German director (a first-time visitor to the region), an opportunity to explore "the still paradise-like conditions and life of . . . the islands" (quoted in Eisner:207). Murnau confessed that he hoped, by so doing, "to catch some of the true unspoiled Polynesian spirit" (quoted in Eisner:207). Among the places the two men visited was Tai-O-Hai, on the island of Nukuhiva, which Herman Melville had described in *Typee: A Peep at Polynesian Life* (1846) (Eisner:210). Aside from having read Melville's South Seas fiction, Murnau brought along on the trip relevant works by Joseph Conrad, Robert Louis Stevenson, Pierre Loti, and Frederick O'Brien (Eisner:210). Clearly, Murnau's interest in Polynesia was as much literary as it was ethnographic. At a local artist's suggestion, Murnau traveled to Ua-Pu, where traditional pearl fishing still flourished. As Eisner recounts the experience, Murnau

> found it one of the most beautiful of all the islands, with a population that was "witty and pure." The young men, handsome in face and figure, upright, energetic, vivacious and polite, invited him to go fishing with them. They dived down to the limpid submarine caves to harpoon fish; they overflowed with joy, everything they did was a game. Although the missionaries had forbidden them . . . to dance, for Murnau and his companions, they performed the ancient ritual dances and sang the Tahitian "Himini." (211)

Murnau compared the sights there to "pictures by Gauguin come to life," and made a pilgrimage to Atuona to visit the artist's grave (211). Eisner sees both men as having "fled the horrors of a baneful civilization" (211).

In Lanavave, on the island of Fauhiva, Murnau found a "dream landscape" of valleys, rivers, thatch-roofed huts, and palm trees (Eisner:211). There, in a native man named Mehao, he thought he had found the lead for his film. Murnau described Mehao, as follows, in a caption he wrote underneath the man's photograph:

> He . . . grew up freely and independently, like an animal in the jungle. A pure-bred Polynesian, of extraordinary physical beauty, slim and strong, with simple, natural movements. The marvellous harmony of his figure makes him look like a Greek god, a model for the Olympic games, a delight of nature. (quoted in Eisner:211–12)

Murnau would, ultimately, choose another individual, Matahi, for the principal role.

In addition to touring idyllic spots (like the Takaroa lagoon, which Murnau called "a marvel of color" [Eisner:212]), he encountered places (like Takapotu, in the Thunder Islands) which, he felt, "had the bitter taste of civilization" about them (212). Such locations had been negatively influenced by Western industry, gambling, consumerism, and popular culture. Despite such disappointing excursions, Murnau was overwhelmingly impressed by the South Seas—which he continued to view within the framework of primitive exoticism. In letters to his mother, he spoke of the "immaterial beauty of the tropics," filled with "mild air, [and] the scent of flowers" (Eisner:213). Clearly, he saw daily life there as naive and simple. As he wrote (glorifying the situation): "There is no work and no worries . . . the shining days go by in games and dancing, bathing and fishing, and the night innocently brings all lovers together" (213). Murnau admits that he was probably "bewitched" by the place (213).

As for the making of the film, Robert Flaherty would provide the broad dramatic line of its narrative; Murnau would supervise direction (with Flaherty as co-director). Floyd Crosby would serve as cinematographer (and would later win the Academy Award for *Tabu*). As David Flaherty acknowledges, although "[Robert] Flaherty led Murnau to [an] island paradise" and "gave him a dramatic story," the German Genius made a "Murnau picture there" (Flaherty:16). Shortly after arriving in Tahiti, the men faced grave production problems. They learned that Colorart was on the verge of bankruptcy and could not continue to finance the film—perhaps a casualty of the Depression economy. Murnau decided to use his dwindling savings to underwrite the picture. From the start, the film was conceived as a mix between fiction and nonfiction—making it a stylistic "half-caste" equal to the racial mélange of islanders the men would encounter. Though influenced by Flaherty's documentary bent, the work would be scripted and rendered from a preconceived plot line.

Evidently, the first story imagined for the project concerned a diver from the island of Avarua. Its text was later published (in a 1959 issue of *Film Culture*) under the title *Turia* and was cosigned by F. W. Murnau and Robert J. Flaherty (Murnau and Flaherty 1959b). In this drama, Tino, who hails from a pristine atoll, dives in a dangerous reef and emerges with a giant oyster and pearl. Rather than sell it to the white traders who visit Avarua on a schooner, he travels with them to Tahiti, where he thinks he will get a better price. Other divers from his island entrust their pearls to him to as well. Tino becomes enamored with a woman on the schooner—Turia, a "half-caste" girl. She accompanies him on his adventure in Papeete—a corrupt city filled with "French, American, Chinese and Jewish" merchants. As bids are made on Tino's extraordinary pearls, he becomes diverted by an accordion which one of the traders uses to distract him. Naively, Tino accepts the man's bid (which is not the highest), since it includes the beloved but worthless instrument. Having made one bad decision, Tino makes others. He allows a Chinese man to stiff him with the bill for a celebratory party that follows the sale of his jewel. Furthermore, Tino permits Turia to control both his money and his stash of island pearls. When Tino begins to gamble, Turia unwisely gives him all the money he requests. Then, when Tino's funds run out, she sells his friends' pearls without telling him. By the end of the day, Tino is penniless and decides he must risk a perilous dive to acquire more pearls with which to eliminate his debt. He returns home and, miraculously, his first dive is successful. But on the second descent, he perishes.

Some, like Eisner, have seen *Turia* as more typical of Flaherty's ideology than the script that was ultimately used for *Tabu*. As she notes: "Flaherty . . . was only interested in the social conditions of the natives, and here the subject is the exploitation of the pearl-divers by the Chinese traders" (216). The reason *Turia* was dropped in favor of *Tabu* was a legal one. When the Colorart deal collapsed, Murnau and Flaherty wanted to make sure that the corporation had no grounds to claim rights to the literary property on which their new film would be based.

The screenplay for *Tabu* (also credited to both Murnau and Flaherty and published in *Film Culture*) tells a related but different tale of Matahi, a pearl diver from the island of Motuvaa. This hero also falls in love, but with a Polynesian woman, Reri, who hails from his own island (fig. 6.2). (Interestingly, though, Eisner claims that the actress who played Reri was a "half-caste" [203]). Shortly after their romance begins at a tropical waterfall, a schooner, captained by a "half-caste," arrives at the island, also carrying Hitu, an old native man who bears a proclamation from the supreme chief of the islands. According to the missive (which invokes the kind of rituals Margaret Mead had documented), the *taupou* or sacred virgin of the region has died and must be replaced by another maiden. Reri has been chosen as her successor. From this moment on, Hitu warns (as we know from Mead's research), no man can desire or touch her without breaking a religious prohibition. Hitu commands Reri to sail with him to another island. As a village celebration of her choice begins (fig. 6.3), Matahi is distraught and dares to approach Reri: they dance together in a sensuous fashion. She is led away to the schooner. In the dark of night, Matahi takes a canoe to the vessel and kidnaps Reri. Eventually, the two are shipwrecked but make their way to another island, one overrun with Chinese traders. For a while, the couple prospers, with Matahi resuming his work as a pearl diver. Like Tino, however, he falls for the ploys of a saloon-keeper who tricks him into signing a receipt for "hosting" a party. Eventually, a ship carrying Hitu lands at the island. When a policeman comes to round the couple up, Matahi bribes him with one of his pearls, assuring the lovers temporary freedom. Reri encourages Matahi to purchase tickets for them on a steamer that will sail to another island. When Matahi goes to town to book their passage, he learns about his "debt" to the Chinese merchant, and the couple's plans to flee are foiled. Matahi vows that he will dive in forbidden, shark-infested waters to acquire a pearl whose value is great enough to solve his financial problems. Meanwhile, unbeknownst to him, Hitu has appeared to Reri, vowing to return soon and take her away. That night, Matahi sneaks off to go pearl-diving and, in his absence, Reri surrenders herself to Hitu. Against all odds, Matahi is successful in his diving feat and joyously returns home, only to find Reri gone. Surmising what has happened, he paddles out to the sailing ship in order to kidnap Reri but, in the process, exhausts himself and drowns.

This second narrative, though incorporating elements of the first, clearly focuses less on issues of Western exploitation than on questions of "native" superstition. While some critics have assumed that the mysterious theme of *Tabu* was indebted to Murnau (known for his interest in the occult), David Flaherty claims that both versions of the scenario were centrally conceived by his brother. This fact, however, did not stop rumors from circulating, following Murnau's death in a car accident a week before the film's New York premiere, that the director's demise was a result of his having violated a series of Polynesian taboos while shooting the movie (Eisner:218–19).

An analysis of the text of *Tabu* reveals its consistency with Primitive/Exotic visions that circulated in the Art Deco era and influenced both its movies and design sense. The opening intertitle of the film informs us that "only native-born South Sea islanders" appear in the picture along with "a few half-castes and Chinese." This statement simultaneously attests to the work's self-conscious claims to exoticism and "authenticity." In a letter to his friend Kurt Korff, sent while making *Tabu*, Murnau discusses how he will "stay away from white actors, and all professionals" in making the film. Instead, he will "experiment" with "people who have never been in front of a camera before" (Eisner:287). Finally, he proclaims (in a remark with racist overtones) that while the players "have all the qualities of the pure native appearance . . . [they will be chosen so as to] appeal to a white audience." He concludes that, "with their childlike charm and grace," his actors "would be a sensation if they entered European or American studios" (Eisner:208).

The character list, which begins the film, stresses the archetypal tone of the narrative, identifying "The Boy," "The Girl," and "The Old Warrior." Such phras-

FIGURE 6.2

The lovers Reri and Matahi
in a tropical Eden (*Tabu*,
1931). (Courtesy Museum of
Modern Art)

FIGURE 6.3

A bare-breasted native
woman dances to celebrate
the new *taupou* in *Tabu*.
(Courtesy Museum of Mod-
ern Art)

ing is highly reminiscent of *Sunrise*, which Murnau deemed a universal "song of two humans," about a man, his wife, and a woman from the city. Subtitled a "story of the South Seas," *Tabu* is divided into "chapters," a structure which highlights its status as a tale. Its first segment, "Paradise," opens with a title that refers to Bora-Bora as a "land of enchantment . . . remote [and] untouched by the hand of civilization." This conception is a familiar one from travel narratives of the era. Eisner finds Murnau's language rife with "painful nostalgia" because the "paradise" he and others conjured up "had already been destroyed long since" (202). Indeed, the consumer objects of the era (with their Primitive/Exotic designs) signaled how the culture of foreign lands had already been commodified.

Tabu opens by displaying the bare bodies of native men engaged in the primal act of hunting; specifically, they carry harpoons with which to spear fish. Thus, the film immediately emphasizes the fundamental element of water: the men not only fish but shower in a forest waterfall. As they dry themselves on the rocks, they notice flowered wreaths cascading down the falls. Upon exploring, they find a group of women bathing there as well (like the chorus girls in the first part of the production number from *Footlight Parade*). It is here that Matahi meets and becomes enamored with Reri.

In this opening sequence, the sensuality of the island people is stressed. On the one hand, their universe is Edenic—with Man and Woman innocently discovering one another in the Garden. On the other hand, it is savagely Primitive. When Matahi first approaches Reri, she physically resists him; but when another woman tries to woo Matahi, Reri attacks her. In the published script for *Tabu*, the scene is described as a "wild fight," with "the girls clawing at each other like tigresses" (Murnau and Flaherty 1959b:27–28).

Following nativist stereotypes, the screenplay conceives the women as wearing "scanty clothing" (28), and in certain scenes some are shown bare-breasted. Such nudity was allowed, of course, only because the movie made certain anthropological claims for itself (coauthored as it was by documentarist Flaherty). Unclad bodies were to be tolerated because the women in question were nonwhite and, therefore by definition, less civilized. Interestingly, the film's heroine, Reri, is always shown wearing a sarong—as though only "extras" could bypass censorship. Furthermore, she is played by a woman who is only "half" Polynesian, so her part-Caucasian virtue must be protected.

The ritual dance counts as one of the more erotic episodes of the film, occurring after Reri has been declared the new *taupou*. Again, such ceremonies had been chronicled by Mead (who dedicated an entire chapter of her book to them). Significantly, in *Tabu* the scene is also one in which several village women are depicted topless. The hedonism of the event is already presaged in the film's scenario, which describes the "ecstasy" of dancers and spectators:

> The audience, really wild now, swaying, chanting takes up the rhythm of the dance. Faster and more sensuous becomes the dance. They stand as though fixed on the spot, swaying their bodies toward each other, their faces coming closer and closer together. The dance has reached its highest pitch. Unable to contain itself any longer, the crowd forms a circle around the dancers, swaying as one with the rhythm.   (Murnau and Flaherty 1959a:31–32)

Clearly, such carnality is seen as tied to the non-Caucasian race. In *Turia*, when the half-caste heroine begins to dance, we are told that it is the exotic element of her genetic heritage that drives her to frenzy: "For Turia it is the call of the blood, the warm, sensuous blood of Polynesia, wild and free. Forgotten is her white blood. . . . One by one she throws her garments off, until she is dancing there . . . primitive and naked" (Murnau and Flaherty 1959b:19–20).

As this passage reveals, within this discourse of carnality Woman holds a special place. Not only is her body displayed more than the men's bodies, but she is also linked to mystery and superstition. Within the world *Tabu* portrays, the anointed woman must be a virgin, and her female purity grants her the power to cast perverse spells on any man who would attempt to violate her. Hence, in archetypal fashion, Woman holds the key to both life and death. Interestingly, in the first version of the scenario, it is the heroine's name—Turia—that titles the narrative, foregrounding her signal role. In the second version, the word *tabu* stands in her stead, managing to equate Woman with life's perverse enigmas and prohibitions.

As part of *Tabu*'s Edenic discourse, natural imagery abounds in the film. Natives frolic amid ferns and fronds; women pick flowers and wear floral necklaces and wreaths; palm trees are silhouetted against the moonlit sky. When noteworthy events occur in the village, a call is heralded on a conch shell. Significantly, the sound synchronized with this last act, in Hugo Riesenfeld's score, is the French horn—the very instrument the composer also used to represent the human voice in the final sequence of *Sunrise*, as European villagers communicate with one another while searching the lake for a body. For, though made some two years after *Sunrise*, *Tabu* is still a silent film, released with only an accompanying musical track. This fact is important; for it is as though Murnau wished to double the theme of primitivism inherent in the movie's content on the level of its technology. While some might claim that the film's silence was tied to its problematic funding or poor production circumstances, David Flaherty states otherwise. As he asserts: "It is not without significance that *Tabu* was made as a silent in the beginning of the era of talkies. This was a deliberate choice, dictated not by economic but by aesthetic considerations. If *Tabu* enjoys a certain universality and timelessness, credit this (for that time) bold decision" (16). Evidently, Murnau also felt some anxiety about being in a remote locale when sound came to the industry (though he had to have known of its imminent arrival when he departed). As he remarked upon his return: "I was far away from civilization when the talkies came in and I must inform myself about the situation and direction in which they are developing" (Eisner:213). Tragically, he never had a chance to obtain this education.

As Eisner points out, *Tabu* was quite inventive in its narrative articulation, using not only standard titles and intertitles but linguistic inserts in the guise of a captain's logbook, a police report, a parchment tribal decree, and a coconut leaf. For Tobing, however, these moments are not only novel but strongly ideological: "Cornered on all sides by written decrees—the texts in the film are written in Tahitian, French, and Chinese, and are translated for the audience into English. . . . Thus this Adam and Eve are trapped in a network of language, writing, and money, and the end result can only be annihilation or perversion" (151).

Eisner sees the finale of *Tabu*, in its "visual perfection," as "the apogee of the art of silent films" (203). And just as Murnau felt nostalgia about the loss of South Seas innocence, he also clearly had regrets about the demise of the silent film. He wrote:

> The talking picture represents a great step forward in the cinema. Unfortunately, it has come too soon; we had just begun to find our way with the silent film and were beginning to exploit all the possibilities of the camera. And now here are the talkies and the camera is forgotten while people rack their brains about how to use the microphone. (Eisner:213–14)

Murnau was not yet comfortable with the acoustic medium and did not "rack his brains" to experiment with it in *Tabu*. Eisner finds it "astonishing that Murnau, who wrote so enthusiastically about the songs of the Polynesians, never thought of recording them" (214). Instead, folk chants are rendered abstractly and by "proxy" in Riesenfeld's musical score.

Eventually, Murnau and Flaherty ran into problems collaborating on *Tabu*. Their personalities were, first of all, utterly opposed: while Murnau was frugal, Flaherty was not (Flaherty:16). Second, while Murnau conceptualized the film as a commercial feature, Flaherty thought of it more in the documentary mode (Eisner:216). According to Richard Griffith, Flaherty felt that Murnau had "Europeanized" Polynesian customs, psychology, and motivation in the film (1959:13). Eventually, Murnau bought out Flaherty's financial interest in *Tabu* and completed it himself. When Murnau ran out of funds, however, and the picture's fate was jeopardized, Flaherty contacted Jesse L. Lasky and convinced him to have Paramount release the movie (Eisner:220). Though Murnau never lived to witness its premiere, *Tabu* proved a profitable picture (Katz 2001:463).

PRECURSORS: *Moana* and *White Shadows in the South Seas*

Significantly, the name of the schooner that brings Hitu to Motuvaa is *Moana*, the title of Robert Flaherty's 1926 film and, quite clearly, an homage to that work. *Tabu* was certainly made in the metaphorical "shadow" of *Moana*. But, on a less figurative note, it was also made in the "shadow" of another more literal shadow—specifically, *White Shadows in the South Seas*, W. S. Van Dyke's adaptation of Frederick O'Brien's travelogue. Both films are relevant for an understanding of *Tabu* and of the era's South Seas fantasies.

Moana (which was commissioned by Jesse L. Lasky of Paramount as "another *Nanook*" [Katz 2001:462]) was shot in British Samoa, then a mandate of New Zealand. On one level, the film takes an ethnographic perspective, as did its predecessor *Nanook*—seeking to introduce sophisticated Westerners to an alien, "backward" world. One of *Moana*'s first intertitles informs us that, "Among the islands of Polynesia there is one where the people still retain the spirit and nobility of their great race." It is this island (alternately referred to as Savaii and Safune by the sea) that we will explore in the film.

However, another opening intertitle in the film quotes Robert Louis Stevenson, stating: "The first love, the first sunrise, the first South Seas island are memories apart." Here, Flaherty reveals that his interest in the region includes both its imaginative address and its heritage in the history of literature. Hence, he will not simply document the islanders' lives but disclose the locale's "drama." Fittingly, *Moana*'s subtitle is "A Romance of the Golden Age"—a phrase that conjoins the concept of ethnographic primitivism with a narrative trope (fig. 6.4).

In its construction, *Moana* shifts fluidly between these two frameworks. An opening sequence depicts a woman "bundling leaves for housekeeping," allowing us to witness indigenous domestic routines. Yet we are introduced to her as though she were the heroine of a dramatic work: "Fa'angase, the highest maiden of the village." Soon, other individuals are "featured": Mother Tu'ungaita and her sons, Pea and Moana (the latter the obvious "protagonist" of the tale). Flaherty

here draws upon techniques pioneered in *Nanook*, where the members of an Eskimo family were known to the viewer by name and treated as characters within an epic struggle.

Other sequences present, in nonfiction fashion, the daily life of the Samoans. We see people picking tarot root (which we are informed is "their bread"), harvesting bananas, and toting mulberry sticks. After we see footage of men setting traps for a jungle animal, the film cuts to images of the sea. Then an intertitle reestablishes suspense by asking: "Meanwhile, what has happened to the snare?" The film then returns to the documentary mode as it presents the capture of a wild boar.

In scholarly fashion, intertitles occasionally present a phonetic version of a native phrase, which is then translated into English. One, for example, reads: "*Taumafa lelei.* Good eating."

Other titles, however, seem drawn from conventional melodramatic rhetoric. Shots of the ocean, for instance, are labeled by the flowery words: "The sea—as warm as the air and generous as the soil." When Flaherty wishes to present the practice of Samoan dressmaking, he initiates his documentary sequence with the

FIGURE 6.4
Native women "by a water-
fall" in *Moana* (1926), a
"romance of the Golden
Age." (Courtesy Museum of
Modern Art)

intertitle: "Mother Tu'ungaita has a dress to make," thus personalizing the event and giving it narrative "motivation." Like good anthropology students, we absorb facts and terminology from the intertitles: that the red clothing dye Samoans use derives from sandalwood seeds; that their native costume is called the *lavalava*, and so on. Images offer views of such quotidian (yet exotic) acts as climbing coconut trees, whittling spears, fishing from cliffs, hunting sea turtles, and cooking breadfruit custard.

Bowing to the narrative imperatives of fiction film, Flaherty then focuses on a young beautiful couple (the heterosexual pair requisite in classical narrative). A title tells us it is "The end of the day for Fa'angase and Moana." They are shown sitting together as she, bare-breasted, puts flowers in a wreath on his head (fig. 6.5). As she rubs ointment into his skin, another title tells us that she is "Anointing [him] with perfumed oil—an age-old rite of the Siva." Both the nudity and eroticism of this sequence are permissible because the film makes an educational claim for itself, and because it deals with nonwhite people who are conceived, within the Western imagination, to be both uninhibited and "innocent" in their sexual pursuits. Moana then dances the "Siva" as Fa'angase laughs and claps. Titles monumentalize both his body and his ceremonial act: "Pride of beauty; pride of strength; the art of worship, the courtship of the race." As these erotic sequences indicate, ethnography meets voyeurism in *Moana*. According to Tobing, these passages depend "in large part on Flaherty's use of a long lens and panchromatic film. According to Flaherty, this technology allowed for better voyeurism, since the Samoan actors were less self-conscious with a more distant camera presence" (140).

An intertitle (directly addressing the spectators) alerts us that, "Everything [we] have seen—the gathering of food, of game, the making of the feast, the Siva—has all been preparation for a great event." Given our conventional cinematic orientation (and the romantic sequence that precedes it), we assume the occasion is a wedding. But it is not. Rather, Flaherty bucks the Western narrative paradigm and focuses upon another act central to Samoan culture—tattooing—the coming-of-age ritual for a young man. We then watch an extended sequence of Moana subjected to this grueling procedure—not as endearing a sight as a nuptial, but one that Margaret Mead documents in her book as well (267). We watch a "witch-woman" make dyes and "keep the devils out." We witness the tattoo artist using bone needles. We learn that the hardest cut to bear is in the knee. We observe the chief drink a celebratory libation. When the three-week process is complete, Moana is *malosi*—an adult man.

After that extended sequence, the film then pays remarkably short shrift to the

traditional climax we had expected all along. Indeed, Flaherty never actually depicts the wedding of Moana and Fa'angase at all, though we do see some women making preparation for it by dressing the bride and arranging her headdress. This relatively brief sequence is followed by a title (which seems to allude to Moana) and reads: "Prestige for his village, honor for his family, the maiden of his desire." The movie closes with footage of people dancing and images of the mountains and sky. In a final nod toward "going native," Flaherty's last title reads: "*Ua Uma Lava*—The End."

In its commercial release, *Moana* was a disappointment. While *Nanook* had been a financial success for Pathé, *Moana* fell short of Fox's expectations. Richard Corliss sees this as related to the lack of drama in the film. As he notes, Moana's life seems an "endless idyll, as opposed to Nanook's epic struggle." And "without the bone-chilling conflict that a situation like Nanook's offers Flaherty," the film "run[s] the risk of degenerating into pretty pictures" (1976:232).

In 1927, Flaherty was asked by Robert Dietz of MGM if he would like to work with W. S. Van Dyke on a filmed version of *White Shadows in the South Seas*. While Flaherty had misgivings about a Hollywood studio project, he signed on to do the film and sailed for Papeete, Tahiti. Once there, however, he was alienated by the army of technicians dispatched to shoot the drama and gather footage of native culture. Obviously, such an assembly-line work method was anathema to an independent filmmaker like Flaherty. Realizing his incompatibility with the endeavor, he resigned and returned home (Calder-Marshall 1963:122–23).

There may have been other reasons why Flaherty felt estranged by plans for the film. While *Moana* had attempted to focus entirely on native characters (seeking to obscure the specter of the Western filmmaker who choreographed their moves), *White Shadows* concentrated on a white male protagonist (a symbolic "stand-in" for author O'Brien). However, while O'Brien's book was a nonfiction travel diary, the Hollywood version creates a fanciful storyline to make the tome's insights more approachable and palatable. Furthermore, the newly invented characters are played by Hollywood stars—not by the indigenous, nonprofessional islanders that Flaherty favored. Despite the film's clear recourse to illusion, it touts its ties to O'Brien's "famous book" by calling itself a "camera record" of his travelogue. Likewise, it boasts of the film's being "produced and photographed on . . . natural locations and with the ancient native tribes of the Marquesas Islands."

White Shadows tells the story of Doctor Matthew Lloyd (Monty Blue), a white physician who has lived for years in the South Seas. Like many works of the late silent era, the film lacks synchronized dialogue but has a sound-on-film track that carries both music and effects. Though intertitles inform us that the island on which Lloyd resides is "fresh from the touch of God," it is also clearly a corrupt place where Western traders have degraded the indigenous society. Hence, we see visions of a town with a bar at its center, where island men drink and girls dance the hula for white men's delight. In case we miss the implications of this scene, an intertitle tells us that "the white man, in his greedy trek across the planet, [has] cast his withering shadow over these islands . . . and the business of 'civilizing' them to his interests began." Distraught by this situation (and "ashamed of being white"), Lloyd has become a derelict drunk who rants and raves around town about the evils of Western influence. A powerful pearl trader (who views Lloyd as a dangerous "native coddler") arranges a trap for him whereby he is set adrift at sea. A typhoon hits his boat and leaves him shipwrecked upon an island where he encounters an indigenous tribe.

They are kind, peaceful people who have never before seen a white man and view Lloyd as a god. In a plot move now familiar to us from other South Seas epics, Lloyd falls in love with Fayaway (Raquel Torres) the virginal *taupou* of the island (fig. 6.6). Though his desire for her is at first forbidden, when he saves the chief's son (who has almost drowned), he is allowed to marry the sacred virgin. All is well until Lloyd discovers that the local oysters bear giant pearls which the natives discard as useless, unaware of their value. Tempted by the profits he envisions mak-

FIGURE 6.6
Fayaway (Raquel Torres)
takes the hand of Doctor
Matthew Lloyd (Monty Blue)
in *White Shadows in the
South Seas* (1928). (Courtesy British Film Institute)

ing, Lloyd lights signal fires each night hoping to attract passing ships. When Fay-away discovers this, she confronts him with her hurt and displeasure. He recants and extinguishes the fire that he has just set. Unfortunately, however, the confla-gration is spotted by the ship of his former enemy. When it arrives on shore, the trusting natives (thinking the crew are all kindly white gods) welcome them. The white men from the ship soon discover the existence of the pearls and set about trading these for worthless trinkets as well as selling the natives bolts of fabric. In trying to warn his people of the danger, Lloyd is shot dead by the sailors. The last image of the film (understood to take place some months later) depicts his beloved island replete with a decadent bar; Fayaway sits sadly apart from the group, wear-ing a Western-style dress.

More so than *Moana* or *Tabu*, *White Shadows* clearly walks a tenuous line between fiction and documentary. The lead "native" character is played by a white film actress (even though in Hollywood she is seen as an "ethnic" figure who stands outside the mainstream). While the broad narrative trajectory of the film smacks of contrived fantasy and melodrama, certain sequences do have an ethnographic quality, especially those showing natives climbing coconut trees, preparing a feast, harpooning fish, and hunting sea turtles. And some of the quasi-documentary footage even has a casual pornographic aspect, as when we see a bevy of female hands (Fayaway's and others') sensuously spread coconut oil all over Lloyd's body. If the film strides uneasily the rift between fiction and documentary, it also takes an untenable ideological stance. As the text (appropriating O'Brien's authorial "voice") decries the venality of civilization as a ruinizing force in tropical lands, we may wonder how it justifies its own encroachment there by a California film crew?

EXOTICISM—HOLLYWOOD STYLE

The truth is that no value was or is attached to maidenhood in all Polynesia, the young woman being left to her own whims without blame or care. Only deep and sincere attachment holds her at last to the man she has chosen, and she then follows his wishes in matters of fidelity, though still to a large extent remaining mistress of herself.
— Frederick O'Brien (1919:109)

While *Moana* and *Tabu* present themselves as quasi documentaries, and *White Shadows* hovers uneasily between fantasy and reality, other movies of the Art Deco era take a standard fictional approach toward representing the Exotic. Like *White Shadows*, these works often focus on a Westerner's encounter with the Polynesian universe—a stance that assures an easy "identification" between movie audience and screen protagonist.

Venus of the South Seas (1924) is a quaint example of this genre, and one of the few which draws tentatively upon elements of the Style Moderne. Made by an independent film company (Vital Exchanges) in the silent era, the film concerns an American father and daughter who live on the island of Manea. John Royal (Roland Purdie) is a pearl and copra trader who helps "to carry on the business of the world." Shona (Annette Kellerman) is his grown child who, under the influence of island life, has become a feisty, independent woman. She is, for example, an expert deep sea diver who polices natives who periodically steal pearls from her dad. While John Royal is represented as an upstanding business-man (whose "right" to the booty he claims is never questioned), Captain Drake

172   STRANGERS IN PARADISE

(Norman French)—whose supply ship regularly visits Manea—is portrayed as an unscrupulous operator who buys stolen pearls from the natives. Annette Kellerman (sister of cinematographer Maurice Kellerman) was a champion Australian swimmer and the Esther Williams of her time,[6] and much of the film is devoted to undersea footage of her in action. (A somewhat controversial figure who allegedly pioneered the one-piece bathing suit, she was reputedly arrested in Boston in 1907 in violation of "community standards.")[7] In the film, however, she is discreetly dressed in shirt and shorts whenever she swims. As the film's narrative progresses, Manea is visited by a luxury yacht owned by the wealthy Robert Quane Jr. (Robert Ramsey), an elegant bachelor and man-about-town. Acting forward (like a native woman), Shona swims out to the boat to see him and a romance blossoms between the two. When Quane sails away, vowing to return, she is lonely and expresses her emotions in a fairy tale she relates to the native children.

What is interesting about her story is that it is illustrated with footage to represent narrative events. The fable concerns Gwytha (played by Kellerman), a princess whose consort is being held captive in chains. In order to release him, she must acquire the Flower of Love, which is found only beneath the sea. Under water, she encounters a mermaid who grows such blossoms and, ultimately, Gwytha procures one for herself, bringing it back to free her lover. What is unique about this sequence is that it is rendered in a lush two-color process (of green and orange) that makes it quite beautiful. Moreover, both the princess and the mermaid are dressed in exotic costumes that resemble the kind of Art Deco theatrical fashions sketched by Erté—for instance, in *Les Bijoux des Perles* (1924) (fig. 6.7). The mermaid wears a striking pearl tiara as well as flowing pearl necklaces and bracelets. Gwytha wears a hat adorned with strings of pearls that extend to cover her arms like sleeves. Furthermore, her skirt is made entirely of jeweled ropes. Significantly, while under water the princess happens upon the mermaid's dressing table, and she marvels at all the wonderful mirrors, cosmetics, and baubles. Later, when Shona completes her storytelling and returns to her rustic cabin, she consults some fashion magazines in order to make herself attractive for Quane's return. For the first time, we see her dolled up in a dress, hat, and jewelry instead of her usual sporty garb. The rough South Seas (albeit Western) female thus becomes an Art Deco woman. Not surprisingly, she eventually gets her man.

6. Esther Williams later made the film *Million Dollar Mermaid* (1952), based on Annette Kellerman's life.

7. Internet Movie Data Base (IMDB), entry on "Annette Kellerman."

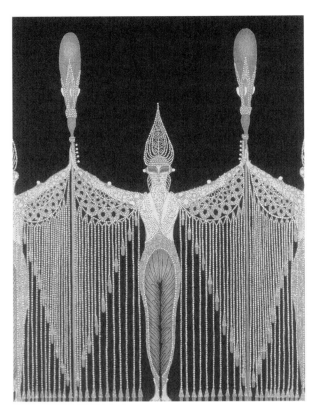

FIGURE 6.7

Les Bijoux des Perles (1924) by Erté. (Courtesy Sevenarts Limited)

Another curious thing about the film is that, even though there are children, we see no other women on Manea, whether Western or native. So when Shona's father dies and she is left alone, she is easily victimized by a native man who attempts to rape her (shades of 1915's *The Birth of a Nation*). But aside from facilitating racial stereotypes (of oversexed primitives), the absence of women—on the screen if not on the island—also guarantees that when Quane arrives he will not be tempted by native beauties, the usual fate of the white male protagonist who travels to the South Seas.

Another (more mainstream) South Seas romance of the twenties focuses upon a female "wild child" raised within Pacific island culture. In *Hula* (1927), directed by Victor Fleming, a young woman, Hula Calhoun (Clara Bow), lives with her father Bill (Albert Gran) on a huge Hawaiian estate. As a title tells us, the Calhouns have been "ranchers, planters and royal spenders for three gin-erations [*sic*]." (Again, as in *Venus of the South Seas*, there is no mother in the picture.) In actuality, however, Hula has been brought up by a part-Hawaiian man, Kahana (Agonstino Borgotao), a ranch foreman who tries to shield her from the influence of her father—a kind but hard-drinking fellow who, in the spirit of the Roaring Twenties, parties with his Western guests day in and day out. When we first encounter Hula, she is bathing in a stream amid tropical fauna—an image that clearly associates her with Nature. (On the other hand, she sports a flapper hairdo—a triangular, frizzy bob.) In demeanor, she is a rough-and-ready tomboy who can ride a horse (even into her father's house) and eat *poi* with her fingers like the natives do. Her seemingly carefree adolescent life is changed, however, when a British engineer, Anthony Haldane (Clive Brook), comes to visit her father before beginning an irrigation project. She is immediately smitten with him and, since she has not been raised according to Western feminine conventions, instantly announces that he is a "beautiful man." Furthermore, she sets a rather bold and outrageous trap for him in order to win his attention. She lets her dog escape and then calls upon Anthony to help find the animal. When the dog dives into raging rapids, Anthony chases after him, almost losing his life by plunging over a waterfall. Interestingly, it is Hula who extends her arm from the

STRANGERS IN PARADISE

shore to save him; obviously, in films like *Way Down East* (1920), the situation is reversed with the heroine rescued from peril by the hero. With her drenched paramour in her arms, Hula audaciously kisses him and declares her love—with no thought for discretion or modesty. When she notices a wound on his cheek, she kisses it and her lips are perversely stained with blood. Hula now assumes that Anthony returns her passion and is puzzled when he avoids her. (Kahana tells her that men from the "mainland" are cold.) One day she sets another daring trap to extract from him an explanation for his aloofness. Playing a bereft Victorian heroine, she lets her horse run off with her astride and purposely falls from the saddle. Anthony comes riding along to save her. Locked in an embrace with her, he confesses that he is married. Rather than be shocked or upset, however, Hula simply asks if he loves his spouse. When he replies that he does not, she says: "Then what difference does it make? Kiss me, love me—please begin!" When she tells him that "even a native knows marriage means nothing without love," he counters: "A native isn't tied by conventions! Gad! I wish we *were* natives!" Despite her willingness to have an affair with a married man, Anthony demurs and spurns her. One night, during a luau at her father's house (in which Anthony is paying attention to a widow, Mrs. Bane [Arlette Marchal]), Hula outrages everyone by living up to her name—donning a grass skirt and joining a performance of the famous native erotic dance (fig. 6.8). (In this respect, she is like Princess Tam-Tam, who leaps to the stage of a Parisian nightclub to dance to the rhythms of the African musicians.) Impassioned, Anthony finally gives in to his impulses and writes a letter to his wife pleading for a divorce. Unbeknownst to him, however, his wife has traveled to Hawaii and soon arrives at the Calhoun estate. She tells Mrs. Bane that she does not love her husband but has come to insure a good financial settlement. To make trouble for Hula (of whom she is jealous), Mrs. Bane tells Mrs. Haldane (Maude Truax) that her husband is about to make a fortune. Suddenly, Mrs. Haldane is interested in a marital reconciliation. When Hula learns of this (and the crass reason for Mrs. Haldane's sudden reversal), she pretends to blow up a dam that is vital for Anthony's irrigation project. Thinking his enterprise ruined, Mrs. Haldane decides to leave and grants her husband a divorce. As the picture ends, Hula and Anthony look forward to a blissful future.

What is interesting about *Hula* is the merging of Clara Bow's "It" girl "flapper" identity with that of the South Seas native female. Clearly, the character of Hula has some of the nontraditional aspects of the New Woman, unconcerned as she is with rigid mores and social pretenses. On the day she first meets Anthony, she runs into his room (to chase her dog) wearing only a Japanese-style kimono. Further-

FIGURE 6.8

Hula Calhoun (Clara Bow), a South Seas "wild child," flirts with Anthony Haldane (Clive Brook) in *Hula* (1927). (Courtesy British Film Institute)

more, to show him an insect bite that she complains about, she opens her robe to expose her naked thigh. As she leaves Anthony's room, Mrs. Bane remarks: "Hula, you can't go into a man's room half dressed. Really—you've lived among the natives so much, you've become as primitive as they are." Hula's sexual forwardness and ease with her body—as Mrs. Bane's comment suggests—cast her as a quasi-indigenous woman—at least as conceived by the Western male imagination. As an opening title informs us, Hawaii is "a land of singing seas and swinging hips—where volcanoes are often active . . . and maidens always are" (shades of Frederick O'Brien's vision of the forward South Seas female!). As we have seen, through exotic Art Deco fashions, contemporary urban women were allowed to engage in such a fantasy of "doubling," seeing themselves simultaneously as sophisticated new women and untamed tropical maidens. Interestingly, after Hula and Anthony have become lovers, she suddenly becomes taken with mainland couture. In one scene, she receives a shipment of a new dress and models it for Anthony. Meanwhile, her father sweats as he looks at his account book with its mounting charges for Hula's wardrobe. Significantly, even at this moment of high style, when she most approximates a metropolitan flapper, Hula's "native" side shines through. When Anthony refuses to embrace her because the dress is "much too splendiferous," she rips off its expensive, organza frills—converting it to a simple sheath.

While *Hula* and *Venus* involve a white woman "going native," other fiction movies again concentrate on the Western male adventurer (as had *White Shadows in the South Seas*). *Bird of Paradise*, directed by King Vidor for RKO in 1932, is a sound-era film which concerns some American men who land on a tropical island and proceed to defy local traditions. At first, the residents are extremely friendly to the strangers. In what has become a "staple" scene of the South Seas picture, happy natives paddle out to the foreign ship in their canoes (here, to the accompaniment of pseudo-Hawaiian music). Unlike the films of Murnau, Van Dyke, and Flaherty, which attempt to be "sensitive" to cultural difference, *Bird of Paradise* immediately wallows in smug ethnocentricism.[8] As the Western crew jests about the natives being "cannibals," they throw ludicrously inappropriate gifts to the islanders (alarm clocks, pipes, hats), obviously enjoying the incongruous joke. Their repartee is also decidedly sexual. One sailor asks whether this is a "virgin island," and another inquires of a female native: "Hey, Baby, anything on for tonight?"

An all-too-predictable note of danger interrupts the merriment when a shark is, suddenly, spotted in the waters. As the natives scurry away, Johnny (Joel McCrea) harpoons the predator, but becomes entangled in the weapon's ropes and falls into the ocean. A native girl, Luana (Dolores Del Rio), cuts the cord with a knife she holds in her teeth, thus saving him. Later, the sailors are welcomed ashore with a festival, replete with beating drums. Once more, ethnocentric humor prevails: when the men are offered some *poi*, they wonder if it is "apple *poi*" or "lemon *poi*." The strangers are soon introduced to the village medicine man who, they are told, "feeds" the local volcano, Pele, with women. In a musical number (choreographed by Busby Berkeley), Luana and other villagers dance and sing. At the end of the ritual, some women are carried off, ostensibly to be sacrificed to the mountain. When Luana faints at the sight, Johnny picks her up but is stopped by the medicine man, who reveals that she is the daughter of the king and taboo to all suitors but the native prince. Again, the tradition that Margaret Mead once documented is treated as an *idée fixe* in cinematic South Seas narratives.

---

8. For a discussion of *Bird of Paradise*, see Hershfield (1998).

Rebellious, Luana swims out to the foreign ship that night. In a balletic sequence shot under water (again, rendered by Busby Berkeley), she looks naked (though the actress is, likely, wearing a sheer body suit). When Johnny spots her, he jumps into the ocean, and the couple frolic in the water and on shore. To communicate, they use sign language: when Luana wants another kiss, she simply points to her lips.

A title (reminiscent of those in Murnau's, Van Dyke's, and Flaherty's films) informs us that, "When flying fish appear, the whole village makes a night of carnival." Here, we have an "ethnographic" excuse for a comical sequence of Johnny attempting to stun fish with his tennis racket. Resuming their flirtation, Johnny and Luana retreat to an area of lush tropical vegetation, but are sobered when an arrow barely misses them. An old woman explains to Johnny that Luana is about to be married to the native potentate.

Once more, we are privy to a spectacle of exotic costumes, dance, and ceremony. Luana appears in an elaborate headdress (fig. 6.9) worthy of a Ziegfeld Girl. When Johnny declares to her that, "White man wants you to stay with him," he is accosted by natives who tie him to a tree. Later, the old woman sets him free and helps him to escape to the ship in return for a phonograph recording of "The Darktown Strutter's Ball." Clearly, this reference purposely negates the difference between Asians and blacks in order to equalize their inferiority as nonwhites. To further blur the racial boundaries, the old woman covers Johnny's body with mud, so he can "pass" for a native and free Luana (a narrative strategy we have already seen in *Roman Scandals*). We then return to the wedding ceremony, as the groom stares lustfully at Luana. She is forced to enact a suggestive dance, made more erotic by a scanty lei that barely covers her breasts. As she performs in a ring of fire, Johnny dashes into the circle and carries her off.

A title proclaims: "Paradise: The secluded island of Lani." As the couple canoes to shore, Luana declares (in her native language) that it will be their "home." In a scene reminiscent of one from *Tabu*, the two happen upon a waterfall and feast on bananas. It is also evocative of Busby Berkeley's production number "By a Waterfall," where chorus girls at first approximate native maidens before being transformed into sequin-capped Deco bathing beauties, outfitted in *moderne* white swim suits. When it rains, Johnny and Luana hide under huge fronds; when they are hungry, she pours coconut milk into his mouth; when they need shelter, he builds her a grass shack. Though, at first, he calls to her with Tarzan-like vocalizations, she is soon speaking broken English. To pass the time, he tells her about such modern conveniences as radio, electric lights, airplanes, and speedboats. She proclaims that he makes "civilization look silly."

When the volcano erupts, the scene shifts to the village, where the natives are highly agitated; they fear that Pele can only be stopped through Luana's sacrifice. Emissaries are sent to find her and bring her back, which they do when Johnny is off hunting. Learning of her disappearance, he paddles his canoe to the village. When a whirlpool threatens his craft, he survives by swinging, Tarzan-style, to the shore on vines. Arriving at the village, he is captured by islanders, who carry him away tied to logs.

When reunited with Luana, who is also restrained and imprisoned, he learns that she will be offered up to Pele for her transgressions (fig. 6.10). After she confesses her love for him (with an inexplicable mastery of American slang: "I thought I only had a yen for you but I love you more than I could ever love any one"), they kiss. With each tied to a pole (in a kitschy romantic scene that smacks of sexual bondage), he recites "The Lord's Prayer" while she prays to her own god.

The two are then carried off, in Christ-like posture. With the natives lusting for human sacrifice, Johnny's cohorts arrive and rescue the couple. As Johnny falls ill with a fever, with Luana by his side, the sailors talk about taking Luana with them but conclude that she cannot be "transplanted." Noting also that Johnny's family would be upset at his liaison with a "native girl," they decide that "East is East and West is West" and should remain so.

As Luana cares for Johnny, further comical scenes mock her unfamiliarity with Western modernity—for example, she has no idea of how to get water from the kitchen tap. On the other hand, her native ways come in handy. When John's illness renders him unable to eat food (in a fairly outrageous sequence reminiscent of Hula's bloody lips), Luana prechews it for him and, like a mother bird, passes it from her mouth to his. Ultimately, to assure Johnny's survival, she offers herself up to the villagers who have pursued her. A final image depicts Luana superimposed over volcanic flames, a clear indication that she has allowed herself to be sacrificed to Pele.

While a standard fiction genre picture (and, therefore, quite unlike *Tabu*), *Bird of Paradise* nonetheless bears certain similarities to the Murnau-Flaherty opus. Though more insensitive in its portrayal, the Vidor film shares with its predecessor a Western, Deco-era fascination with the Asian/Exotic. Furthermore, it evinces a similar focus on primitive "superstitions." Like *Tabu* (and also *White Shadows*),

FIGURE 6.10

Johnny (Joel McCrea) con-
fronts South Seas villagers
over his love for Luana
(Dolores Del Rio) in *Bird of
Paradise*. (Courtesy Museum
of Modern Art)

its narrative entails the violation of native religious edicts involving prohibitions against women. Joanne Hershfield has seen this plot device in *Bird of Paradise* as conveniently preventing any marriage between Johnny and Luana—thereby maintaining clear racial separation and upholding Western cultural sanctions against miscegenation (7–8).

What is perhaps most fascinating about comparisons between *Bird of Paradise* and *Moana* or *Tabu* is their respective engagement of point of view. In the latter works, the white man is, largely or entirely, absent from the screen. *Moana* concentrates completely on the world of the residents of Savaii; it is only they who are depicted in the film. Of course, the intertitles (which lecture us on the ways of the islanders) are a clear indication of Flaherty's authorial voice (posing as the Voice of Knowledge). Furthermore, there is obviously a Western, voyeuristic eye behind the camera, the ever-absent reverse shot. In *Tabu* the specter of the European presents itself in the "half-caste" captain of the ship *Moana*, which arrives on the island carrying Hitu. Significantly, it is this halfbreed's navigational act that sets Matahi's world in chaos and that leads to the couple's tragedy.

Alternately, in the fiction/adventure genre (as we have seen previously in *White Shadows*), there is often a white male who travels to an exotic locale and serves as the protagonist of the film—thus making the Western perspective more obvious. In *Hell Harbor* (1930), Bob Wade (John Holland) sails to the Caribbean in order to buy pearls. In *Trader Horn* (1931), the title character (played by Harry Carey) travels through Africa to acquire ivory. A similar quest motivates Harry Holt (Neil Hamilton) in *Tarzan and His Mate* (1934; directed by Cedric Gibbons and Jack Conroy). Clearly, the men who voyage to remote locales are not simply Westerners, but businessmen who intend to exploit the natural resources of foreign locations. In fact, many of their prized acquisitions (pearls, ivory, animal pelts) are precisely the coveted materials of Art Deco jewelry, coats, or chryselephantine sculptures. In rare cases, it is a woman who arrives in alien territory. In *East of Borneo* (1931), Mindy Randolph (Rose Hobart) voyages to the Orient to find her lost husband; and in *Trader Horn* the hero encounters a woman, Mrs. Trent (Olive Carey), who is looking for a lost white girl. These are different situations from what we found in *Hula* and *Venus of the South Seas*, where white women have been born into an exotic culture.

In *Tarzan and his Mate*, aside from hunting, Holt is also interested in "rescuing" his former girlfriend Jane (Maureen O'Sullivan), an English woman who has remained in the jungle with her lover, the "wild child" Tarzan. Hoping to seduce Jane back to Europe, Holt brings her Art Deco-era accoutrements: expensive fragrances, sheer stockings, and Paris gowns. As he tells his traveling companion: "I thought if she saw some of the latest dresses, got the feel of silk, the scent of perfume," she would come home; "women are funny about things like that." In some respects Jane is a bit like Shona of *Venus of the South Seas* or like Hula, other white women "gone native" who develop a sudden interest in Western fashion. In the scene of Jane trying on the modish clothing, Holt also plays for her a popular phonograph recording. His lascivious friend, Martin Arlington (Paul Cavanagh), ogles her, remarking that she is "a fascinating little savage," and the first woman he has had to "coax *into* a gown." But while Jane actually resides in Africa, the women back home who have bought Art Deco exotic fashions hope, if only symbolically, to gain a little of the "savage" for themselves. As though to show the connection between "savage" and "animalistic," the chimpanzee Cheetah appears wearing one of Jane's new hats. Clearly, in this campy fashion sequence, we see the influence of Cedric Gibbons, a codirector of the film.

As with *Bird of Paradise*, most Deco-era Hollywood adventure films are shameless in their racism and ethnocentrism. In *East of Borneo*, one Westerner refers to a local potentate as "moderately civilized." In *Trader Horn*, a Westerner claims that the Africans are "happy, ignorant children." Also in that film (as in *Tabu*), native women are shown bare-breasted, like illustrations from *National Geographic* magazine. Furthermore, in a trailer for the film, the lost Caucasian girl (grown into womanhood) for whom Mrs. Trent searches is deemed a "White goddess of paganism; [a] she devil Queen of [the] Jungle." Some films also reveal a curious disregard for any illusion of accuracy. While *Trader Horn* was actually shot in Africa and, ostensibly, used native residents as "extras," other films (like *Tarzan and His Mate*) clearly use black Americans for the role of Africans. Hence, throughout the film, character accents are "off," and, in one scene, a native chant sounds more like a Negro Spiritual. Similarly, though *Hell Harbor* is supposedly set in the Latin Caribbean (somewhere near Cuba), the black men and women who play the island natives speak in a distinctly American Southern patois.

While, in the fiction South Seas film, the Western view is obvious, it is also present in Flaherty and Murnau's more "politically correct" work. In *Tabu* we found evidence of the notion that the tropical world is a new Eden, a representation made even more literal in *Bird of Paradise* when Johnny and Luana settle on a deserted island. Likewise, *Tabu* and *Moana* imagine the primitive human as being highly corporeal—whether it be Matahi's athletic build and physique, Moana's tattooed torso, or Reri's sensual midriff. Surely this is why Marianna Torgovnick finds anthropological discourse riddled with a "keyhole vocabulary" that turns the scientist into a "Peeping Tom" (4). Moreover, the primitive human is not only characterized by embodiment in these films but also by excessive eroticism. While in *Tabu* we are privy to Reri's rather restrained hula, in *Bird of Paradise* we are treated to Luana's campy production number. Alternately, in *Trader Horn* a native ritual dance becomes an occasion for mass frenzy. Furthermore, the same educational tone that we find in the titles of *Moana* and *Tabu* appears in the fiction films. *Trader Horn* (directed W. S. Van Dyke) opens with a title proclaiming how MGM is indebted to the Territory of Tanganyika, the Protectorate of Uganda, the Colony of Kenya, and the region of the Belgian Congo. Finally, *Tabu* is marked by the very dichotomies that Torgovnick finds typical of Western representations of the primitive, which it sees as "by turns gentle, in tune with nature, paradisal, ideal—or violent, in need of control" (3). Murnau and Flaherty maintain respect for the traditions of the South Seas islands, but they treat the religious edict that haunts *Tabu* as a pernicious superstition. The sequence that recounts the lovers' escape is entitled "Chapter II: Paradise Lost" and proclaims: "Feeling the vengeance of the tabu the guilty lovers fought their way over leagues of open sea seeking some island . . . always driven on by fear, fear of the avenging tabu." Hence, though in its own technological bow to "primitivism," *Tabu* is a silent film, it clearly articulates a series of Western, judgmental, and modern utterances. As Torgovnick notes (in language that bears an uncanny relevance to the Coming of Sound): "The primitive does what we ask it to do. Voiceless, it lets us speak for it. It is our ventriloquist's dummy—or so we like to think" (9).

In addition to "speaking" for the jaded Westerner's hallucinatory longing for an imagined primitive past (especially in the Depression era), the South Seas films of the Art Deco era express a particular vision of the female. For the South Seas maiden is a figure rife with contradictions, being blatantly erotic but hopelessly taboo. Hence, she is consonant with other "schizoid" representations of the Art Deco Woman—be it the desirable but transgressive Garbo heroine, the sensual but "backward" Baker *danseuse*, or the feminine but androgynous chryselephantine figurine.

7. ARCHITECTURAL EXOTICISM & THE ART DECO PICTURE PALACE

LEISURE AND COMMODIFICATION

In chapters 2 and 3, I discussed Art Deco's relation to modern American consumer culture—and delineated the material objects that the design style sold. What I did not mention, however, was the ways in which the movement was also tied to the commodification of leisure time. According to Don Slater, following industrialization capitalists feared that workers would choose to use their income to buy themselves free time rather than work additional hours to acquire more material goods (1997:29). In response to this anxiety, businessmen learned to "sell" leisure time in a variety of ways. As Slater comments, "Amongst the most adventurous pioneers . . . were the entrepreneurs of leisure; they organized activities such as sport, theatre and entertainment, assemblies, balls and masquerades, leisure and pleasure gardens and so on into commercial events, with fee-paying admission by ticket or subscription" (19).

Obviously, the cinema functioned as part of this economic dynamic, with a price tag attached to a ticket to a film. I have shown in chapters 4, 5, and 6 how the costumes and mise-en-scène of movies promoted and packaged the Art Deco style, in a productive interaction between cinema and material culture. But the attraction of filmgoing in this era was not only based on the picture that one went to see but also on its architectural environment. As John F. Barry and Epes W. Sargent make clear in 1927, the American movie theater of the period was sometimes an architectural jewel that allowed the audience to spend time in a place of "romance," away from the harsh, dull surroundings of quotidian life. Curiously, they also claim that the space enabled the public a respite from the "com-

If you understand why patrons visit the motion picture theatre, you understand why architects plan as they do. People come to the motion picture theatre to live an hour or two in the land of romance. They escape from the humdrum existence of daily life.

—John F. Barry and
Epes W. Sargent (1927:110)

mercialized" world—this despite the fact that the movie theater was the site of rampant economic exchange. Part of what the viewer paid for was a taste of luxury. As Barry and Sargent note: "Watch the bright light in the eyes of the tired shop girl . . . as she sighs with satisfaction walking amid furnishings that once delighted the hearts of queens" (110). Hence, in purchasing her ticket, the spectator bought access not only to a motion picture but to a "shrine of democracy" (110). Furthermore, she purchased entry into a therapeutic environment, a "playland" that could "stimulate the imagination of tired minds and re-create the strength of weary hearts" (110).

AN "ART DECO PARADISE"

Newcomers [today], unexpectedly transported by the [Oakland] Paramount's Art Deco paradise, gaze with open mouths and wondering eyes just as those did opening night in 1931. —Peter Botto, manager of the Oakland Paramount Theatre's restoration (quoted in Stone 1991:9)

As I have shown, Art Deco was associated with many aspects of the cinema: its sets, its costuming, its stars, its themes, and its generic modes. But it was also a movement linked to the architecture of the movie theater since it was in the Deco era that the most extravagant American "picture palaces" were built. In this chapter I focus on one such building whose design style had ties to the Primitive/Exotic strain of the Art Deco style—one we have just examined in chapter 6.

Of course, not all movie theaters of the era were influenced by modernism. Many (like those designed by C. W. and George L. Rapp of Chicago, or by Thomas W. Lamb of New York City) were baroque or classical in appearance, creating for the American public the impression of visiting an Ancient Greek or Roman temple, or a historic European castle. Here one thinks of Rapp's *Chicago* or *Tivoli* Theaters (built in Chicago in 1921), or of Lamb's *Loew's State* (built in St. Louis in 1924), or of Lamb's *Poli's Palace* (built in Worcester, Massachusetts, in 1926). Other architects, like John Eberson, were known for their incorporation of elaborate special effects into movie theater design. In such "atmospheric theaters" as the *Tampa* or the *Olympia* (both built in Florida in 1926), a patron had the sense of inhabiting an open-air amphitheater, seated beneath a dark night sky or a blanket of clouds and stars (Margolies and Gwathmey 1991:18).

One of the major goals of such monumental theaters was, clearly, to make moviegoing an impressive experience, worthy of its escalating price of admission.

As Marcus Loew said: "We sell tickets to *theaters*, not movies" (Margolies and Gwathmey:17; emphasis added). In a similar vein, Barry and Sargent noted that, while "programs come and go . . . the theatre alone remains" (111). Such an edifice also encouraged moviegoers to indulge their desire for elegance. Thus, George Rapp conceived his theaters as populist spaces in which "the wealthy rub elbows with the poor" (Margolies and Gwathmey:17). This sentiment is apparent in an excerpt from a brochure published by the San Francisco *Fox* theater (built by Lamb in 1929) touting its glamorous atmosphere:

> You enter the wide swinging doors of the great Castle of Splendor and behold: The silent magic of life's mirror, the Screen, in creations of its finest magicians . . . the thousand throated organ, now whispering in gentle melody, now reverberating in mighty thunder . . . the Orchestra, trained musicians . . . in moods of exquisite harmony . . . a myriad of multicolored lights . . . architectural beauties; . . . soft miles of carpeted wonder in lounge and foyer . . . the vast magnificence of the palace of a King. (Stone:13)

The ascendancy of the picture palace was related to the growth of the American economy in the 1920s and to the rise of film's popularity as a middle-class entertainment. Its demise, however, came swiftly in the early thirties, as the Depression took its toll. The same forces that produced a drop in magazine advertising and in the consumption of Art Deco fashion led to a decline in movie patronage as well. The final nail in the picture palace's coffin was the coming of sound. While the need for musical accompaniment had created the setting for gala orchestral productions and stage shows, the "talkies" sleekly wedded sound to film. Hence, any modest theater with an adequate amplification system could present its patrons with a highly sophisticated musical score—packaged courtesy of the film studio and rendered automatically by the movie projector's sound head. No extravagant hall or cast of thousands was required.

The Oakland (California) Paramount, one of the last grand theaters of its era, opened against all odds in 1931 (Stone:13). Susannah Harris Stone deems it "a gilded fantasy brought to life in the midst of Depression-era poverty" (11). With its 3,408 seats, it was also "the largest art deco palace ever built on the West Coast" (Naylor 1981:164). Its Depression-era context was made clear in a newspaper headline of December 1930 which, in announcing the theater's groundbreaking ceremony, focused more on the jobs it created than on its potential for film exhibition: "Local Labor Employed in the Building of Great Moving Picture Palace" (Stone:13). The total cost of the theater was $1,184,000, not including the land (Levin 1991:4).

The Paramount was what Harold B. Franklin (writing in 1928) deemed a "De Luxe First Run" theater—one that would cater "to the pleasure of an entire metropolis . . . [and would be] situated in some central district, such as the main business or shopping zone. On its program [would] be found a feature [and] . . . a number of short subjects" (2002:116). Like most such theaters, the Paramount was a "combination" house: in addition to playing movies, it was equipped for accompanying stage presentations and full-fledged vaudeville productions (Stone:11). When it opened its doors on December 16, 1931, it presented not only a series of films (*The False Madonna* plus a newsreel and cartoon) but an elaborate theatrical performance—sister and brother dance team Fanchon and Marco's "Slavique Idea"—a forty-minute revue enlisting dancers, comedians, acrobats, and a female chorus line (Stone:19).

The Oakland Paramount was designed, in high Art Deco style, by architect Timothy Pfleuger (1892–1946) of the local Miller and Pfleuger firm. Though not primarily known for movie-theater construction, Pfleuger had already built several others in the San Francisco area: the Spanish Baroque *Castro* (1922), the Moorish *Alhambra* (1925), and the *El Rey* (1936–1938). By the end of his career, he had designed eight original theaters (including the Paramount) and had renovated an equal number (Levin:5). Significantly (given the ties between Art Deco and the department store), Pfleuger was also the architect for the I. Magnin emporium on San Francisco's Union Square. Pfleuger was a builder with a notably aesthetic orientation. In fact, he later helped to found the San Francisco Museum of Art and served as president of the San Francisco Art Institute for many years. While it was fairly common for architects to commission original works for monumental buildings—as Pfleuger had done when he hired Diego Rivera to paint a mural for the San Francisco Stock Exchange (Levin:5)—it was less usual to do so for movie theaters. Yet this is precisely what Pfleuger did, hiring (among others) Charles Stafford Duncan to execute some of the Paramount's murals; Gerald Fitzgerald to render drawings for its marquee, Grand Lobby, and auditorium walls; Robert Boardman Howard to sculpt bas-reliefs in its Auditorium and lobbies; and Michael Goodman to design the stage curtain, valence, and lighting effects (Stone:20). Beyond the latter specific tasks, Goodman also served as the "idea man" for the enterprise, and his pictorial vision had a great impact on the project's ultimate realization (Levin:31). To some degree, collaboration of this kind is characteristic of the Art Deco aesthetic, which sought to mount projects in an organic fashion. Art historian Elayne Varian notes that

> The stability and grandeur of Art Deco architecture was the product of careful planning that resulted in totally harmonious units. All the artists,

architects, painters, sculptors, and designers were commissioned at the inception of each building and worked together to create a synthesis that involved every last detail of the external and internal structure." (Quoted in Levin:8)

The Oakland Paramount boasts many architectural elements associated with the Art Deco style. Stone describes its exterior as "austerely . . . functional," with a rectangular marquee bisected by a 100-foot-high vertical projecting sign.[1] Framed in chromium-plated brass and lit by neon tubing, the marquee and its "attraction board" were a vision of simplicity. Inside the theater, geometric and curvilinear modes—so prevalent in Art Deco design—abound. The doors leading from the lobby to the ticket booth are made of rectangular panels of etched glass arranged in assymetric rows (Levin:15); the chromium banisters of the Grand Lobby Stairway are rendered as "curving ribbons of silvery metal" (14); the tall internal windows of the lobby form a V pattern (as does a light fixture in the Lower-Level Men's Lounge); the borders of the Grand Lobby's metal filigree ceiling are done in a zigzag mode; the back-lit aluminum "Columns of Incandescence" (Naylor:168) framing the Auditorium's stage look like pillars of pure illumination; the lighting fixtures in the Mezzanine Foyer are comprised of etched glass rectangles with rounded corners (Levin:19–20); and chandeliers in the Mezzanine Public Lounge are rendered in tiered, ziggurat style (Levin:23).

Beyond its abstract elements, the Paramount "followed the art deco creed of seeking to integrate technology and art into an ideal architectural style. All services were combined within the building's structure. The unending variety of lighting fixtures are all incorporated into the decoration, with some completely hidden from view" (Naylor:168). Hence, Pfleuger managed to "camouflage all the mechanical operation of the building with art deco glitter" (168, 170). The elaborate, galvanized-iron grillwork ceilings of the Auditorium and Grand Lobby—which Pfleuger referred to as "silvery metal fins" (Stone:66)—hide a system of reflected light and air-conditioning. Moreover, Pfleuger concealed the protruding front of a Wurlitzer organ in the Auditorium's wall by utilizing a plaster screen decorated with scrolled "volutes." In addition to functionalism, the Paramount was characterized by a modern use of technology. As Stone notes, "Pfleuger took full advantage of . . . the freedom . . . of the Art Deco approach (which included the recognition of lighting engineering as a 'new science') . . . with . . . no thought for energy conservation" (25).

1. The original marquee was replaced in the mid-1960s for subway construction (Levin:11).

As evidence of this, the reflecting chamber above the Auditorium's ceiling utilized 150 lamps whose light was tinted by colored rondels (Stone:78).

But, for our purposes, the most intriguing aspect of the Paramount's style is its instantiation of Art Deco's fascination with the Exotic and the Primitive. These themes (just discussed in the preceding chapter, on the era's adventure films) are woven into the theater's overall architectural design. This orientation is clearly apparent in Pfleuger's earlier Deco picture palace, the *Tulare*, built in California in 1928. According to David Naylor, that theater resembled "a back-lot-desert fortress, thus earning its tag 'Fox Foreign Legion'" (164).

MANSIONS AND PALACES

One of the main questions which engages the attention of a large number of architects at the present is: How can a building communicate meaning?
—Michael H. Mitias (1994:121)

For the Oakland Paramount, however, Pfleuger moved in a different direction from the one he took with the Tulare. Michael Goodman reputedly urged him to consider a theme suggested by W. H. Hudson's novel *Green Mansions*, first published in 1904. Subtitled "A Romance of the Tropical Forest," its narrative concerns the adventures of a young Venezuelan man, Abel Geuvez de Argensola, who flees political upheaval in Caracas to hide in the country's interior, south of the Orinoco, in the Guayana region. There he befriends the Masquiritari tribe of indigenous people and lives with them in the wild. Near their encampment, he discovers a lush rain forest into which the Indians refuse to venture because they believe it inhabited by a dangerous female spirit (whom they call the "daughter of Didi"). Evidently, years earlier, a brave had traveled there and, when he shot a hunting arrow, was killed when it "magically" reversed itself and hit him. Since then, the forest has been forbidden territory. Thinking this tale mere "savage" superstition, Abel journeys into the woods, which he deems a "paradise" (45). As he muses: "What a wild beauty and fragrance and melodiousness it possessed above all forests" (74), with its "precious woods and fruits and fragrant gums," its wild animals and birds, and its "wide-spreading plants[s], covered with broad, round polished leaves" (74–75). There he encounters a mysterious and ethereal young woman named Rima (a "wild solitary girl") whom, he realizes, the Indians have mistaken for a phantom (81). She appears and disappears so quickly that he wonders whether she is, in fact, a "dream" or an "illusion" (80.). Almost immediately, he falls in love with the blithe spirit. As he ruminates: "To keep her near me or always in sight was, I found, impossible: she would be free as the wind, free as the butterfly, going and coming at her wayward will, and losing herself from sight a dozen times every hour" (123). Abel contrasts Rima with his girlfriend in Caracas, a "daughter of civilisation and of . . . artificial life," who "could never . . . return to nature" (153). After trekking with Rima and her "grandfather," Nuflo, back to Riolama (the place of Rima's birth), some Indians, emboldened by Abel's forays into the forest, return and slay her. Though set in Latin America (versus Polynesia), there are certain parallels between the story of *Green Mansions* and many of the South Seas fictional epics I discussed earlier. All involve a white man's encounters with primitive indigenous peoples and his romance with a magical female figure surrounded by taboos.

As one tours the Oakland Paramount Theatre, its theme of the Exotic (so central to *Green Mansions* and the South Seas adventure films) is boldly visible. If, as Stone has noted, the theater's exterior is "austere," its façade is "a perfect foil for what it cloaks [inside]: . . . a wealth of artistic detail on walls of silver and gold leaf, an amazing and enduring tribute to the world of the imagination" (16). In conceiving the theater as a paean to fantasy, Pfleuger addresses what Barry and Sargent deem "the psychology of the theatre-goer" who has a "love of adventure and [a] craving for the beautiful" that excites in him or her a "spirit of romance" (110). Significantly, in the whimsical universe that the Pfleuger fabricates for the Paramount, notions of the Exotic, the Tropical, and the Primitive constantly intermingle.

In its broad architectural plan, the theater evinces a focus on Nature, which, as we have seen, is a staple of the South Seas drama and documentary. As Stone remarks: "Each detail of the Paramount partakes of an overall theme in which Nature is celebrated in outlines that range from the classical Greek to the stylized modish Moderne. Particular forms—the shape of a leaf, the arch of a fountain or rainbow, the sinuous curve of a vine—are echoed, now accurately, now geometrically, on all sides" (20). The Grand Lobby, with its "tropical yellows and greens . . . has the ambience of a rain forest" (39). Its metallic filigree ceiling (made of galvanized metal strips riveted together and suspended by steel cables) is lit by hidden green reflecting lights which suggest a "curtain of foliage" (39) or a canopy of forest leaves. Here again, we are reminded not only of the (implied) greenery of films like *Moana*, *Tabu*, or *White Shadows in the South Seas* but of Abel's description of the woods in *Green Mansions*. As he notes:

> Even where the trees were largest the sunshine penetrated, subdued by the
> foliage to exquisite greenish-golden tints, filling the wide lower spaces with

tender half-lights, and faint blue-and-grey shadows. Lying on my back and
gazing up, I felt reluctant to rise and renew my ramble. For what a roof was
that above my head! Roof I call it, just as the poets in their poverty sometimes describe the infinite ethereal sky by that word; . . . How far above me
seemed that leafy cloudland into which I gazed! (45)

Significantly, Hudson even invokes the subject of architecture in Abel's response
to the rain forest canopy. Clearly, Pfleuger intended to overcome, in the Paramount, the very lighting limitations that Abel assumes inevitable. As Abel muses:

Nature, we know, first taught the architect to produce by long colonnades
the illusion of distance; but the light-excluding roof prevents him from getting the same effect above. Here Nature is unapproachable with her green,
airy canopy, a sun-impregnated cloud—cloud above cloud; and though the
highest may be unreached by the eye, the beams yet filter through, illum-
ing the wide spaces beneath—chamber succeeded by chamber, each with
its own special lights and shadows. (45–46)

In Abel's later references to the forest canopy's "tangle of shining silver threads," its
twists of "anaconda-like lianas," its "huge cables," its "airy webs and hair-like
fibres," we are, uncannily, reminded of Pfleuger's "silvery metal fins" (46).

The "tropical jungle" theme is further articulated by the Grand Lobby's extraordinary "Fountain of Light" (see plate 11)—a tall 40-foot construction, located above
the entrance doors, comprising twelve planes of scalloped, etched, and sandblasted
glass which seem to "billow . . . foam and erupt" in an amber-lit glow (Stone:34;
Levin:19). In addition to mimicking a fountain, the construct is reminiscent of a
waterfall, another staple of Art Deco imagery that we have seen in musicals like
Footlight Parade and in numerous South Seas epics. The fountain motif also calls
to mind the water imagery of *Green Mansions*, with its exotic rain forest locale.
Light, too, is central to the novel's shimmering, sylvan milieu. At one point, we are
told that the "western sky was now like amber-coloured flame," while "the vegetation still appeared of a uniform dusky green" (186–87). This passage suggests both
the color scheme of the Fountain of Light and the serenely green illumination
Pfleuger chose to light the Grand Lobby's ceiling, in imitation of a forest canopy.

Even the lobby's carpeting echoes the tropical rain forest theme. Woven in subtle shades of terra cotta, beige, and deep earth-greens, it employs abstract motifs of
leaf, vine, fern, and flower—images repeated throughout the theater. (Tellingly, Abel
compares Rima to such "beautiful things in the wood" as "flower, and bird, and butterfly, and green leaf, and frond" [138]). Finally, the metal ornamentation of the

balustrades of the Grand Stairway is done in a "palmette pattern" (Levin:14), an iconography extended to the mirrors of the Mezzanine Foyer, which are affixed with palmette crests (20). Again, we are reminded of Hudson's portrait of a lush, emerald Eden: his mention of "the feathery foliage of an acacia shrub," the "stems and broad, arrow-shaped leaves of an aquatic plant, and [the] slim, dropping fern fronds" (81). It is precisely this paradisal sense that attracted filmmakers to the South Seas landscape.

Exotic nature symbolism is prevalent in other areas of the building, and much of it engages a floral motif. The lights on the Auditorium's balcony overhang are realized in a shape suggesting lotuses or water lilies, and the hall's seat upholstery—made of a pale green and gold velour—is decorated with a vine and blossom pattern. The Auditorium's exit doors are routed and painted in a geometric floral pattern; likewise the stage curtain is decorated with huge pyramidal leaves (see plate 12). As illumination filters through the Auditorium's metal filigree ceiling, it is said to approximate a "sea of flowers beneath a ceiling of stars" (Levin:30; Stone:23).

Floral imagery also appears in the etched glass panels of the theater's Twenty-first Street doors (Levin:16), as well as in the vaulted ceiling panels of the Mezzanine Lounge (which, additionally, depict deer, vines, and sun). Throughout the building, plaster bas-reliefs ornament the walls and door-frames. A silver-leaf vine-and-flower-covered trellis adorns the entrance to the Mezzanine Women's Lounge, and stenciled *fleurs-de-lis* "accentuate the suggestion of an arbor" (Stone:47). Extending the theme, the walls of the adjoining Cosmetic Room are papered in a pale green floral design (Stone:46–47). In the Lower-Level Women's Lounge, a saucer dome at the center of the ceiling contains a large plaster medallion of stylized foliation. Beyond its particular ornamentation, the luxuriousness of the Paramount's Women's Lounges reminds us that a "customer in a Movie Palace was always intended to feel special, even when visiting the restrooms. A trip to the ladies lounge was an experience not be missed. It was almost worth going a few hours early so as to have ample time for primping in a parlor worthy of an Egyptian princess or a lady of the royal court" (Pildas 1980:23).

Even the Paramount's furnishings and trappings are crafted with the theme of Exotic Nature in mind. This informs the type of materials used, which include such rare woods as Malaysian teak. A small table in one of the building's lobbies advances Pfleuger's floral motif. As Stone describes it:

> On an ebony-based table with a marble top, colorful enameled flowers nestle in such out-of-the-way places that they are seldom seen. . . . The pattern of those enameled flowers is precisely reproduced in the metallic ends of the sofas, whose "tabletops" are veneered with Balinese rosewood in a radiating sunburst design. (49)

Vegetative detail extends even to the shape of the air vents, one of which has a floral design (Stone:49).

Pfleuger would surely have found inspiration for this theme in Hudson's *Green Mansions*. While wandering through the woods, Abel comes upon a rare and mysterious Hata flower. As he notes:

> The following day I went again, in the hope of seeing it still untouched by decay. There was no change; and on this occasion I spent a much longer time looking at it, admiring the marvellous beauty of its form. . . . It had thick petals, and at first gave me the idea of an artificial flower, cut by a divinely inspired artist from some unknown precious stone. . . . The next day I went again, scarcely hoping to find it still unwithered; it was fresh as if only just opened; and after that I went often . . . and still no faintest sign of any change. . . . Why, I often asked, does not this mystic forest flower fade and perish like others?   256–57)

He later learns from the Indians that a strange legend surrounds the flower's mysterious essence:

> They said that only one Hata flower existed in the world; that it bloomed in one spot for the space of a moon; then on the disappearance of the moon in the sky the Hata disappeared from its place, only to reappear blooming in some other spot, sometimes in some distant forest. And they also said that whosoever discovered the Hata flower in the forest would . . . obtain all his desires, and finally outlive other men by many years. (257–58)

Clearly, the lore surrounding the flower resounds with Hudson's sense of the mystery of Nature and its power to enrich forever the human soul.

But, as noted above, not all of the Paramount's tropical imagery engages floral motifs. Some of it draws upon an aquatic theme—an element that was central to South Seas lore as well. A mirror in the area of the men's and women's bathrooms is placed on a base of frosted glass panels that echo the water imagery of the Fountain of Light. In the Auditorium, the figure of Poseidon is rendered in metal filigree on the ceiling above the proscenium arch. Furthermore, the volute design of the Wurlitzer organ's grill-screen suggests both a waterfall *and* an ocean wave (Stone:23).

Other aspects of the theater's design look to the animal world, which we have seen represented in South Seas epics. The silver-leaf door-frames to the men's and women's bathrooms display peacocks posed under a half-disk of sun. The entry doors to the Paramount's Auditorium are crowned with carved images of parrots perched atop sinuous vines—all rendered in gold leaf. As Stone notes, these figures contribute greatly to the "tropical-paradise theme" of the Paramount's overall décor (58). Not surprisingly, in Hudson's *Green Mansions* Abel hears "parrot screams and [the] yelping of toucans" (55). Finally, in another nod to the Exotic, an elaborate mural in the Mezzanine Cosmetic Room depicts "Moorish castles . . . adrift behind cloud-like mountains in a palmy paradise" (Stone:47).

THE GOLDEN MAIDENS

The [Tahitian] women are of middle size, with lines of harmony that give
them a unique seal of beauty, with an undulating movement of their bodies,
a coordination of every muscle and nerve, a richness of aspect in color and
form that is more sensuous, more attractive than any feminine graces.
—Frederick O'Brien (1921:49)

On some level, the Paramount's insistent focus on Nature can be seen as "feminizing" its space, since traditional thought has identified Woman with that pole in contradistinction to Man's association with Culture (Ortner 1974:72). But the Paramount ultimately extends and literalizes this gender orientation through an obsessive fixation on the female body throughout the theater's décor.

The importance of gender in the Paramount's overall architectural plan is announced by the building's façade. In addition to its marquee, attraction board, and vertical sign, the front of the theater boasts a huge tile mosaic. The vertical sign, in fact, bisects not only the marquee but also the mural—so that one side depicts a man, the other a woman. Here is how the theater's 100-foot-high, 70-color mosaic (designed by Pfleuger and Gerald Fitzgerald) is described in the Historic American Building Survey of the theater:

> The left-hand panel represents a maroon-robed male figure frontally posed
> against a gold background. . . . The hands, crossed across the chest at their
> wrists, each hold three gold puppet strings. . . . Except for the hair, softer
> lines of the face, details around the neck and more slender hands, the
> female figure on the right-hand panel is precisely like its male counterpart.
> Each figure manipulates four tiers of puppets costumed in a multiplicity of
> bright colors. (Levin:11)

One of Pfleuger's press releases states that the mural symbolizes "man and woman—representing the guiding part of the theatrical and motion picture indus-

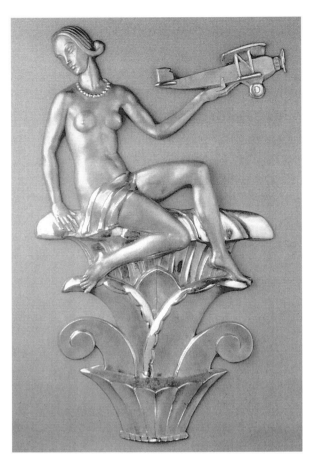

try" (Levin:11). For Stone, they are also "deities of the new art, Cinema—puppeteers, offering the world an unprecedented variety of amusements" (31). Though the figures pictured in the mural evince a brand of androgyny quite prevalent in Art Deco, their composition nonetheless divides the world into male and female sectors.

Within the theater, however, it is the feminine pole that rules (though the male is not entirely absent). This is most forcefully articulated in the Grand Lobby, where, below the high, back-lit internal "windows," there is a railing entirely sculpted of female figures (see plate 13). These "golden maidens" (now rendered in 120 layers of Dutch metal, aluminum, and variegated gold leaf) "beckon [the moviegoer] in toward the foyer" (Stone:40, 42). Even the process of "leafing" has implications for Exotic and Primitive themes, since the technique is thought to have originated in ancient Egypt (Stone:42). A trace of the Egyptian is also apparent in the "blocking" of the maidens, though their major stylistic influence comes from the South Seas. As Stone notes: "Their skirts are vaguely Polynesian, their angular poses faintly Egyptian. . . . They set the tone of the strange, the mysterious, the faraway" (40). Here, clearly, in the very design of the Oakland Paramount Theatre, we have the architectural equivalent of the South Seas maidens we have seen in the documentaries and adventure films of the period. Yet despite the primitive exoticism of the theater's "golden maidens," Stone finds "their streamlined faces startlingly modern" (40). In fact, from a certain vantage point, they resemble a contemporary chorus line—precisely the kind that might have performed in the stage shows at the Paramount. In this mix of the Modern and the Primitive (as centered on the female form), we are reminded of a provocative Art Deco object of the period—a plaque crafted by Mario Moschi in 1926 which depicts a woman sitting on a huge tropical frond holding an airplane in her hand (fig. 7.1) (Kaplan 1995:163).

The "female principle" reigns in other areas of the theater as well. On the walls of the Mezzanine Foyer are several plaster bas-reliefs thought to depict the Greek goddess Artemis (or Diana, in Roman mythology). In some of these, this goddess of chastity, hunting, and the moon stands nude; in others she rides a

FIGURE 7.2

A plaster bas-relief of
Artemis on the wall of the
Mezzanine Foyer of the
Paramount Theatre. (Cour-
tesy Paramount Theatre of
Arts)

mountain ram (surrounded by Saturn and the stars). Artemis is also pictured in a large silver bas-relief above a sofa in the Lower-Level Women's Lounge—rid-ing a ram and blowing a horn, surrounded by shooting stars (fig. 7.2). Indeed, this very image became the logo of the Oakland Symphony Orchestra, which performs in the Paramount to this day. Elsewhere, on a lobby table, stands a sculpture of Diana; and in the Ladies Smoking Room (a fairly controversial social space for 1931) are several murals depicting female forms as realized by Charles Stafford Duncan. One (rendered in gold, vermilion, green, and white, against a black lacquer background) presents the goddesses of theater and music: one deity holds the masks of drama (comic and tragic), while the other muse holds a lyre.

Such mythological imagery, found throughout the Paramount, conforms to the qualities—academic, classical, allegorical—that Edward Lucie-Smith identifies with Art Deco painting (1990:8). In fact, the "golden maidens" resemble the female figure in a painting done in 1925 by Raphael Delorme—*The Columns* (aka *Girls and Pigeons*)—that is included in Lucie-Smith's book (8). This picture depicts a scantily clad woman posed against a background of Greek columns and holding a bird. The folds of her skirt are like those of the "golden maidens," but she is also reminiscent of W. H. Hudson's Rima, often described as a "bird-woman."

As Lucie-Smith notes, Art Deco's interest in neoclassicism allowed it to explore "the trappings of modernity," while "shy[ing] away from genuine radicalism" (8). Thus, its iconography is "leavened with irony" and is "given a typically ambiguous twist, so that the viewer [is] left uncertain whether it [is] meant to be taken at all seriously" (8). Lucie-Smith's observation is here clearly relevant to Deco's association with "kitsch." A third large mural on the central wall of the Ladies Smoking Lounge depicts three women and a man seated under a tropical tree, picnicking by a body of water. Abstract hills are visible in the distance. The blocking of these figures evinces the kind of "mannered pos[ing]" that Lucie-Smith finds characteristic of Deco painting (8).

But the Paramount's *tour de force* space for the female form, its crowning glory (as well as being the most important locale in the theater itself), is of course the Auditorium (fig. 7.3). As part of the elaborate grillwork ceiling, five enormous panels repeat a huge filigree image of a woman. Some claim she represents the Egyptian goddess Isis—a fertility figure who controls all aspects of life. (Clearly, this mythic vision has ties to the South Seas *taupou* whom we have seen depicted in so many films of the era.) Amid immense pyramidal leaves, the Paramount's goddess is shown lifting the sun—a fitting icon for a movie theater (which, after all, depends on the projection of light). According to Stone, the "legend [of Isis] tells of the sun overwhelmed by night and then reborn with the new day" (66), thus suggesting the tension between light and dark that obtains within a movie theater. Alternately, Steven Levin sees the female figure depicted on the ceiling as a vision of W. H. Hudson's Rima (31).

But the most extraordinary aspect of the Paramount's Auditorium is its use of figural bas-reliefs on both the walls and the ceiling (on strips alongside the central grillwork paneling). Created by Gerald Fitzgerald and sculpted by Robert Howard (with a molded intaglio technique), they comprise five panels, each of which depicts "five subjects arranged in as many as five tiers flanked by very wide borders. The subjects include various trios of female nudes in differing poses amid lush tropical vegetation, and a sword-bearing horseman clad only in a laurel wreath" (Levin:26). These panels continue onto the ceiling, extending both the floral ornamentation and the female figuration. The bas-reliefs of native women even surround the light fixtures, which have been described by some as "bulbous . . . beet-shaped pendants" (Levin:30). Levin, again, sees here a literary influence: "There is evidence that this auditorium, with its suggestions of tropical vegetation, joyous figures in a state of nature, and the lone female figure in

each section of the ceiling grille . . . was inspired in part by W. H. Hudson's *Green Mansions*" (31).

Essentially, with its themes of Woman, Nature, and the Exotic, the Paramount represents a decidedly feminized space. If, as Stone would have it, the Paramount is "Pfleuger's Art Deco fantasy," it is a decidedly woman-centered one (8). Though monumental, it is also "uterine"—with its omnipresent maternal goddesses as well as its ubiquitous symbols of fertility and vegetation. Some of its fixtures manage even to suggest the female body: the lights on the ceiling of the Auditorium (described elsewhere as "beet-shaped") also resemble breasts, and those on its balcony overhang (described elsewhere as resembling "water lilies") also favor female genitalia.

Its overall "feminine" quality is proven by nothing so much as the one clear exception to the rule: the Lower-Level Men's Lounge. Here, significantly, in a space marked as "male," we find the influence of the abstract/linear strain of Art Deco in the room's plain square-paneled, veneered walls; its geometric terrazzo floor (fashioned after the pattern of Native American Indian blankets); its plain leather chairs; its rectangular air vents; its simple molding. As Stone notes, its

FIGURE 7.3
The Auditorium of the Paramount Theatre with its flower-like ceiling light fixtures, its bas-relief tropical scenes, and its vine-and-leaf-patterned upholstery. (Courtesy Paramount Theatre of Arts)

elements are severe, "but their austerity shows off the streamlined modernity of the Art Deco style" (53).

THE MOVIE THEATER AS PLAYLAND

Entry to [Graumann's Egyptian] theater requires passage through a forecourt lined with tall, rough-cut mock tombstones. During the show, an Egyptian guard marched back and forth across the roof parapet, rifle in hand. Inside the theater, a metallic vulture looms over the screen. —David Naylor (1981:83)

As we have seen, the Oakland Paramount offers the public not only a movie theater but a "themed" space—a world constructed so as to conjure a South Seas tropical universe. If we imagine that some of the films discussed in chapter 6 may have actually played there, we can conceive the total environment as a kind of cinematic Theme Park. Of course, the film industry would not literalize this concept until 1955 when Disneyland opened in Los Angeles, offering the public amusement park rides and settings derived from the studio's major films (e.g., *Pinocchio, Alice in Wonderland, Dumbo,* etc.). But cinema had long been tied to the fairground. One of the first public demonstrations of the Vitascope (a cinematic projection device patented by Thomas Armat) took place at Atlanta's Cotton States Exposition of 1895. Similarly, a turn-of-the-century Edison movie captured (Eugene) Sandow the Strongman, a sideshow entertainer like those who appeared at American fairs. Furthermore, amusement parks were favored sites for early filmmaking, be it in the newsreel or dramatic modes. For example, Edwin S. Porter made *Rube and Mandy at Coney Island* in 1903, relating the antics of two fictional "hicks" visiting New York City. Interestingly, Coney Island first opened to the public in 1895—the same year that traditionally marks the birth of cinema. Finally, in the same way that international expositions had built "themed" areas devoted to diverse regions of the world, so movie theaters were named for exotic locales and designed to reflect their influence. Los Angeles had its Egyptian, Mayan, and Chinese theaters; San Francisco its Alhambra; and San Antonio its Aztec.

One would not want to push the analogy too far between the "themed" movie theater and the amusement park. But as the Oakland Paramount mirrored the South Seas movie genre, so the various geographical areas of Disneyland would later reflect assorted categories of film. Thus, Frontierland mimicked the western; Tomorrowland, the science fiction film; Adventureland, the action movie; and

Fantasyland, the children's picture. Finally, in its numerous themed restaurants and hotels, the Disney corporation eventually invoked the South Seas genre as well. Here one thinks of the Enchanted Tiki-Room at California's Disneyland or the Polynesian Village Resort at Florida's Walt Disney World.

Clearly, like a theme park, the American picture palace of the 1920s and 1930s was a space of supreme illusion. As John F. Barry and Epes W. Sargent stated back in 1927, there were "few other places in the . . . commercialized world where [people could] get mental rejuvenation and imaginative play at so small a cost" (110).

PARADISE LOST—AND REGAINED

By the late 1920s, along with everything else, the movie theater boom began to go bust. So many had been built that there were suddenly not enough patrons to fill the seats . . . With the Great Depression, the movie palace era began to skitter to an end. Theaters became smaller and more efficient.
—John Margolies and Emily Gwathmey (1991:20)

While the Oakland Paramount was an architectural jewel of its era and a playland for its customers, its fate was not a happy one. Built at precisely the wrong historical moment, it closed its doors in June of 1932 after only six months of operation, unable to meet its $27,000-a-week expenses. It reopened in May 1933 as a dedicated movie theater, having done away with its stage shows. To save money, much of the theater's high-tech lighting was scaled down or eliminated. The Paramount shut its doors temporarily in 1967 (for Oakland subway construction) and finally closed as a movie theater on September 15, 1970. It remained boarded up until 1972 when it was purchased by the Oakland Symphony Orchestra for its performance hall. The orchestra's management sought to accomplish a full restoration of the facility—making it the sixth such picture palace to be "retrieved" in the United States. According to Stone: "An . . . obstacle to the restoration . . . was the fact that Art Deco had not yet been given the full measure of appreciation it later received as an architectural style. The idea of authentically restoring an Art Deco movie palace was, for these reasons and on the surface of it, highly improbable" (Stone:31). Yet funding for the project materialized, and work began in earnest on December 20, 1972. True to the principles of restoration (versus the less ambitious goals of "conversion" or "renovation"), an attempt was made to repair all elements of the theater that remained but had deteriorated (e.g., the leafing on the bas-reliefs), and to replace with exact replicas that which had disappeared (e.g., the original curtain, carpeting, and seat upholstery).

The Oakland Paramount reopened as a restored professional arts center on September 22, 1973 (after having won a listing on the National Register of Historic Places in August of the same year). On August 26, 1975, the City of Oakland assumed its ownership; and on May 5, 1977, it was declared a National Historical Landmark. Presently, the Paramount is "one of the finest remaining examples of Art Deco design in the United States" (Levin:4).

While, as Stone remarks, at one point Art Deco architecture had gone out of style (making the restoration of the Paramount unlikely), by now the timelessness of the mode has been acknowledged and its lessons are relevant once more. Thus, like *Green Mansions*'s Hata flower, Art Deco continues to blossom while other design movements die.

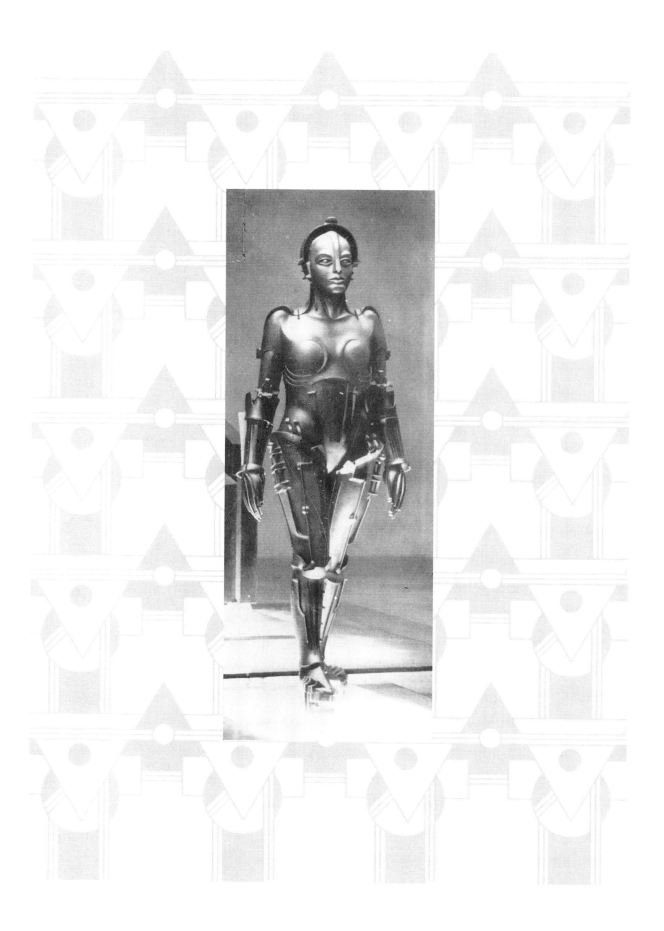

8. MADAME SATAN

Fantasy, Art Deco, and the Femme Fatale

THE DEVIL IS A WOMAN

Cecil B. DeMille's *Madame Satan* (1930) is a sophisticated MGM romantic comedy that tells the tale of Angela Brooks (Kay Johnson), a wealthy, married woman whose husband Bob (Reginald Denny) stays out all night carousing with his friend Jimmy (Roland Young) and carrying on with Trixie (Lillian Roth). When Angela, who is rather staid and conservative, gets wind of Bob's antics, she insists that they separate. He, in turn, justifies his adulterous behavior by claiming that while he craves warm affection from her, all he gets is "frozen justice." As he sardonically remarks: "Love can't be kept in cold storage." Upon learning that Jimmy will host an extravagant costume party aboard a moored zeppelin, Angela decides to shed her traditional demeanor and appear at the celebration as "Madame Satan," a fictitious but provocative French femme fatale. On the night of the event, she arrives at the high-tech site (designed by Cedric Gibbons and Mitchell Leisen) masked and adorned in a revealing Art Deco evening gown (created by Adrian) whose black, white, and silver flame appliqués barely cover her erogenous zones. Bob is entirely captivated by this "hot," mysterious, and outrageous woman who flirts with him and seems eager to scandalize the gathering. Only when a storm hits and the aircraft becomes untethered does Bob realize that the beguiling Madame Satan is his allegedly frigid and inhibited wife. Clearly, in *Madame Satan*, the notion that "the devil is a woman" is treated wryly—and Angela's Art Deco status only augments her appeal. But, as I shall demonstrate, when we turn to the more fantastic films of the era—those of the *horror*, *fantasy*, or *science fiction* genres—the sense of the demonic Art Deco Woman takes on a weightier and more dreadful valence.

Although her origins are literary and pictorial, the femme fatale has a special relevance in cinematic representation, particularly that of Hollywood insofar as it appeals to the visible as the ground of its production of truth.

—Mary Ann Doane (1991:1)

To approach this topic, I will once again explore the rich and intricate connections between the European and American conceptions of the Art Deco style. As I have noted, the movement began in Paris in the 1920s with an exposition that influenced one of Hollywood's nascent set designers, Cedric Gibbons. Furthermore, I have charted how much of the American press reacted enthusiastically to Art Deco's Continental innovations: how a certain Francophilia reigned in the pages of women's magazines, with their focus on French fashions and their romance with beauty products and department store salons graced by Gallic names. I have also analyzed the importance of Greta Garbo's status as a European star, since her opposition to the All American Girl allowed her to be a daring Art Deco icon. Moreover, I explored the appearance in French films of American performer Josephine Baker, a likely outcome of her Parisian stage success and France's interest in things "African." If Josephine Baker was an Art Deco "American in Paris," so Erté proved to be a modernist Frenchman in Hollywood, contributing to films like *The Hollywood Revue of 1929*. Finally, in my chapter on the exotic adventure film, I investigated the collaboration between a European director and an American director: F. W. Murnau and Robert Flaherty.

In a similar transnational vein, it is necessary to begin my discussion of the era's Art Deco fantasy female with reference to a seminal European work—Fritz Lang's *Metropolis* (1926). Though Lotte Eisner has called it an "encounter of Expressionism and Surrealism" (1977:86) (a phrase that highlights the broad and tangled roots of the Style Moderne), it is also a monument to Art Deco design.[1] Significantly, before turning to the cinema, Lang was both an architect and a graphic artist. Given Art Deco's melding of European and American influences, it is intriguing to note that Lang claimed his idea for *Metropolis* stemmed from his initial impression of the New York City skyline, first glimpsed in 1924 (Ott 1979:124). Moreover, Lang eventually migrated to the United States where he continued his directorial career and brought his European sensibility to the American screen.

"FANTASTIC, FUTURISTIC, AND FATALISTIC"

Going down into the streets of a modern city must seem—to the newcomer, at least—a little like Dante's descent into Hades. —Hugh Ferris (1929:18)

---

1. Only a few critics have specifically mentioned Art Deco in relation to *Metropolis*: see Coates (1991:45) and Mandelbaum and Myers (1985:166).

Metropolis is a futuristic fiction (allegedly set around the year 2000) that depicts life in a modern city. While the opening process shots (utilizing model work, forced perspective, and optical tricks) portray a (still) astounding and dazzling up-to-date municipality (with aerial train bridges connecting skyscrapers), as the film's narrative begins we realize that the world depicted is a dystopian universe ruled by the social and economic inequities of the past. As a 1927 Paramount advertisement for the film proclaims, its universe is "Fantastic, Futuristic, and Fatalistic" (Borst 1992:20). At the heights of Metropolis (with access to its stadiums, gardens, views, and fresh air) live the wealthy, led by industrialist Joh Fredersen (Alfred Abel), the "Master of Metropolis." In its middle ground stand Fredersen's factories and machines. In its bowels live the workers who toil in Fredersen's plants. While, in many texts of the Art Deco era, the machine is valorized as a social liberator (as it was in such art movements as Constructivism and Futurism), in *Metropolis* it is demonized, as it would later be in Charles Chaplin's *Modern Times* (1936). As Andreas Huyssen has noted, this view is more consonant with the tenets of Expressionism, which has an equal stylistic pull on the text. That movement "emphasizes technology's oppressive and destructive potential" (Huyssen 1986:67). Thus, in Metropolis, the clock is a tyrant that rules the workers with its fragmentation of time. Elevators take them from the city's sunny surface to its gloomy depths. Thermometers register the inhumanly high temperatures in which they must toil. And, at one moment (as seen from a subjective point of view), a giant industrial machine literally takes the shape of the Middle Eastern god Moloch, devouring workers in its colossal, fiery orifice. With its formidable modernist set designs (created by Otte Hunte, Erich Kettlehut, and Karl Vollbrecht), *Metropolis* portrays the city of the future as a worker's prison camp—a place in which they can only be incarcerated, not reside.

As part of the drama, Fredersen's son Freder (Gustav Fröehlich) becomes aware of the injustices of Metropolis and of the grim laborer's world from which he has previously been shielded. (It is he, in fact, who envisions his father's industrial technology as a monster.) He first becomes curious about the laborers' domain after encountering Maria (Brigitte Helm), a working-class young woman who has escorted some children to the surface of Metropolis to enjoy its gardens. Later, journeying to the underworld in search of her, Freder observes an employee who must control the dial of a huge gauge by standing before it with his arms outstretched, frenetically adjusting its hands at each instant (and often assuming a Christ-like pose, as though "crucified" by the mechanism). When the man faints with exhaustion, Freder changes clothes with him and takes over his job, personally experiencing the horrors of menial work in his father's business. As the narrative develops, it becomes clear that the lower classes of Metropolis are regularly meeting to protest their persecution. A factory foreman loyal to Joh Fredersen shows him some "strange plans" he has uncovered that make reference to the city's ancient catacombs (down below the workers's quarters). Still underground and dressed in worker's attire, Freder is informed of a secret assembly that will take place. Interested in the event (and now sympathetic to the laborers' plight), Freder stumbles into a cavelike space outfitted as an ersatz church in which Maria leads a service for her compatriots in front of a series of abstract wooden crosses. She recounts to them a version of the story of the Tower of Babel, stressing how the powerful men who designed the structure had no concern for their crew, while the slaves who built it did not understand the purpose of their own construction. The parallels to Metropolis are clear, especially since the Tower of Babel sequence that illustrates her sermon for the viewer looks like a modern skyscraper. She postulates how, in the future, the power of the "mind" and "hand" will be mediated by a leader with a "heart," and urges those congregated to be patient for "he will surely come." As Siegfried Kracauer has noted, Maria serves as a "comforter of the oppressed" (1966:163), thereby tempering any revolutionary message in the film with a biblical overlay—one that argues conservatively for forbearance versus action. As Maria holds the workers rapt, Joh Fredersen and his cohort, the mad scientist Dr. Rotwang (Rudolph Klein-Rogge), spy on her.

Realizing that Maria is revered by the workers (and fearing their insurrection), Joh Fredersen asks Rotwang, who is currently experimenting with robots, to create one that resembles Maria and then switch the two personae—unleashing the automaton on the workers in order to control them and subvert their radical plans. Joh hopes that the robot will incite the agitators to rebel, at which point he will order the police to retaliate and eliminate the firebrands. Rotwang pursues Maria through the catacombs, shining a searchlight on her in the dark that self-reflexively resembles a film projector's beam. He eventually captures her and, in a struggle that mimics attempted rape, takes her away. Freder (who has become enamored with Maria) hears her screams of distress and searches for her, but he becomes trapped in Rotwang's house. Meanwhile, in the mad scientist's laboratory—a space replete with futurist neon coils, glass beakers, and electric sparks—Maria lies in a glass, coffin-like box, restrained by metal semicircular cables. She is attached by wires or tubes to a rather feminine-looking robot (fig. 8.1) seated upon a chair (whose marvelous metallic costume was designed by Aenne Willkomm). Moreover, the robot's hard metal face resembles a sculpture (entitled *The Clown*) by Gustave Miklos, a modernist artist whose work showed at the Paris Exposition of

1925.[2] Gradually, in a show of high-tech special effects (involving lightening bolts and bands of light), the robot is transformed into a false version of Maria, as the true Maria remains inert on the table. Ironically, the robot becomes animate after rings of light move up and down her body—seeming to mock the quasi-religious "halo" with which the real Maria has been metaphorically encircled.

The eyes of the false Maria are made up darkly to signal a certain decadence at her core. (Again, the Paramount ad deems the film "Erotic, Exotic and Erratic" [Borst:20].) Danger is also communicated by the false Maria's slouched stance and her lascivious gestures. In a close-up, she executes an ominous one-eyed wink, as though to invoke her perverse duality (the other eye being open). When Freder escapes from Rotwang's house, he observes Maria flirting with his father. Thinking her to be the real Maria (and unaware of her doubling by a robot), he suffers an Oedipal crisis and has a breakdown—a phenomenon portrayed through an abstract montage of shapes, effects, and obsessively repeated images. Hysterical, he takes to bed and is tended by physicians.

In a scene which follows, Dr. Rotwang formally presents the robot Maria to a crowd of male citizens. As he does so, she emerges from a giant avant-garde urn—appearing as an Art Deco goddess. The men gape at her as she is silhouetted in light, like a contemporary figural lamp. Wearing a strange, crescent-shaped headdress, a revealing "hula" skirt, and "pasties," she performs a sensuous dance for them, gyrating licentiously. Finally, holding a chalice, she is raised up and posed astride a pedestal adorned with a seven-headed monster (like some bizarre chryselephantine sculpture). This entire structure is supported by male statues of the seven deadly sins (which are, clearly, morally associated with her). Here, as Tom Gunning has noted, we have a "whore of Babylon" who conceals "the mechanism of modernity" (81).

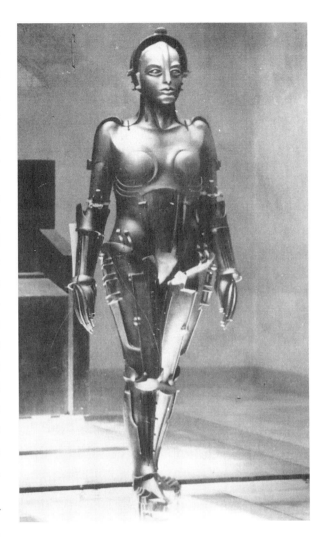

FIGURE 8.1

The high-tech robot Maria in *Metropolis* (1926). (Courtesy British Film Institute)

---

2. Miklos (1888–1967) was born in Hungary but worked in France and collaborated with such Art Deco craftsmen as Jean Dunand. A reproduction of *The Clown* is pictured in Menten (1972:139).

Obeying Joh Fredersen's instructions, the false Maria—acting as a rabble-rous-ing demagogue—speaks to a crowd of workers. Freder, returned to health and now aware of the false Maria plot, tries to warn the workers that this is not the true Maria who, earlier, had spoken instead of peace. But the false Maria, looking more depraved than ever, with her dress fallen off her shoulder and her eyes shooting cyn-ical, knowing winks, eggs the crowd on. The now unruly mob attacks Freder and follows the robot Maria's call to riot against their exploiters. They explode the indus-trialist's machines and flood the underground city—clearly a self-destructive act.

In the meanwhile, the true Maria has escaped from Rotwang's clutches. She sounds the alarm in the worker's quarters, thereby warning them of the impending calamity. By so doing, she saves countless children from the deluge. When the laborers realize that the woman who has led their revolt is not the true Maria, they declare her a witch and go in search of her. They find "Madame Satan" at a tony nightclub in the upper realms of Metropolis. There, in an Orientalist, Art Deco setting, she dances, transformed into a robot flapper. The workers capture her and burn her at the stake. As she expires, her lewd expression melts, and the flames turn her back into a machine. At the end of the drama Freder, his father, and the true Maria are reunited on the steps of the city's huge cathedral. Freder convinces Joh Fredersen to shake hands with a worker, and Maria deems Freder the "heart" that will mediate society's head and hand, thus joining the capitalist with the worker.

Tom Gunning has called *Metropolis* Lang's "most blatantly allegorical work" (55), and Siegfried Kracauer has noted how the film is "rich in subterranean con-tent" (163). Clearly, much of the film's symbolism focuses on the figure of Woman, the most intriguing aspect of which is the trope of the two Marias—one that draws upon German Expressionism's romance with the doppelgänger (Coates:41). Many critics have sought to interpret this dualistic sign. Paul Coates, for example, sees the true and false Marias as embodying the familiar female stereotypes of the vir-gin and the vamp. He finds, however, that the eerie strangeness of even the *real* Maria shows the "dangerous resemblance" of the two figures, proving that Victo-rian morality was "on the verge of collapse" (51). In a similar vein, Huyssen sees a certain similarity between the polar versions of Maria. While the true Maria might seem an entirely benevolent figure (who advocates nonviolent protest), it is she who actually initiates the chaos that befalls Metropolis by luring Freder to the workers' lower depths. Moreover, Huyssen sees both Marias as fundamentally mas-culine projections: "in both forms, femininity, imagined as it is from the male per-spective, poses a threat to the male world of high technology, efficiency, and instrumental rationality" (72). Taking a more psychoanalytic approach, Roger

Dadoun sees the true Maria as a highly maternal emblem. He points to the fact that she is frequently surrounded by children (be it playing in the upper gardens or fleeing from the underworld floods). Moreover, she is associated with the workers' underground quarters (which he likens to a womb) and with the catacombs, an even deeper uterine space (1986:143). On the other hand, the false Maria (in her hard, metallic robot form) is "part phallus" and "assumes the paternal functions of tyranny, repression, and punishment" (also associated with her "benefactor," entrepreneur Joh Fredersen) (146).

We might also see the robot Maria (with her metallic skin) as associated with modernity, while the true Maria (in her soft, folksy white-collared dress and shawl) is linked to tradition. In a famous Art Deco poster for the film (credited to Heinz Schulz-Neudamm in 1926), the female replicant (in her synthetic shell) stands at the base of a geometrically rendered city, with its angular high-rises and electric lights. The bone structure of her forbidding face quite literally blends into the edges of the buildings. Furthermore, the robot in the film is associated with the Machine, tying what is normally a male symbol (and, in *Metropolis*, one linked with patriarch Joh Fredersen) to the female. Significantly, when Rotwang speaks to Joh of his experiments with an automaton, he talks of how he will make it "in the image of man." Yet when he shows his prototype to Fredersen, it has a distinctly feminine appearance (with large hips and proto-breasts). From this perspective, Freder's vision of the industrial machine as a spike-toothed Moloch (a male god) is also interesting. For, on another level, the monster seems posed like a female Sphinx, with its teeth a version of the "vagina dentata"— a threat not only to workers but to all men. Hence, in *Metropolis* the monster is decidedly female (despite her phallic overtones). While in Linda Williams's classic reading of the horror film we must work to see the monster as feminine by interpreting the narrative in a convoluted way (for example, construing the male King Kong as a double of his victim, Ann Darrow [Fay Wray]), in the Lang film female malice is apparent on the surface. For Huyssen, the fact that, in *Metropolis*, the mechanical Devil is a Woman makes clear the merging of two male fantasies and fears: that of technology and that of femininity. As he notes, in the period in which the film was made: "Woman, nature, machine had become a mesh of significations which all had one thing in common: otherness; by their very existence they raised fears and threatened male authority and control" (70).

While, on one level, the false Maria's associations with Rotwang's laboratory (filled with metal coils, sparks of electricity, and abstract tubes and beakers) would seem another link to modernity, on a different plane it is a bridge to the past. For, as Gunning has observed, Rotwang's world is a medieval one, with his home an antique cottage in the midst of a contemporary city (63). Also associated with the archaic are the catacombs and the cathedral, both sites in which the real Maria triumphs. Thus, as Gunning makes clear, *Metropolis* seems to argue that "the gothic exists in the core of the modern" (65).

But aside from being tied in a general way to modernity, the pernicious woman in the film is specifically imagined as an *Art Deco icon*—a fact not mentioned by any of the critics. Thus, the robot Maria is an avant-garde metallic figure who bears a notable resemblance to Cedric Gibbons's later Oscar statuette (this, despite the gender difference between the two). Moreover, even beyond the robot, much of the world of corruption in the film (the upper realms of Metropolis) is also tied to the Style Moderne. While the film is set some seventy-five years in the future, Joh Fredersen's environs resemble those of 1926. His office is filled with up-to-date gadgets and its walls are designed with modish geometric murals (as are those of Freder's bedroom, which also boasts some Art Deco lamps). Furthermore, the nightspot in which the bad Maria is eventually captured is an Orientalist Deco club worthy of patronage by Josephine Baker or Astaire and Rogers.

Here we are reminded of certain aspects of fantasy that have particular relevance to our project. As Lucie Armitt indicates, "We are unlikely to be surprised by the fantastic's *spatial concerns*" (7; emphasis added). As she continues, the "determining sense [in the genre] of the 'outside-of-place' confirms what we already suspect; it is the spatial that determines the realm of textual dynamics . . . in the context of fantasy forms" (5). This conclusion is also supported by Sigmund Freud's work on the "uncanny," which focuses on the etymological source of the German term for the phenomenon, *unheimlich*. Freud begins by analyzing the derivation of its opposite and root word, *heimlich*, which means that which is "familiar." His full documentation of dictionary sources, however, reveals another sense for the term which has more spatial implications, that of "belonging to the *house*" (1958:125). Hence the notion of a concrete, architectural dwelling is referenced in one sense of the phantasmagoric: that which does *not* "belong to the house." In keeping with her interest in fantasy's spatial elements, Armitt privileges the Gothic subgenre of the mode, with its emphasis on a weird and inhospitable edifice (e.g., a haunted mansion). As she notes: "Like metamorphosis, [the genre] takes the everyday and forces it into a grotesque relationship with the body—here the body of the house" (7). In *Metropolis*, as in other works to be considered, part of what seems uncanny in the text is the very *spatial dimension* in which the narrative transpires—simultaneously familiar to the viewer (as the cutting-edge style of the 1920s), but innovative enough to be somewhat alien and eccentric.

In the spellbinding scene of *Metropolis* in which the false Maria dances at her lecture debut, she appears in an exotic costume and hat, emerging from what seems a huge Art Deco urn; she ends her routine perched on a sculptural base like a twenties figurine. Lotte Eisner alludes to the film's Art Deco status obliquely through her mention of the word *kitsch*, drawing upon the movement's later associations with camp. As she notes: "The *kitsch* reaches its extreme in the dance of the false Maria. . . . Yet as soon as Lang escapes from the arts and crafts stylisation and the kitsch emotionalism and 'sophistication,' the 'architect' Lang takes over, triumphantly" (89). Here, her use of the term "arts and crafts" seems to stand in for "Art Deco," an inheritor of the earlier aesthetic.

In two other scenes of the film, we observe the kind of women who reside in the upper spheres of Metropolis: modish females dressed in outlandish fashions. They look, in fact, as though they might be headed for the zeppelin costume party in *Madame Satan*. In one episode, these women gallivant at a nightclub, dancing along with the false Maria. In another scene, set in the city's opulent "pleasure" garden, Freder frolics with a contemporary woman who is costumed in a bare-backed leotard and shorts outfit, accessorized with a dramatic chapeau. In fact, he is about to kiss her when, through a pair of *moderne*, patterned doors, comes the true Maria (whom he sees for the first time), surrounded by children. He immediately drops his "flapper" and is drawn to Maria, pursuing her through the gates—like Lewis Carroll's Alice into a worker's "Wonderland." So again the true Maria is counterposed to the Art Deco female, this time a modern Metropolis maiden. Even in the workers's quarters, Freder is not safe from the clutches of the Art Deco Woman, who appears again as the false Maria (and is once more associated with Joh Fredersen's world). This dichotomy between good and bad females in the film is made even starker by the fact that the underground domain seems devoid of women. Until the final moments of *Metropolis* (when we view some laborers' wives in the crowd of escapees), all we see are male workers and (eventually) their children. Hence, the figures of the two Marias stand in for *all* women—reduced to an archetypal formulation.

The fact that, in a dystopian fantasy like *Metropolis*, the perverse female is linked to Art Deco is of no surprise to us, given what we have seen earlier of the ambivalent portrayal of bold modern women (e.g., Greta Garbo's melodramatic heroines). Neither are we astonished that such a female would be contrasted with the motherly woman, the Art Deco diva's nemesis. Finally, it is precisely the *fluidity* of these poles—the possibility that the conservative woman will "turn into" the modern maiden (like Maria morphs into the robot), or that we will not be able to detect any clear "difference" between the two—that so troubles a patriarchal culture in the midst of feminist change (suffrage, birth control, workplace rights, and sexual freedom).

The obvious successor to the false Maria in the modern American horror cinema is the bride of Frankenstein, another famous heroine of the era. In linking these two figures, the connections between Art Deco, Expressionism, and the broader Style Moderne are, once more, made clear. While a comparison between the robot and the monster's bride occurred to me independently of any reading, it is one that many critics have made. Interestingly, Eisner takes a contrarian approach, denying the relation between the Lang and James Whale films. In describing Rotwang's studio, for example, she remarks: "We are far from the grotesque laboratories of the old Frankenstein films. [In *Metropolis*] the futurist fantasies are masterly, controlled, credible" (86). Others, however, have noted the similarities between the two works. John Baxter claims that "Universal's designers working on *The Bride of Frankenstein* [1935] copied the metal-banded machine with which Rotwang vivifies his creation [in *Metropolis*]" (1970:31). Roger Dadoun notes how the Whale film uses "the same battery of signifiers . . . : electrical charges and discharges, light waves, ringlike forms, mechanical motions of the robot gradually changing to more supple human movements, and so on" (149). Thus, the bride of Frankenstein—with her dramatically white-streaked, frizzy hair (piled high like that of the Egyptian Nefertiti) can also be seen as an Art Deco diva (fig. 8.2). This fact seems clear from information proffered in a documentary on the making of Frankenstein (*The Frankenstein Files: How Hollywood Made a Monster* [*Frankenstein* 1999]), in which a contemporary cosmetician states that, in being prepared for filming, Elsa Lanchester was given the same "glamour makeup" that might have been utilized for a romantic female star of the era. Hence, the easy shift between good woman and bad is made apparent. While in *Bride of Frankenstein* (as in *Metropolis*), the evil of modernity is not *entirely* linked to the female (since Dr. Frankenstein [Colin Clive], Dr. Pretorius [Ernest Thesiger], and the monster [Boris Karloff] are also to blame), in both works, a woman is its most novel and intriguing incarnation.

Finally, even the look of Frankenstein's monster himself is, in part, derived from modernist graphics—making him a travesty of the Art Deco male. Mary Wollstonecraft Shelley's 1818 novel says the following about his appearance:

> His yellow skin scarcely covered the work of muscles and arteries beneath; his hair was of a lustrous black, and flowing; his teeth of a pearly whiteness; but these luxuriances only formed a more horrid contrast with his watery eyes that seemed almost of the same colour as the dun-white-sockets in which they were set, his shriveled complexion, and straight black lips. (Shelley 1996:34)

If we examine Chevalier's engraving of the monster that served to illustrate the 1831 edition of the novel, his representation looks little like Shelley's description or Karloff's incarnation exactly one hundred years later. Rather, the reclining creature resembles an ordinary man, though his head is strangely askew and his musculature and bone structure are rather overpronounced (Florescu 1998:150). Similarly, if we consider the cover of a program for a nineteenth-century theatrical adaptation of *Frankenstein* (written by R. B. Peake and enacted by T. P. Cooke), the creature is pictured as not only human but attractive. Furthermore, if we assess the image of actor Fred Leslie, who appeared in an 1887 London production of *Frankenstein*, he is made to seem a rather normal, bowler-hatted urbanite (Forry 1990:56). Even in the case of a more phantasmagoric rendition of the creature (as seen in Paul Bedford's 1850 London stage interpretation), the monster is portrayed quite differently than in the screen versions of the 1930s—tapping into colonialist visions of a savage (and perhaps African) native (Forry:60). Moreover, an illustration from a 1922 volume of *Frankenstein* (published by Cornhill in Boston) avoids representing the ogre at all by showing merely his skeleton (Glut 1984:6–7). Finally, none of the myriad nineteenth-century political cartoons which picture the monster bear much relation to Karloff's later film incarnation (Forry:43–78).

In contrast, if we contemplate certain graphic prints of the 1920s and 1930s realized by Danish artist Sven Brasch (1886–1970), we see parallels to the demeanor of Karloff's monster. In a 1922 film advertisement for *Manden fra Sing-Sing* (*The City of Silent Men*), Brasch depicts the figure of a prisoner with an entirely squared-off jaw and profile. Similarly, in other Brasch posters of the era (representing Wallace Beery, Buster Keaton, and Wallace Reid), the actors' faces are angularly rendered like some geometric construction. Significantly, Brasch exhibited his prints at the Paris Exposition of 1925 (Dailey 1990:20). Furthermore, if we examine a wood engraving of the monster created by Lynd Ward for a 1934 book edition of *Frankenstein*, it favors Karloff and bears the mark of abstraction that typifies the Art Deco style (Florescu:159).[3]

---

3. In Florescu's book (159), this edition is credited to Harrison Smith and Robert Haas.

This shift from Victorian to modern conceptions of the monster seems highlighted in Mel Brooks's film parody *Young Frankenstein* (1974), set (like Whales's movie) in the 1930s but, obviously, unlike Shelley's novel. Here the creature (Peter Boyle) is presented to the public at a formal lecture (as is the robot Maria in *Metropolis*). For the occasion, he incongruously dresses up in top hat and tails and, once on stage, dances to the strains of "Puttin' on the Ritz," clumsily imitating Fred Astaire. Similarly, when Dr. Frankenstein's fiancée (Madeline Kahn) has sex with the well-endowed monster, her hair (whitened and standing on end) transforms into the coif of Frankenstein's bride.

SEX AND DEATH

[*She* is] a novel full of the kind of half conscious sexual symbolism possible only in an age of pre-Freudian innocence and which can be interpreted as an allegory of man's ordeal in the face of threatening female sexuality.
—Patrick Bade (1979:32)

Clearly, in the case of *Metropolis* we find the classic femme fatale transposed to an Art Deco aesthetic. While, in general, the movement's iconography avoids the portrayal of Woman as entirely sinister, traces of this vision survive from Deco's predecessors. At the turn of the century, in both Art Nouveau, Symbolism, and Secessionism, painters conceived the female in a rather forbidding fashion. Patrick Bade links this conception to the nineteenth-century male's association of sex and death (due to the scourge of syphilis) and to his intimidation by advances women had made on the social front (9, 22). Thus, Austrian artist Gustav Klimt (1862–1918) rendered such threatening visions of Woman as *Pallas Athene* (1898), and German painter Franz von Stuck (1863–1928) depicted rather daunting biblical figures—for example, in *Salome* (1906). Finally, Edward Munch (1863–1944), in his series *The Frieze of Life* (1890s), portrayed a virtual catalog of malignant femme fatales. *Vampire* (1893) depicts a woman biting a man's neck; *The Heart* (1896) portrays a woman holding (and seeming to devour) the specified organ; and *Madonna* (1893–94) pictures a sexualized and deathly version of the Holy Mother.

According to Bade, Klimt was the last major painter for whom the femme fatale was a significant theme. By the beginning of the twentieth century, the figure's reign declined:

The downfall of the femme fatale was hastened by her astonishing popularity. By the end of the nineteenth century, the femme fatale was a stock cliché in art and literature, often cheapened almost beyond recognition. This trivialisation, combined with changing social conditions, eventually discredited her in the eyes of serious artists. The subject was repeated *ad nauseam* by the hordes of artists exhibiting in the Salons and Academies of Europe, always eager to latch on to a fashionable theme and to water down the innovations of more radical artists for easy public consumption.   (Bade:28)

While the femme fatale's currency may have waned in the sphere of high art, her appeal survived in the realm of popular culture, though her perversity and villainy were tamed in Art Nouveau and further muted in Art Deco.

It is clear that a mass art (like commercial cinema), devoid of pretensions of genius, often revives the stereotypes that earlier generations or media have discarded. This is certainly the case in the two American film versions of *She* that were produced in 1925 and 1935. Both were based on an 1887 novel by British author Henry Rider Haggard—a classic work of the femme fatale genre.

The twenties variant (directed by Leander de Cordova and G. B. Samuelson) concerns a British scholar, Horace Holly (Heinrich George), who is visited by an elderly friend on the verge of death. The old man reveals that he has a son and asks Holly to be the boy's guardian once he is gone. He gives Holly instructions for his child's education and for opening a box on the boy's twenty-fifth birthday. The camera then focuses upon an hour glass (which signals the passing of time). The fateful day arrives and Leo (Carlyle Blackwell) finds, within the box bequeathed to him by his father, a letter from an ancient female ancestor who claims to have discovered, along with her husband, a magical "Pillar of Fire" ruled by an immortal queen named She-Who-Must-Be-Obeyed. The epistle speaks of how the monarch (also known as Ayesha) slew the author's husband, Kallikrates, out of jealousy and desire for him. The writer asks her descendants to avenge the crime. Leo, Holly, and a friend named Job (Tom Reynolds) decide to take up the challenge and sail to Libya, where (as a title informs us): "She-Who-Must-Be-Obeyed has, with undying youth, watched and waited for the re-incarnated Kallikrates—her loved one." When the three arrive, they are confronted by spear-toting natives who take them to Ayesha (Betty Blythe). Among the indigenous group is Ustane (Mary Odette), a woman who falls in love with Leo and refuses to leave his side. Villagers perform a hasty marriage rite to seal their union. Leo falls ill and Holly asks Ayesha for help. Once in her presence, he requests that she remove her black veil so that he can see her. She warns him that looking upon her face "may be [his] undoing." When he finally views the queen's visage, he seems both smitten and alarmed. When he later humbly prostrates himself before her, she says: "I wondered how long it would take to bring you to your knees." Before Ayesha comes to Leo's bedside, she stops at the underground tomb of her dead lover Kallikrates. When she visits Leo, she is shocked to apprehend that he is the reincarnation of her deceased paramour. She immediately becomes jealous of Ustane and orders her death. As though by magic, Ustane disappears into thin air. With Ustane gone, Leo is suddenly attracted to Ayesha and ensnared by her amorous powers. She takes him to the tombs where he gazes upon her dead lover and realizes that the man is a double for himself. Ayesha promises Leo that he will soon stand "in the place of life and bathe in the fire," after which he will achieve immortality along with her. To reach the flame, Leo, Holly, Job, and Ayesha climb a huge precipice and leap over a cavernous abyss, then enter a cave in which the "fire of immortal life" blazes. To give Leo courage, Ayesha offers to stand in the flame first. As she does so, however, she evaporates into the smoke. Suddenly regaining his senses, Leo flees with Holly and Job. A final intertitle (ostensibly in Ayesha's voice) warns us that she will "be reborn . . . with greater beauty."

In its theme of a death-defying queen, *She* taps into primordial conceptions of the female as having magical command of the life process. If woman can give birth, such superstitions reason, she can also master death—a power that makes her a frightful opponent. According to psychoanalysts Frieda Fromm-Reichman and Virginia Gunst, for example, such a view informs a famous Persian legend:

> In that myth a woman creates the world, and she creates it by the act of natural creativity which is hers and which cannot be duplicated by men. She gives birth to a great number of sons. The sons, greatly puzzled by this act which they cannot duplicate, become frightened. They think: "Who can tell us, that if she can give life, she cannot also take life." And so, because of their fear of this mysterious ability of woman, and of its reversible possibility, they kill her. (1977:88)

While *Metropolis* is an avant-garde work, *She* is far more traditional in its narrative structure and visual style and, unlike Lang's masterpiece, it is a most average film of its time. Ayesha's world has an Egyptian aura about it, a very common occurrence in fantasy films of the period following the discovery of King Tutankhamen's tomb. Hence, the rooms of her palace are decorated with statues that look like the exterior of mummy cases. In the film's emphasis on Ayesha's white or black veils (which, in varied light, alternately display or obscure her face), we see evidence of the era's fascination with the Salome figure. Similarly, Ayesha's unruly mane (which she frequently combs) is another stock feature of the femme fatale character. As Bade notes, her "hair was her most effective and lethal weapon" (13) Significantly, in *The Frieze of Life*, Munch includes a painting entitled *Man's Head in Woman's Hair* (1899). In Ayesha's exotic and elaborate costumes, we see evidence of the period's stylish Orientalist fashions, once more giving the femme fatale a decidedly contemporary look at odds with her allegedly "ancient" heritage. But Ayesha's couture does not match the modernist outfits of Garbo's silent films. The most interesting aspect of the queen's dress is not, in fact, its design but its extremely risqué nature. In one scene, her thinly veiled bodice clearly reveals her breasts and nipples below and, in another, her bosom is barely covered by a meager brassiere made from two shells. In almost all scenes, her naked legs are emphatically present. Not surprisingly, some of this imagery would later be muted by the Production Code of the 1930s.

It is, however, in the 1935 version of *She*, directed for RKO by Lansing C. Holden and Irving Pichel, that the nineteenth-century femme fatale and her fantastic environs receive the full Art Deco treatment. One of the first images we see on the screen announces that the picture has been approved by the Production Code (recently strengthened in 1934)—and, here, the queen's costumes (though more innovative and artistic) are less decolleté. In many respects the story is similar to that of the 1925 film (and Haggard's original). Again we have Horace Holly (Nigel Bruce) whose old and ailing friend—here John Vincey (Samuel S. Hinds)—must confess a secret to a relative, this time his nephew Leo (Randolph Scott). John tells Leo that, as a man of science, he has attempted to battle humanity's enemies: time and death. He opens a box and shows John a letter from a female family member of some five hundred years earlier. In it, she claims to have traveled with her husband to Muscovy to find "the flame and she who stands there in triumph over death." John takes Leo and Holly into his laboratory (which looks like Dr. Frankenstein's) and explains that he has been trying to reproduce the "flame of life." He suspects that its potency has something to do with radioactivity and that, perhaps, at high enough temperatures, fire grows benignly cold instead of fatally hot. He then shows his cohorts a small gold statue of a woman engulfed in flames and says that it is an heirloom from his ancestors' ancient voyage. Significantly, we see the artifact in an insert close-up and realize that (like the nude female figure in *The Torrent*), it resembles Art Deco pieces of the era.

Holly and Leo decide to take up the challenge and go in search of the "flame of life." This time, however, the region in which they must travel is one of icy glaciers rather than tropical deserts. What is most perilous about the trip is that they must cross a huge mountain barrier that has deterred earlier explorers. In order to scale the range, they enlist the help of an arctic guide, Dugmore (Lumsden Hare), who insists on taking his daughter Tanya (Helen Mack) with them. On the journey through luminous, surreal, craggy vistas (resembling those in Maxfield Parrish's 1926 *Romance*), Dugmore perishes and Leo and Tanya fall in love. Finally, the group enters a fantastic cave in which crystals sparkle and volcanic mists rise. A primitive tribe finds them and takes them away. As the natives are about to kill them for a cannibalistic feast, a group of warriors arrive to save them. In contrast to the pelt-wearing Neanderthals, these men are garbed in modernist-looking variants on the Roman helmet and toga. The trio is taken to Kor where Queen Hash-A-Mo-Tep (or She-Who-Must-Be-Obeyed) reigns supreme (fig. 8.3).

When we first glimpse the matriarch (Helen Gahagan), she is enshrouded in smoke at the top of a long, modern, ziggurat set of stairs. When she glimpses Leo, she calls him John Vincey, her long-lost and "dearest lover." Later, she woos Leo in her modernist-primitive bedroom (with its chic table and ottoman, and its sculpted niches). When she learns that some of the "Cave People" have tried to harm him, she sits on her throne (in a black, streamlined outfit, hooded with a balaclava capped by a spiked Lucite crown) and sentences them to death. She claims that she must be cruel in order "to rule by terror." In a second scene in the queen's boudoir (this time adorned with a modern vase filled with cherry blossom branches), she tries to make Leo remember his ancient past. She tells him to gaze into a pool; he does so and sees a reflection of his double—the venerable John Vincey. With Leo in shock, the queen takes him through huge, abstract, modernist doors to a tomb where her dead lover lies on a geometrical marble slab. Leo recognizes the man as his alter-ego. Hash-A-Mo-Tep reveals to Leo that, centuries ago, she killed her beloved because he refused to leave his wife for her. When Leo succumbs to the queen's erotic advances, she informs him that, following a ritual sacrifice, he will join her in immortality. Excited, Leo returns to Tanya and Holly to announce that he will soon view the secret "flame of life." Jealous, Tanya tries to denigrate Hash-A-Mo-Tep, asking whether she's grown "good" as well as young. She claims that, in contrast to a magical and endless life, she can give Leo something more prosaic: the promise of two people living together, laughing at small things, sharing with each other, and growing old as a couple. "That isn't much to offer," she says, "compared to power and a kingdom." Leo, however, chooses Hash-A-Mo-Tep and attends the Festival of the Sacred Well.

What follows is a virtual "production number" inserted into a fantasy film. It is staged on an elaborate set graced by huge, ancient-looking male statues that are placed around the room; despite their exoticism, they have a modern feel to them. Inside the room is a huge urn with cut-outs designed in a contemporary flame motif. Within this ceremonial site, men dance in masks, headdresses, and cos-

tumes that seem a cross between Kabuki, avant-garde, and Native American modes. Hash-A-Mo-Tep sits on a throne with an Orientalist background and wears a modernist metal helmet. Musicians arrive wearing costumes decorated in geometric patterns: lines, squares, and triangles. A veiled maiden is brought forth for the sacrifice and poised on the rim of the urn. Leo realizes that she is Tanya. Tossing her over his shoulder (like a limp sack of potatoes), he and Holly flee, moving through caves, abstract arches, and mountain precipices. Eventually they make their way to a modernist-looking cave that is the queen's temple. In its look, the structure reminds one of Hugh Ferris's description of the city of the future in *The Metropolis of Tomorrow* (1929:124):

FIGURE 8.3
Hash-A-Mo-Tep makes her wishes known in *She* (1935). (Courtesy British Film Institute)

> Buildings like crystals.
> Walls of translucent glass.
> Sheer glass blocks sheathing a steel grill.
> No Gothic branch: no Acanthus leaf: no recollection of the plant world.
> A mineral kingdom.
> Gleaming stalagmites.
> Forms as cold as ice.

Upon entering Hash-A-Mo-Tep's temple, Leo declares that he wants nothing from her. She reminds him that while she will remain forever lovely, Tanya will grow old: "Her eyes will loose their brightness; her cheeks will wrinkle and her limbs will wither." Seeking to convince Leo to stand with her in the "flame of life," she offers to go first. When she enters the conflagration, however, rather than prevail, she fades, growing older and older with each burst of fire. Finally, she turns into a white-haired, wizened old hag. "I die," she cries; "have pity on my shame." As the film ends, we find Tanya and Leo back in England, by the fireplace of Holly's traditionally appointed study. Tanya opines that the real flame of life resides in the hearth of a home in which two people truly love each other.

With sets conceived by Van Nest Polglase (and decorated by Thomas Little), the world of Kor is an Art Deco wonderland—with its bare sculpted walls (simultaneously primal and modern), its pedestaled urns, its ziggurat staircases, its chic boudoirs, its Orientalist accents, and its Cubist temples. Again, confirming Armitt's sense of the import of space in the fantasy genre, the *moderne* universe of Kor is an exotic world through which the hapless traveler wanders (as does Freder in *Metropolis*). Set off by a mountain barrier, it is a separate land that only some may enter, a factor which emphasizes the region's foreignness. Alternately, there is something "familiar" about Kor, a fact that seems symbolized by the notion that Leo is his own ancestor reincarnate. Thus the text reveals the tension between the alien and the familiar that Freud saw as central to the uncanny. Significantly, Art Deco style manages to fulfill both semiotic requirements. It is somewhat recognizable as a contemporary style, but extraneous enough (in its elite, avant-garde associations) to be exotic.

In its ties to the unsettling and ageless queen, the film clearly links Art Deco design to a world of desire, hubris, and youth. In costumes created by Aline Bernstein and Harold Miles, Hash-A-Mo-Tep parades around Kor in floor-length elegant tunics adorned with modernist borders; accenting these, she wears Deco-inspired jeweled breastplates and avant-garde headdresses. Counterposed to the queen (like von Stuck's painting *Innocence* [1889] to his canvas *Sin* [c. 1906]) (see plate 4), Tanya is the good woman of the drama. Significantly, she is forced to wear exaggerated dress only when she enters Kor, the realm of the pernicious matriarch. If Hash-A-Mo-Tep is ambitious (in her wielding of power and her hope for eternal love), Tanya is quite modest in her search for a "home for two" with the man she adores. With this 1935 version of *She*, released within memory of the Roaring Twenties and halfway through the treacherous Thirties, it is Tanya who represents the nation's conservative feminine ideal. Clearly, a passive Angel-of-the-House is preferable to an Art Deco Female-Who-Must-Be-Obeyed.

One day [my wife] accompanied me . . . into the cellar of the old building
which our poverty compelled us to inhabit. The cat followed me down the
steep stairs, and . . . exasperated me to madness. Uplifting an axe . . . I aimed
a blow at the animal . . . But this blow was arrested by the hand of my wife.
Goaded, by the interference, into a rage more than demoniacal, I . . . buried
the axe in her brain. —Edgar Allan Poe, "The Black Cat" ([1843]; 1976:14)

Earlier, I mentioned Boris Karloff's roles in the Frankenstein films, but these were
not the only horror movies to showcase the actor in the 1930s. In between making
the two adaptations of Mary Shelley's fiction, he starred in another work, *The
Black Cat* (1934), directed by Edgar G. Ulmer for Universal Pictures. Like the
Whale films, this was based on the work of another nineteenth-century author,
Edgar Allen Poe, though the final script had almost nothing to do with the writer's
original.[4] As with *The Bride of Frankenstein*, the female is not the principal representative of evil in *The Black Cat* (as she is in *Metropolis* or *She*), but is nonetheless a crucial accessory to crime.

The film concerns American newlyweds—author Peter Alison (David Manners) and his wife Joan (Jacqueline Wells/aka Julie Bishop)—who board the Orient
Express in France to travel to Gombos, Hungary, a honeymoon resort near Vizhegrad. Again, as in other works of fantasy, the protagonists voyage to a faraway place.
As Armitt notes, if the genre "is about being absent from home . . . then the inhab-
itant of the fantastic is always the stranger" (8). As the train departs, a conductor asks
them to share their compartment with a rather melancholy European man, Dr.
Vitus Werdegast (Bela Lugosi), who they learn is a psychiatrist. Werdegast tells the
couple that he is traveling to visit an "old friend," then remarks how Joan reminds
him of his deceased wife (thus, in keeping with the genre, she is familiar yet
strange). Werdegast recounts how his spouse died while he was away fighting in

4. In the original story (first published in 1843), a man is haunted by the specter of a
black cat whom he has killed. When an almost identical black cat appears at his house, he
chases it into the cellar, accompanied by his wife. When his wife restrains him from killing
the second cat, he is enraged and murders her instead. He then hides her body behind the
cellar wall but is undone when the police come to inspect the premises and hear a strange
noise muted in the background. It turns out that he has buried the black cat along with his
wife and that the animal's plaintive cries lead the detectives to solve the mystery of the
woman's disappearance.

World War I and then interned in a prison camp. At the appointed station, in the midst of a rainstorm, the Alisons, Werdegast, and the doctor's manservant disembark from the train and board a rickety bus. Werdegast directs the driver to the home of Hjalmar Poelzig. As the new acquaintances journey together, Werdegast points out that the countryside has been the locale of many wartime battles; he finds it horrifying that people now live on the site of such carnage. He tells the Alisons that Poelzig has built a mansion overlooking Fort Marmorus ("the greatest graveyard in the world"). As the storm worsens, the bus skids off the road and careens into a ravine. The driver is killed and Joan is knocked unconscious. The three men carry her to Poelzig's home. In the house, they are greeted by their host, a middle-aged, unattractive man (Boris Karloff) who sports a strange, jagged widow's peak and wears a black kimono. Accompanying him is his sullen, mute housekeeper (Egon Brecher). Concerned about Joan's condition, Werdegast injects her with a strong sedative. As the men await her recovery, Werdegast confides his hatred of Poelzig who, during the war, had been the commander of Fort Marmorus and was suspected of betraying Hungary to the Russians. Furthermore, Werdegast reveals that, while he was a prisoner of war, Poelzig informed his wife Karen that he had died and then married her himself. Werdegast has returned to Vizhegrad to learn the fate of his ex-spouse and daughter. When he confronts Poelzig, he is suddenly unsettled by a black cat that walks through the room. He cowers, drops his drink glass, and throws a knife at the animal, killing it off-screen. Poelzig explains that, although Werdegast is a psychiatrist, he suffers from a phobic fear of felines. Right then, Joan, who has awakened from her stupor, glides strangely into the room—as though hailed by the creature's demise. Werdegast deems her "mediumistic." The newlyweds retire and, as they do, we find Poelzig in bed with an unidentified, beautiful young woman (who seems incongruous as his mate); she lies there almost comatose. During the night, Poelzig descends to his basement and regards a series of transparent glass display cases in which are suspended the bodies of numerous nubile dead women, preserved in a pristine state. As he looks at them, he strokes the fur of a black cat he holds in his arms. He then makes his way to Werdegast's bedroom where he orders the doctor to follow him down below to the old chart room of the fort (whose wall is done in a graph paper motif). There he shows Werdegast yet another "diorama," this one containing the deceased body of his wife Karen, whom Poelzig stole away. The woman's hair seems to stand erect (like that of the Bride of Frankenstein). Poelzig informs the doctor that his daughter has also expired. As Werdegast pulls a gun on Poelzig, we see the shadow of a black cat slink by, rendering the doctor impotent. When Poelzig returns to his quarters, we realize that the young woman in his bed is a look-alike of Werdegast's wife. He calls her

"Karen" and tells her to remain in her room all the next day, revealing to her that Werdegast is her father. Poelzig retires to bed to do some light reading: *The Rites of Lucifer*. The next morning, Poelzig makes preparations for a Satanic ceremony that will be held at his home that night. Realizing that his host intends to hold Joan captive, Werdegast engages him in a game of chess to win her freedom. Meanwhile, Joan awakens with no recollection of the day before and convinces Peter that they should leave immediately. When the couple tries to depart, however, Poelzig's servant (at his master's instruction) lies and tells them that the car is not functioning. Peter tries to make a phone call but finds the lines suspiciously out of service. Trying to flee, Joan faints and is taken away by Poelzig's henchmen; Peter is knocked out and imprisoned in the basement. Soon, Poelzig's thugs dress Joan in a white gown, preparing her for ritual sacrifice; they tie her up and bring her to the diabolical service. Elsewhere, Peter escapes and Werdegast and his servant manage to rescue Joan. On their way out of the mansion, Werdegast discovers his daughter on what seems to be an operating or embalming table. Fearing that Poelzig intends to harm her as well, he fights with the architect and ends up restraining him in hanging handcuffs. As Werdegast skins his captive (an act that we see only in shadow), Peter shoots him and the couple flees. Meanwhile, the dying Werdegast finds a lever on the wall that will blow up the mansion. He pulls it and, as the Alisons escape, they see the estate explode. Some time later, on a train to Budapest the couple reads the newspaper reviews of Alison's newest novel, which some critics find overblown with "melodramatic imagination." They laugh to themselves, knowing his tale recounts the truth.

While, on one level, *The Black Cat* (fig. 8.4) seems a standard and clichéd horror film (with its Carpathian setting, its mysticism, its menacing villain, its drugged female victims, its ghoulish servants, its occult and semi-incoherent plot), it bears one point of interest that both distinguishes it from other works of the genre and makes it relevant to our study. The House of Horrors in which the Alisons and Werdegast find themselves is a jewel of the Style Moderne. With sets designed by Charles D. Hall, the mansion in which Hjalmar Poelzig resides is one worthy of coverage in *Architectural Digest* of 1934. Indeed, Peter Alison remarks, upon entering Poelzig's home, that it is a "very tricky house" with an "interesting atmosphere." While Werdergast admits that the building is a "masterpiece of construction," and Poelzig's "chef d'oeuvre," he claims its ambiance is one of "death." Later, Alison seems to agree, noting that if he wanted to build a "nice cozy insane asylum," Poelzig would be the man to hire.

To make the question of style even more emphatic, Poelzig is said to be a well-known Austrian architect (Vienna being the site of great modernist architectural

FIGURE 8.4

Dr. Poelzig (Boris Karloff)
and Dr. Werdegast (Bela
Lugosi) visit Joan Alison
(Jacqueline Wells) in a *mod-
erne* bedroom in *The Black
Cat* (1934). (Courtesy British
Film Institute)

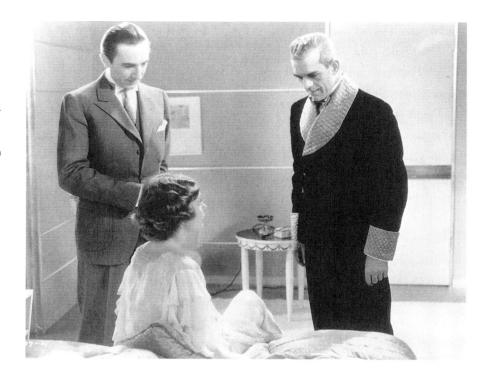

activity in the 1920s and 1930s involving the Secessionist group).[5] More tellingly, Hjalmar Poelzig is not the only one to have hailed from Vienna—so did the film's director, Edgar G. Ulmer. Born there in 1904, he studied architecture at the Academy of Arts and Sciences and later worked as an assistant stage designer for Max Reinhardt. When he came to the United States he was an art director for the Broadway theater and later for Universal Pictures. Ultimately, he worked with F. W. Murnau on two pictures: *Sunrise* (at Fox) and, later, *Tabu* (Katz 2001:1382). So, here again, in the case of *The Black Cat*, an Art Deco mise-en-scène is allied to the touch of a European émigré director working in America (as it was in *The Kiss* to the hand of Jacques Feyder).

Beyond aspects of the broader Style Moderne, there are numerous Art Deco design elements associated with the alien space of Poelzig's nefarious abode.[6] The

---

5. Significantly (as John Belton informed me), there was a real architect by the name of Hans Poelzig, a German artist remembered for his Grosses Schauspielhaus (1919), an auditorium in Berlin that is one of the finest architectural examples of German Expressionism. (For entry on "Grosses Schauspielhaus," see *Encyclopedia Brittanica* (online version) at www.search.eb.com.

6. Howard Mandelbaum and Eric Myers include mention of *The Black Cat* in their book *Screen Deco* (1985).

entrance hall (with a black glossy floor fit for Astaire and Rogers) is an open room which includes a circular staircase (with chrome railing) whose wall is paneled in a gridlike, geometric manner. The foyer's ceiling is dropped and illuminated by lights hidden behind translucent panels. The chimes at the front door are modernist in style, as is a divider with circular, "porthole" openings. All over the house are large rectangular picture windows, subdivided into smaller square panes. The room in which Joan rests includes a modernist bed and vanity, upon which are various Art Deco objects (including a female figurine on a pedestal). The mirror that surrounds the dressing table is also done in a contemporary mode, as are the tumblers that stand on her night table. The walls of her bedroom (and many others in the mansion) are ornamented with a linear metallic trim, as are many of the house's doors; and most of home's upholstered furnishings are fashioned in the rounded Art Deco style. Peter Alison's bedroom sports a cutting-edge digital clock and is divided by an asymmetrical, triangular interior wall. Elsewhere in the house stands a screen (in the Japanese mode) constructed of rice paper. Even the film's invocation of cats has reverberations for Art Deco design, since (in homage to Egyptian iconography) figural representations of felines (especially Siamese) were hugely popular in the era. Most notable were the cat statues, lamps, and bookends created by Arthur Frankenberg under the Frankart label. In Poelzig's bedroom, there is a porthole opening illuminated by a neon light strip. On the desk of his study is a modernist lamp; a contemporary torchère stands on the floor. A Deco female statuette is located on his desk, while another is positioned elsewhere in the room. Significantly, when Joan enters Poelzig's study after recovering from her faint and embraces her husband, her host inexplicably grips a female figurine, as though disturbed by the couple's show of affection. His gesture is highlighted by its close-up framing in the foreground of the shot. Here again (as with the female figurine in Joan's bedroom) an Art Deco sculpture seems, self-reflexively, to emphasize the gender politics of the film.

Poelzig clearly has a horrific "woman problem," which is displaced here onto his ominous grasp of the Art Deco statuette. Certainly, he has "held" other women captive, embalming them and preserving them as trophies in glass display cases (like the true Maria kept in a vessel in Rotwang's laboratory). Hence, the difference in *The Black Cat* between a live female (Joan) and her inanimate representation (the statue) is minimized, making the two almost coequal. This seems significant in an era in which the popular design mode so frequently harnessed the female body for a static decorative motif. Additionally, through his necrophilic display of women, Poelzig is not only an architect but an "artist" whose deathly creations mimic the favored Art Deco mode. While, obviously, a man is the villain of *The Black Cat*, it is through female taxidermy that his depravity is registered. Furthermore, in Joan's strange behavior (which seems vaguely linked to the appearance of a black cat), a sense of the "mediumistic" potential of the female is advanced. Karen, Werdergast's daughter, also seems locked in a malign spell (like some baleful Sleeping Beauty).

But the clearest link in the film between the Style Moderne and evil is the Satanic Mass at which Poelzig officiates. In his cellar "chapel," he is surrounded by angular, canted, Constructivist crosses reminiscent of those framing the two Marias in the catacombs of Metropolis. The crosses are mounted on a ziggurat-tiered platform and surrounded by abstract towers that seem a mix of obelisks and skyscrapers. Here again, in the lower depths of an avant-garde edifice (like the bowels of Metropolis, or the caves of Muscovy), the distressing moral valence of modernism is disclosed. Once again, it is, in part, associated with the body of woman—here as the sacrificial lamb of Poelzig's demonic zeal.

DRAGON LADY

[Myrna] Loy was the perfect Deco subject: a white woman able to pretend to the role of oriental. Deco style seems to imitate Loy because Loy is a Deco mold, a Deco figurine in lines and poses. —Mark Winokur (1996:206)

The Mask of Fu Manchu (1932)—one of many movies based on the novels of British author Sax Rohmer—is another fantasy film of the Art Deco era that, like *Metropolis* and *She*, involves an evil heroine. Here, the villainess is Fah Lo See (Myrna Loy), daughter of the criminal Doctor Fu Manchu (yet another role for Boris Karloff). In *Fu Manchu* (which falls broadly within the science fiction genre), Deco design takes an Orientalist bent (which is logical since most of the narrative is set in China). In so doing, the film taps into a strain of Art Deco already referenced in my earlier discussions of melodrama (e.g., *Mata Hari, The Painted Veil*) and the adventure film (*Bird of Paradise*). As it happens, setting *Fu Manchu* in Manchuria was a highly topical move at the time, since China was then struggling to rid the nation of Japanese influence.[7]

---

7. The so-called Manchurian Incident occurred in 1931. Japanese troops seized the city of Mukden (now Shen-yang in China) "which was followed by the Japanese invasion of all of Manchuria and the establishment of the Japanese-dominated state of Manchukuo in the area. See entry for "Mukden Incident" in the online version of the *Encyclopedia Brittanica* at www.search.eb.com.

228   MADAME SATAN

The Mask of Fu Manchu begins in England where agent Nayland Smith (Lewis Stone) sends archaeologist Lionel Barton (Lawrence Grant) on a mission to the Gobi Desert to retrieve the mask and sword of Genghis Khan from the tyrant's long-lost tomb. (In its explorative theme, the story bears obvious comparison to the narrative of *She*.) There is a special urgency to Smith's request because he has learned that the infernal Chinese doctor Fu Manchu is set on garnering the objects for himself in order to achieve world domination. Unhappily, on his way from a meeting at the British Museum, Barton is abducted by Fu Manchu's thugs and taken to the doctor's palatial estate in Liangchow. There, Barton is subjected to the infamous bell torture in order to make him reveal the location of Genghis Khan's tomb. Meanwhile, Barton's daughter Sheila (Karen Morley) has been informed of her father's fate. She and her boyfriend Terry Granville (real-life football hero Charles Starrett) decide to undertake the expedition themselves, hoping to find both Barton and Genghis Khan's resting place. They are accompanied on their journey to China by Smith and two other men, Von Berg (Jean Hersholt) and McLeod (David Torrence). The group succeeds in finding the tomb and unearthing the coveted mask and sword. Before they can safely dispose of the valuables, however, Fu Manchu's henchmen come after them and kill McLeod. Terry decides to venture to the doctor's palace in order to exchange the treasures for Barton's freedom. Once there, it is apparent that Fu Manchu's daughter, Fah Lo See, is attracted to Terry (fig. 8.5). When Fu Manchu tests the sword that Terry delivers (with a Tesla–coil-like contraption), he finds it to be a fake, and Terry is taken away for punishment. At Fah Lo See's command, he is brutally whipped and then placed on a divan where she begins to sexually ravish him—which her father deems her "customary procedure." Later, Terry is subjected to a form of experimental "surgery" at Fu Manchu's hands whereby he is injected with the serum of snakes and tarantulas to render him entirely under Fah Lo See's control. As Fu Manchu proceeds, his daughter (in a series of intercut close-ups) gleefully looks on. Meanwhile, at their hideout, Sheila, Smith, and von Berg await Terry's return but, when they answer a knock at the door, find Barton's dead body on the ground. Smith decides to take Genghis Khan's real sword and mask to Fu Manchu's hideout to gain Terry's release. Upon entering the doctor's domain, however, he falls through a trap door and finds himself suspended above a pit of ferocious alligators. Having placed Terry under Fah Lo See's control, Fu Manchu sends him back to his colleagues to lure Sheila and von Berg to the palace. When the group arrives, von Berg is sent to the Room of Slim Silver Fingers where he is positioned in the middle of a spiked vice that slowly closes. Sheila is dispatched to the Room of the Golden Peacock where (like Ustane and Tanya in the two versions of *She* and Joan in *The Black Cat*) she is prepared for ritual sacrifice at a ceremony that will hail Fu Manchu as the heir to Genghis Khan. Before Sheila is taken away, however, she manages to break the spell that Fah Lo See holds on Terry by reminding him that he really loves her. Fortunately, Smith escapes from the vicious alligators and saves Sheila from her demonic fate. The two rescue Terry from a second mind-altering surgery and then pry von Berg loose from the jaws of death. The group finds Fu Manchu's bolt-firing ray gun and aims it at the doctor and his subjects, who have assembled for Sheila's sacrifice—wreaking havoc on them all. In the final sequence of the film Smith, Sheila, Terry, and von Berg are on shipboard, sailing safely to the West. Smith throws the sword of Genghis Khan into the ocean to prevent another demagogue from acquiring it.

Certainly, the world of evil in the film is associated, in a racist and xenophobic fashion, with the East. As noted, this tendency had particular historical coordinates at the time since Japanese imperialism was feared as a continuing force. But the Oriental world depicted in Fu Manchu's mansion is not merely an ancient one, as one might suppose from the film's reference to Genghis Khan. Rather its atmosphere is highly modernist and tinged with an overlay of Art Deco sensibility. This should not surprise us, as the film was developed by MGM (the same studio that produced *Madame Satan* and the silent melodramas of Greta Garbo) and was made under the supervision of both Cedric Gibbons and Adrian. The design world associated with Fu Manchu differs tremendously from that linked to Smith and Barton, who are seen in highly traditional European settings (symbolized by the British Museum). It also is distinguished from other Chinese locales glimpsed in the film—a bazaar, a restaurant, and an opium den—all of which look rather old and shabby.

Certain aspects of Fu Manchu's manor are noteworthy for their Chinese Contemporary look: its stark ebony black pillars, its abstract leaded-glass windows, its throne (mounted on a modern tiered pedestal). Several rooms, in particular, stand out for their hyperbolic Art Deco touches. When Terry is made Fah Lo See's love slave, he is placed on a modern divan positioned beneath a circular frame containing a curtain adorned with Japanese-looking representations of tree branches. The room seems more like a 1930s movie star's boudoir than a Chinese torture chamber. Later, when Terry is dragged to the operating room, he is forced to ascend a huge, winding, ziggurat-like set of black stairs which are seen in stark silhouette against a white background. When Terry is finally readied for his surgical ordeal, he is chained to a rectangular marble slab in a large, vacant, circular room whose only design feature is a white wall whose lower section is entirely black. Standing to guard him around the room are a series of huge, bare-chested African-

American males with polished bald scalps and muscular folded arms (looking for all the world like living prototypes for Gibbons's Oscar statuette). Similarly, the Room of Slim Silver Fingers is boldly spare and modern. All one sees (against its white wall) are the sharp dark lines of the spikes as they close in on von Berg's body. Finally, given the film's science fiction veneer, the scenes of Fu Manchu's experiments (testing the authenticity of the sword; operating on Terry) are replete with beakers, test tubes, and bolts of electricity—all of which convey the look of high modernity. Even more than the film's sets, however, the costumes are deliciously over-the-top. Both Fu Manchu and Fah Lo See wear outrageous Oriental headgear—alternately trimmed with what appears to be excessive lamp fringe or incongruous pom-poms.

It is within this audaciously camp Art Deco mise-en-scène that Fah Lo See presides. With long, clawlike artificial nails on her pointer fingers, she is a visual incarnation of the Dragon Lady. This perverse impression is underscored by

FIGURE 8.5

Fu Manchu (Boris Karloff) and his daughter Fah Lo See (Myrna Loy) entertain Terry Granville (Charles Starrett) amid Chinese-modernist splendor in *The Mask of Fu Manchu* (1932). (Courtesy British Film Institute)

close-ups that show her frequently lit from below, giving her face an ominous, shadowed angularity. It is she, not Fu Manchu, who has a vision of the doctor as the reincarnation of Genghis Khan, and it is she who proclaims the patriarch a leader of the "East against the world." It is also she who takes especial pleasure in the sadism of torture, telling her henchmen—in a frenzy of desire that is simultaneously shocking and hilarious—to whip Terry "faster and faster!" As Mark Winokur notes, "Loy plays the classic dominatrix in an era that desires her" (215).

Significantly (like Hash-A-Mo-Tep), her preferred exercise of power is an erotic one—making her captors "boy toys." She is also a kind of prostitute, since her father trades her carnal services for favors from powerful men. As though to fore-shadow the connection between Asian women and sensual danger, we recall that when Smith and company first locate the tomb of Genghis Khan, they open two sets of doors to find his mask and sword: both decorated with relief sculptures of bare-breasted Oriental females. While Fah Lo See—the Asian Art Deco Woman—foists her physicality on men, the white woman is seen as man's helpless prey. As Smith tells his companions (in reference to Sheila's presence in China): "Do you think for a moment Fu Manchu doesn't know we have a beautiful white girl with us?" Again, in this film, as in other fantasy works of the era, the "good" heroine's looks and demeanor are contrasted with those of a "bad" temptress. Although Sheila is clearly a modern maiden here (dressed in jodhpurs and pith helmet), she is no Art Deco vamp like Fah Lo See.

It is important to note, of course, that the cruel Asian woman in this film is played by a Caucasian actress (as were the native heroines in *White Shadows in the South Seas* and *Bird of Paradise*). Clearly, this casting practice merely liter-alizes an aspect of the Art Deco aesthetic which "provides a vehicle within which whites can play out a fantasy of otherness" (Winokur:212). For Winokur, this linkage of marginalized ethnicity and seductive femininity accomplishes yet another purpose: it "enables an aesthetic/psychic economy" by creating "two tar-gets of repudiation in one person" (220). He also finds that the yoking of white and Oriental races in the film (in the form of a heinous female) bespeaks the real-life tensions of assimilation in America at the time: "As Anglo woman play-ing ethnic, Loy is a dominatrix punishing the desire to be Anglo, to be equal." She is also the female Other with whom the white male may cavort if he will risk being "punishe[d] for that transgression" (Winokur:222). Only through a coun-terfeit vision of the Oriental woman can such a cultural ideology be advanced. For, as Winokur remarks (referencing Anna May Wong, a Chinese-American actress of the period):

[Her] version of Art Deco does not work because she is authentically Asian; history begins to creep back into her character with an unacceptable realism, a history that would, by the 1920s, include the Chinese Immigration Exclusion Act, the ill treatment of Chinese in the United States, the special exclusion of Chinese women, and the subsequent picture bride and prostitute phenomena. . . . Wong's career must fade in a climate in which Loy's can flourish. (212)

Interestingly, though Loy's persona is coded as hateful (through costume, lighting, dialogue, and characterization), her theatrical enactment of the role is, ultimately, rather bland and unconvincing (perhaps revealing its synthetic nature). As rendered by Loy, Fah Lo See's malevolent status seems purely "semiotic" and lacking in passion. There is a restraint and stiffness to her performance that prevents our reacting viscerally to her character with the dread we feel toward Brigitte Helm's robot Maria. The same might be said of Helen Gahagan's realization of Hash-A-Mo-Tep in *She*, which softens the hard edges of the character's awesome persona.

DARK QUEENS OF THE COMICS

[Outer] space or science fiction has become a dialect for our time.
—Doris Lessing[8]

While feature films like *The Mask of Fu Manchu* skirt the generic borders of science fiction and exotic adventure, many serials of the period fit squarely within the first category. Among the most popular was the Flash Gordon cycle, based on a comic by Alex Raymond first published 1933. In 1934, Universal Pictures bought the screen rights to the material and, in 1936, released *Flash Gordon: Space Soldiers*, a 13-episode series directed by Frederick Stephani, starring Larry "Buster" Crabbe in the title role. The head of Universal's serial department, Henry McRae, allocated some $350,000 to the project to assure a high-tech décor and ample special effects—an unprecedented amount for a chapter play of the time (*Flash Gordon* 1996). Given the science fiction atmosphere of the Flash Gordon story and its fanciful nature, it was ripe for an Art Deco treatment.

---

8. Cited in *Columbia World of Quotations* (1966; online version). See Entry #35495 at www.bartleby.com/66/43/35495.html.

The works eventually produced, however, remain—in contrast to feature-length films—low-budget products of questionable quality, with their implausible plots, stock characters, awkward use of miniatures, and poor acting. While touches of Art Deco design are apparent (in their futuristic cityscapes—reminiscent of something out of Ferris's *The Metropolis of Tomorrow*—streamlined rocketships, gadget-laden research laboratories, exotic costumes, and whimsical settings), they show no evidence of the kind of artistry that typified the work of Deco artists like Cedric Gibbons, Van Nest Polglase, or Adrian.

Flash Gordon begins as Earth is experiencing strange atmospheric conditions (hurricanes, typhoons, earthquakes, etc.) that throw the planet into a worldwide pandemonium (portrayed in a montage of newsreel excerpts). Flash Gordon (the son of a science professor) is flying home on an airplane when a bizarre storm hits and he and a female passenger, Dale Arden (Jean Rogers), must bail out of the craft in parachutes. On the ground, they encounter Dr. Hans Zarkov (Frank Shannon), a rocket scientist, who informs them that environmental catastrophes are occurring because the planet Mongo is set on crashing into Earth. Flash and Dale decide to accompany Zarkov on his intergalactic voyage to Mongo in order to thwart those plans. Once there, they encounter every sort of enemy, beginning with giant lizards. The trio is captured by armor-suited soldiers (who look like warriors from the Middle Ages) who take them to an evil leader, Emperor Ming (Charles Middleton). Though he has an Oriental name and mustache, he is obviously played by a Caucasian actor (as was Fu Manchu by Boris Karloff and Fah Lo See by Myrna Loy). Ming orders his troops to take Zarkov to a laboratory where he will be forced to work on ventures for Mongo instead of for Earth. Ming also commands that Flash be thrown into an arena where, in Roman Circus fashion, several primitive tusked men are released to brutalize him. Luckily, Ming's daughter, Princess Aura[9] (Priscilla Lawson), who looks more Middle Eastern than Chinese in her halter tops, bare midriff, and filmy skirts, immediately lusts for Flash (as had She-Who-Must-Be-Obeyed for Leo, and Fah Lo See for Terry). She tells Ming that if Flash survives the carnage, he is hers. Meanwhile, displaying a similar interracial longing, Ming is attracted to Dale Arden, whom he calls his "pretty one." Like Sheila in

9. Princess Aura also appeared in a Flash Gordon comic strip ("The World in Danger") where she opposed her father and became enamored with and an ally of Flash. In the comic, she wanted her father to marry Dale Arden so that the earth woman would no longer be a rival for Flash's affections. See Gelman (1974: no pages in volume).

The Mask of Fu Manchu, Dale is taken away to serve the whims of the alien. As in so many films of the era, cross-cultural desire is made to seem automatic, fiendish, and unnatural.

As Flash fights the protohumans, Aura looks on excitedly (as had Fah Lo See at Terry's thrashing). Finally, she bolts into the arena to save him with her ray gun. This begins a series of escapades in which Aura and Flash run away, encountering numerous traps set by Ming (attacks by shark-men, giant octopuses, claw-handed dragons, etc.). Whenever Flash remembers Dale and shows concern for her fate, Aura becomes agitated, asking whether he "likes the Earth woman" better than her. Jealous and punitive, she threatens that he "will never see Dale Arden again." Here, once more, we have a dichotomy between the passive good woman (who can only scream, faint, and gape) and the active bad one (who totes pistols, plots escapes, defies her father, and expresses erotic desire). Again, the bad woman (who is, of course, dark-haired instead of blonde) is conceived in high style—with ornate Orientalist harem costumes that harken to Art Deco fashion. Similarly, her malevolent father is clothed in a fanciful, high-collared, starkly designed cape bordered by geometric motifs. While the brief glimpses of Earth that we see (of scientists attempting to communicate with Dr. Zarkov) show a traditional décor, the world of Mongo is both futuristic and exotic, simultaneously modern and antique. A room in which Dale is imprisoned boasts a statue resembling an Egyptian mummy case as well as some Sphinx figures. However, another room in which she is held sports a modern bed that is shielded by a transparent plastic curtain. While some of the drama takes place in the futurist "city in the sky" with its up-to-date high-rise buildings, other segments occur in caves that suggest the catacombs of *Metropolis* or the cellar tombs of *The Black Cat* and *She*. As Howard Mandelbaum and Eric Myers have stated: "No attempt was made [in the Flash Gordon films] to explain how Roman-style helmets could co-exist with disintegrating-ray guns. It was all pure fantasy, cheerfully amalgamating thirties styles with Oriental, Ottoman, medieval, operetta, and what have you" (169).

As in *The Mask of Fu Manchu*, the Art Deco Woman (who here is, quite literally, associated with the concept of an "aura") controls her male object of desire by obfuscating his consciousness. Hence, Flash is given a pill for "forgetfulness," after which he temporarily loses all memory of Dale Arden (as had Terry of Sheila). When Aura later offers him a marital choice between the Earth woman and herself, he looks at Dale and inquires: "Is this someone I should know?" While Aura is set up to be the bad woman of the drama, her characterization (unlike that of Fah Lo See and Hash-A-Mo-Tep) is not insistently abhorrent. She continually seeks to save Flash from the aggressive acts of her father and, aside from attempting to steal Dale's man, does no harm to the Earth woman. Furthermore, by the end of the film (after the presumed death of her father), Aura gives her blessing for Flash and Dale's departure and promises that Mongo will no longer be hostile to Earth. Thus, the Art Deco Woman seems, once more, defanged (as she was in *The Mask of Fu Manchu* and the 1935 *She*)—encoded as sinister but drained of her potent venom.

This depletion of power is continued in the second series, *Flash Gordon's Trip to Mars* (1938), directed by Ford Beebe and Robert Hill (fig. 8.6). In some fifteen episodes (made on a budget of only half the original), we learn that Mars now poses a threat to Earth (*Flash Gordon's Trip to Mars* 1996). While we had presumed that Ming had expired at the end of the first cycle, he actually escaped to the Red Planet where (as again portrayed by Charles Middleton) he is in league with the evil Azura, Queen of Magic (Beatrice Roberts).[10] She is embroiled in a war with the Clay People (other residents of Mars) and now aims a powerful Nitron beam on the Earth to deprive it of its atmosphere. Once more, Flash Gordon, Dr. Zarkov, and Dale Arden (all played by the same actors as in the 1936 version) are dispatched into outer space to save the day. Evidently, the character of Azura made only one appearance in the original Alex Raymond comic strip in 1935. There she is a gorgeous vamp who, as she enters the narrative, is dressed provocatively in a bikini and a transparent cape. The following text accompanies her first appearance:

> Flash and his companions are blinded by a livid flame in which a spectral figure appears . . . Azure [*sic*], Queen of Magic! The group becomes paralyzed by the sudden vision that seems suspended from the sky . . . They hear a strange laughter which is multiplied by the echo! The blood freezes in their veins! (Gelman 1974:n.p.)

While in the comic Azure is called the "witch-queen" and is a decidedly vicious figure (who orders one of her female guards to flail Dale Arden with an electric whip), in the film rendition her depiction is radically muted. Although she is associated with the fanciful world of outer space (with its modernist and stylized Art Deco touches), her demeanor seems more like that of a fairy princess than an Art Deco diva or evil spirit. Furthermore, while in the original strip she, like her predecessor Aura, is erotically desirous of Flash (drugging him to be a love slave; forcing him to be her royal consort), in the film version she seems to have no sexual presence whatever. (In the comic strip, Dale becomes so jealous of Azure that she

---

10. In the film her name is spelled "Azura," while in the comic strip it is spelled "Azure."

calls her a "hussy.") Finally, while Azura begins the film series as a ruthless hero-ine, bent both on oppressing the Clay People and on destroying Earth, she ends it by admitting the error of her ways. Interestingly, this confession comes on her deathbed—a fate that other more provocative Art Deco villainesses had been spared. (Even Hash-A-Mo-Tep threatens to return from the grave!) In the comic strip, while Queen Azure eventually relents and helps Flash Gordon and his friends to escape, she manages to survive.

Significantly, Azura's power (that of invisibility) is achieved by her owner-ship of several secret, talismanic jewels. Throughout most of the episodes, her possession of a black sapphire is emphasized, and various characters (Ming or Flash) sequentially wrest it from her. On her deathbed, however, she reveals that she is also the proprietress of a white sapphire and that by combining the powers of the two stones the spell on the Clay People can be lifted. We then see Flash place the two jewels in a glass box and fire an electric current between them. On some level, this action seems symbolic—as though to signify that, by

FIGURE 8.6
Flash Gordon (Buster Crabbe) stands before Emperor Ming (Charles Mid-dleton) and Azura, Queen of Magic (Beatrice Roberts), in a laboratory on Mars in *Flash Gordon's Trip to Mars* (1938). (Courtesy British Film Institute)

the end of the 1930s, the "dark" Art Deco Woman could no longer survive as a popular figure but had to be tempered by her "light" and complementary female double. Hence, Queen Azura's power of disappearance seems relevant not only to her but to the broader embodiment of the pernicious Art Deco female.

This "fade-out" is enacted in another famous science fiction cycle of the era—*Buck Rogers* (1939), directed by Ford Beebe and Saul Goodkind and starring Buster Crabbe in the lead role. Evidently, the comic strip on which it was based, "Buck Rogers in the 25th Century" (conceived by Phil Nowlan and drawn by Dick Calkins), first appeared in 1929. The 12-episode film begins in the present day, with our hero and his sidekick, Buddy Wade (Jackie Moran), flying in a dirigible—the same icon of modernity we encountered in *Madame Satan*. (In a book on modern art Moholy-Nagy, significantly, includes a photograph of a zeppelin across the page from a sculpture by Alexander Archipenko and states: "Engineering assemblage . . . has had a fundamental influence on the new sculptural creation" [1932:101].) While Buck and Buddy are in flight, an ice storm ensues and the dirigible's passengers and crew realize that they will soon crash. Through communication on the ground, they are told to release a special gas from a tank on the aircraft that will "suspend animation" and preserve them from harm until they are rescued. Following the disaster, a montage informs us that some five hundred years have passed and that it is now 2440. A spaceship lands and some men discover the now antique dirigible encased in ice. They manage to defrost and revive Buck and Buddy. Once aware of how long they have been unconscious, the men learn that Earth is threatened by a powerful and wicked man, Killer Kane (Antony Warde), who leads a band of former racketeers. General Huer (C. Montague Shaw), who resides in the "Hidden City," is fighting Kane and trying to gain assistance from other planets. Unfortunately, his spacecrafts are continually intercepted by Kane's militia, which has created a blockade. Worse yet, when the malevolent leader captures enemy soldiers, he holds them prisoner in his palace's Dynamo Room where he turns them into robots by forcing them to wear mind-altering helmets. Always heroic, Buck Rogers volunteers to go to Saturn to solicit that planet's help in the campaign against Killer Kane. He is accompanied on his journey by Buddy and by a female pilot, Wilma Deering (Constance Moore). When presented to the Saturnian council, Buck tries to convince them to join forces with Earth against the threatening villain. But Killer Kane has also sent his representatives to the planet and manages to convince the councilmen that Buck and his cohorts are dangerous revolutionaries. Buck, Buddy, and Wilma barely escape and the Saturnians send

Prince Tallen (Philson Ann) to Earth to sign a treaty with Killer Kane. Eventually, Buck manages to befriend Tallen and to show him the prison in which Killer Kane houses the oppressed automatons. The sight of them convinces Tallen to ally Saturn with Buck, Dr. Huer, and the forces of Good. The rest of the chapters detail various exploits in which Buck, Wilma, Buddy, and Tallen infiltrate Kane's realm and eventually defeat him only after surviving a series of battles, challenges, emergencies, and close calls. An alliance with Saturn is formed and Earth is saved.

Once more, the design of the series is highly modernistic, with fewer elements than in the *Flash Gordon* films that hark back to antiquity (though the leaders of Saturn do look a bit like monks, and Prince Tallen resembles a medieval warrior). Although the prince is, at first, aligned with the forces of evil, he is ultimately an ally—which is interesting, given that he is played by a Japanese-American actor at a moment when China and Japan were at war and the United States was wary of Asian imperialism. In general, the mise-en-scène of *Buck Rogers* seems more influenced by Art Deco than its predecessors. Here one thinks of the geometrically shaped rocketships; the circular, tubular capsule that "beams" people from one point to another; the angular, glass "taxi" that transports individuals around Saturn; Dr. Huer's high-tech laboratory (with its television screen) and his office (with its white desk, evocative of contemporary furnishings of the 1930s); the skylines of the Hidden City and of Killer Kane's domain, with their soaring, linear towers, their tiered terraces, and their aerial highways; the futurist/minimalist costumes that characters wear (versus the Roman armor, wings, and headgear worn by characters in the *Flash Gordon* series). Furthermore, Killer Kane's mansion is one of the most fanciful spaces in the film, with its hyperbolic design patterns and flourishes (on walls, floors, windows, furniture, costumes) reminiscent of Art Deco's whimsy and excess (as seen, for example, on the Venetian set of *Top Hat*). Finally, what is most interesting about the Buck Rogers series (coming at the end of the 1930s) is the complete absence of a female villainess associated with the Art Deco style. If, as we have seen, this figure was progressively subdued in the years between *Metropolis* and *Flash Gordon*, she becomes invisible in *Buck Rogers* (as though zapped by Queen Azura's invisibility spell). In her stead is Wilma Deering, a pilot of the future who, despite her radical job assignment, is colorless, innocuous, and holds no interest for us at all. What is even more curious about the film's gender politics is that, aside from Wilma, there are no women present on either Earth or Saturn. Thus, by the time of *Buck Rogers*, the heroine stands alone and the female population seems to make up the ultimate "hidden city" of the drama.

If people would forget about utopia! When rationalism destroyed heaven and decided to set it up here on earth, the most terrible of all goals entered human ambition. It was clear there'd be no end to what people would be made to suffer for it. — Nadine Gordimer[11]

If most of the fantasy films of the 1920s and 1930s present dystopian views of the universe, a few raise the possibility of a benign alternative. In part, of course, *She* had already done this, since the villainess promised her lovers a world of eternal youth. However, her perversity so overwhelms the drama that it is more a work of despair than of hope.

America in the 1930s was, however, full of utopian fantasies—this, despite the Depression and the impending war. One arena in which such visions were concretely realized was the institution of the world's fair, which significantly drew upon a modernist aesthetic. As Eva Weber notes: "Almost all of the era's major architects, artists and designers—many of whom were prominent producers of art deco works—were involved to a greater or lesser degree in the planning of and the execution of ideas for these extravaganzas" (1985:163). A major exposition took place in Chicago in 1933–34, with others in San Francisco and New York City in 1939–40, and each event had its own special conception and perspective. The Chicago fair trumpeted "A Century of Progress" and focused on advances in science and business technology. As the program stated: "Chicago . . . ask[s] the world to join her in celebrating a century of the growth of science, and the dependence of industry on scientific research."[12] Certainly there was a corporate and consumer bias to the fair's dream of the future. Firestone Tires had its own building and the Hall of Science included an exhibit on foot care by Dr. Scholl's. Some of the amusements were reminiscent of the realms of Flash Gordon and Buck Rogers. The Towering Skyride provided fairgoers a whirl on a "rocket" suspended on cables some two hundred feet above ground. Furthermore, certain aspects of the fair had resonant implications for the vision of Woman. One of the official posters for the event displayed a masked woman (looking like a cross between Madame Satan and the robot Maria) dancing hedonistically atop a globe poised between such icons of modernity as skyscrapers and airplanes. Similarly, a cartoon

---

11. From *Burger's Daughter* (1979), cited in *Columbia World of Quotations* (1966; online version). See Entry #25643 at www.bartleby.com/66/43/25643.html.

12. See the Century of Progress Exposition Web site at www.members.aol.com/chicfair.

FIGURE 8.7

Postcard for "A Century of
Progress" from the 1933
Chicago World's Fair. (Cour-
tesy of John Findling)

A CENTURY OF PROGRESS! — CHICAGO 1933

postcard for the exposition (fig. 8.7) mocked the notion of progress by showing, in one frame, an image of a naked woman bathing by candlelight in a tin basin and, in the next, a naked woman bathing in a modern shower stall (Rydell, Findling, and Pelle 2000:86). Clearly, recipients and viewers of the postcard were meant to understand that, although designs and styles might change, male voyeurism prevailed through the ages. Furthermore, many of the fair's buildings "incorporated a variety of art deco motifs, including skyscraper style setbacks, Cubist-influenced volumes and cylindrical shapes, decorative geometric surface patterning, stylized relief sculpture, innovative use of glass and other machine age materials, and modernist interiors" (Weber:166). Finally, even many of the fair's souvenirs were classic Art Deco objects. Glass salt and pepper shakers had colored rings around them that looked like the electric coils in Dr. Frankenstein's laboratory; and their overall shape was reminiscent of two rocketships about to be launched.

Alternately, the Golden Gate International Exposition of 1939 (which celebrated the completion of the Bay Bridge in 1936 and the Golden Gate Bridge in 1937) was a fanciful enterprise that demonstrated both a "practical and romantic interest in the lands of the Pacific Basin" (Neuhaus 1939:2). The more romantic and poetic formulation was everywhere apparent in the names of the varied fair sites: the Court of the Pacific (designed by the Oakland Paramount's Timothy Pflueger), the Portals of the Pacific (fig. 8.8), the Arch of the Winds, the Court of Flowers, the Court of the Seven Seas, the Towers of the East, and the Court of Reflections. Significantly, one of the exposition's official posters also foregrounded

PORTALS OF THE PACIFIC
1939 World's Fair on San Francisco Bay

FIGURE 8.8

The Portals of the Pacific (c. 1938–39) at the 1939 Golden Gate International Exposition on San Francisco Bay; artist unknown. (The Mitchell Wolfson Jr. Collection, Wolfsonian-Florida International University, Miami Beach. *Photo:* Bruce White)

the female image: a graphic by Vanderlaan pictures a woman's huge, abstract head (Zim and Rolfes 1988:27).

Finally, the New York World's Fair of 1939, called "The World of Tomorrow," was the most futuristic of the three, with its modernist perisphere and trylon— iconic sculptures fashioned according to Art Deco's geometric preference. As Weber notes, the fair "apotheosized the streamlined phase of art deco architectural design" (172). Interestingly, the exposition's poster was entirely abstract and shunned the human image entirely (be it male or female). Many aspects of the fair bore the traces of a science fiction aura. A sculpture in front of the Westinghouse pavilion echoed in its structure the electric rings that encircled the robot Maria as she was given human form. And the popular General Motors building offered fair-goers the experience of "Futurama." Here is how novelist E. L. Doctorow describes the ride in *World's Fair* (1985):

> In front of us a whole world lit up, as if we were flying over it, the most fan-tastic sight I had ever seen, an entire city of the future, with skyscrapers and fourteen-lane highways, real little cars moving on them at different speeds.

. . . Cars were regulated by radio control, the drivers didn't even do the driving! This miniature world demonstrated how everything was planned, people lived in these modern streamlined curvilinear buildings. (324)

While fairs of the past had often favored traditional and monumental styles of architecture, the American expositions of the 1930s embraced the contemporary mode. As Paul Greenhalgh (1988) indicates:

> Classical form gave a look of power, solidity, and permanence; it suggested a certain stature. . . . It was only in the 1930s, when European fascist states employed classicism to very different ends, that policies switched to representing America with various modernist forms. Republicanism was then more closely identified with progress of the free world, making forward-looking constructions more appropriate to classical ones. (129)

Hence, in the case of American expositions, modernism bore distinctly political and idyllic overtones.

Lost Horizon (1937), directed for Columbia Pictures by Frank Capra, is a major utopian cinematic text of the era. Based on British author James Hilton's 1933 novel, the stance of the film is apparent in its opening title, which asks: "In these days of wars and rumors of wars—haven't you ever dreamed of a place where there was peace and security, where living was not a struggle but a lasting delight?" This notion would doubtless have appealed to audiences of 1937, who daily were reading about turmoil in Asia and Europe (including the Sino-Japanese conflict, the Spanish Civil War, and Hitler's rearming of Germany and the Rhineland). Focusing on the Eastern theater, *Lost Horizon* tells the tale of Robert Conway (Ronald Colman), a British diplomat stationed in China. When unrest and strife break out in the region, Conway is ordered to evacuate Americans and Europeans in a series of airlifts from Kabul. When the last plane arrives, he, his brother George (John Howard), and a few others take flight for Shanghai, where they hope to find safety. At some point during the long overnight trip, one of the passengers realizes that the plane is traveling in the wrong direction. When Conway taps on the cockpit window, he finds an unknown, armed, Asian pilot there instead of the Western flyer he had expected. The group soon discerns that they are being kidnapped and taken to an undisclosed location. The airplane refuels somewhere in Tibet and then flies on, ultimately crashing into the snowbound Himalayan mountains when it runs out of gas. Although the pilot dies, all the passengers survive. The next day, some Tibetan men appear at the disaster site, led by a man named Chang (H. B. Warner). They escort the stranded party to a lamasery in a place called Shangri-La. When

Conway and the others inquire as to how they might contact home, they are told that Shangri-La lies beyond the reaches of any communication devices. The only contact the community has with the rest of the world comes through porters who arrive there every few years to bring supplies. Before long, the group realizes that their arrival at Shangri-La was not an accidental rescue but part of the original hijacking plot. They also understand that Chang has no intention of releasing them. As time goes by, many members of the group become contented with their days in Shangri-La and abandon their impatience and rage. Paleontologist Alexander Lovett (Edward Everett Horton) happily gives classes to the natives; swindler Henry Barnard (Thomas Mitchell) relinquishes his plans to steal gold from the community and excitedly decides to help the people install a plumbing system; Isabel Jewell (Gloria Stone), who arrives there terminally ill, recovers her health; and Robert encounters Sondra (Jane Wyatt), who questions his worldly ambitions and gains his love. The only person to remain angry and disheartened is George, who continues to plan an escape. In discussions with Chang, Robert learns that Shangri-La was founded in 1713 by a Belgian priest, Father Perrault. Robert also ascertains that, in Shangri-La, people live without want or conflict and enjoy extreme longevity and near-perfect health. Moderation and restraint rule the day, and people behave in a kind and generous fashion. When Robert inquires what happens if a man wants the woman of another, Chang informs him that good manners dictate that the second man concede to the first. Chang also reveals that, in Shangri-La, art and culture are highly valued, which explains why the lamasery is a repository for ancient objects and rare books. Chang asks Robert to meet with the High Lama, and when Robert arrives for his interview he realizes that the man is Father Perrault (Sam Jaffee), still alive after 214 years. The High Lama explains that Robert has been brought to Shangri-La as his successor. Later, Robert hears from Sondra that it is she who has suggested him as the community's new leader—having followed his career and realizing that, although his life was empty, he had progressive hopes for the future. When Robert informs George what he has learned about Shangri-La (its idealized morality, its promise of immortality, his own place in its order), George concludes that Robert has gone insane. He vows to leave Shangri-La with the help of Maria (Margo), a young woman who loves him and has offered her assistance. Robert warns George that he knows that Maria came to Shangri-La in 1888 and will "fade away like an echo" as soon as she leaves its magical terrain. George is incredulous and remains determined to flee. In a protective, brotherly gesture, Robert reluctantly agrees to accompany George and Maria on the dangerous trek through the Himalayas. The three depart, guided by Mongolians who soon abandon them and laugh at their plight. When an avalanche kills the porters, the three trek on, but Maria becomes too weak for the journey and must be carried. As he lifts her, George is horrified to find that she has turned into a haggard old woman and expired. Made hysterical by this vision, he falls off a mountain peak to his death. Robert travels on. The scene then shifts to London where newspaper headlines declare that Robert Conway has been found in Tibet suffering from amnesia; he is headed home on the SS *Manchuria*. Another headline then announces that Conway has recovered his memory and has spoken to his fellow passengers about the mystical kingdom of Shangri-La. The newspaper also reports that, shortly thereafter, he jumped ship, never to be seen again. The final shots of the film disclose Robert alone in the Himalayas, trying to make his way back to Shangri-La. As bells ring and we glimpse a vague, distant view of the lamasery, it seems likely that he is about to realize his dream.[13]

Various aspects of *Lost Horizon* are intriguing for a study of modernism and its figuration of Woman. The film begins with a scene of contemporary international strife, with World War II looming on the horizon. Airplanes, those emblems of technology, evacuate people from a combat zone. Various up-to-date means of communication inform the West of the plight of Conway's party: newspapers, typewriters, radios, telephones. In contrast to this chaotic universe stands Shangri-La, which is cut off from the outside world (again revealing the spatial imperative of fantasy fiction). When Chang tries to convince Robert to stay there, he contrasts the slow pace of the community with the frantic tempo of the rest of humanity—its orgy of brutality, power, and greed. Clearly, the geography of Shangri-La also augments its remoteness. The Himalayan peaks are so forbidding that even the most current technology can barely penetrate its perimeters. Because of this, Shangri-La seems, on one level, to reside in the primitive past, with its pelt-costumed natives who craft their own pots and draw water from a well. In this regard, its icy domain seems to be the polar opposite of the tropical realm (which we have seen in the South Seas adventure film), although both regions provide Westerners with alternative (but coequal) views of the Exotic. Propelled into the American imagination of 1937, Shangri-La offers a cinematic fantasy of escape from the political, economic, and technological struggles of the contemporary world. As Charles Maland (1980) notes, Franklin Delano Roosevelt would later call his Maryland retreat—now Camp David—Shangri-La (98–99).

---

13. According to the "Alternative Ending" section on the DVD for *Lost Horizon*, the original closing (which was forced on Capra and ran for only for a few weeks in March 1937) gave a more definite sense of Conway's arrival at Shangri-La. In that rendition, we see Sondra looking into the mountains, discovering Robert there, and dispatching men to rescue him. The ending that now stands is far more ambiguous.

While certain aspects of Shangri-La seem to harken to the past (its timeless aura, its collection of museum artifacts, its 214-year-old patriarch), other elements point to the future. It is significant that, as conceived by art director Stephen Goosson, the world of Shangri-La is, in part, a modernistic one—though one with an Oriental flavor popular in the Art Deco era. Evidently, the first designs for the film imagined a lamasery with a traditional appearance. These plans, however, were scotched in favor of an edifice that resembles a cross between a Bauhaus and a Frank Lloyd Wright building. In fact, if one skims through architectural history books, one notices similarities between the film's lamasery and several other structures of the era: the Pavillon d'un riche collectioneur from the 1925 Paris Exposition (Scarlett and Townley 1975:36); the "Brick House" and the "Florida Tropical House" from the Chicago World's Fair of 1934 (Raley 1934:26, 52); and I. M. Pei's 1937 design for an aquarium (Bush-Brown 1976:28). Alternately, Graham Greene saw the structure as favoring a movie actor's home. As he notes: "This Utopia closely resembles a film star's luxurious estate in Beverly Hills," and the activities taking place there seemed appropriate to a posh California lifestyle: "flirtatious pursuits through grape arbors, splashing and divings in blossomy pools under improbable waterfalls" (quoted in Mandelbaum and Myers:170). Constructed on the Columbia ranch, Goosson's creation was ninety feet tall and required 150 men to build over a two-month period (169). *Variety* of March 10, 1937, reported that it cost some $2,500,000 to erect (Abel 1937).

In its appearance, the lamasery is a "white, floodlit building with broad flights of stairways, terraces and colonnaded pavilions" (Albrecht 1986:164). The greenery that surrounds it has a decidedly Japanese feel to it, with its stark branches of cherry blossoms silhouetted against blank walls. In truth, there are aspects of Shangri-La (built in southern California) that seem a blueprint for the architecture of the Golden Gate International Exposition (built in northern California) some two years later. Eugen Neuhaus (who published a book about the fair on the year of its opening) called the Treasure Island site a "magic city" (15), and Eva Weber some forty-five years later deemed it an "Oceanic Shangri-La" (171). Even Shangri-La's Valley of the Blue Moon reminds us of the lyrical names for locales at the San Francisco fair: the Tower of the Sun or the Court of the Moon and Stars. If Shangri-La had its reflecting pool, the fair boasted a Lagoon and a Court of Reflections. Thus, both settings took their inspiration from the East. Several structures at the fair blended Oriental and modernist vocabularies (e.g., the Court of Flowers, the Tower of the East, and the Pacific House). While eschewing the "cubistic" excesses of contemporary design, the fair nonetheless adopted aspects of modernism, especially its lack of exterior ornamentation in building style (Neuhaus:16, 19).

While much of the interior of *Lost Horizon*'s lamasery is decorated with antiques (old wooden chairs, wrought-iron candelabras), it has a decidedly modernistic ambience. Here, one thinks of a rounded, biomorphic sculpture in the corner of the dining room; a huge rectangular decorative window that stands atop the building's majestic stairway; its minimalist sliding doors (that resemble Japanese rice paper screens); its numerous bare marble pillars; the door to Father Perrault's quarters, with its abstract, Oriental motif. While in the novel the lamasery is not specifically described as a modern building, its use of contemporary fixtures is referenced.[14] As James Hilton notes, the

> appointments of Shangri-La had been all that he [Robert] could have wished. . . . That a Tibetan monastery should possess a system of central heating was not, perhaps, so very remarkable in an age that supplied even Lhasa with telephones; but that it should combine the mechanics of Western hygiene with so much else that was Eastern and traditional, struck him as exceedingly singular. The bath, for instance, in which he had recently luxuriated, had been of a delicate green porcelain, a product, according to inscription of Akron, Ohio. Yet the native attendant had valeted him in Chinese fashion . . . " (1936:85).

Thus, according to the logic of *Lost Horizon* (and, some might say, Art Deco), paradise seems a beneficent blend of ancient and current modes.

On the other hand, the film leads us to question whether Shangri-La is paradise at all. Clearly, Maria (who has achieved immortality there) nonetheless wants to leave, giving the lie to Chang's notion that all its residents are content. Furthermore, we suspect that Conway may be as "mad" as his brother George believes him to be. In the concluding shots of the film, when Robert glimpses a vision of Shangri-La, we are unsure whether he has sighted a real locale or a hallucinated mirage.

Finally, like so many other modernistic fantasy films of the era, the portrayal of Woman in *Lost Horizon* is both problematic and intriguing, especially for its play with familiar binaries of feminine representation. On the one hand, we have Sondra, the idealized female of the future. Though she wears modern tunics with fashionable Oriental accents, she is no Art Deco dame. For her first several scenes, she says nothing at all, and we begin to wonder if she is mute. She does, however, occasionally laugh, like some garden sprite or blithe spirit. An innocent child of Nature

---

14. Hilton describes a "grand tour" of Shangri-La in which its numerous rooms and courtyards are mentioned as well as its fabulous library. Also described are its "recognized treasures that museums and millionaires alike would have bargained for" (1936:114).

(like the one in Maxfield Parrish's 1926 *Stars*), she bathes nude in a stream, as Robert looks on. However, his view of her, like ours, is so distant that her body is entirely obscured. (This contrasts starkly with Hedy Lamarr's infamous and provocative swim scene in 1933's *Ecstasy*.) Like the good Maria of *Metropolis*, Sondra is frequently surrounded by children: in one scene, she leads them in a verse of "Lullaby and Goodnight." Significantly, one of the lines of the song speaks of baby being a "mother's delight," cementing Sondra's association with the maternal. If she is linked to Nature and to children, she is also tied to the animal world (like Rima in *Green Mansions*). When Robert inquires about the eerie choral music that he hears in the Valley of the Blue Moon, she reveals that it is produced by flutes that she has attached to the tails of birds. Though Sondra discloses that it is she who campaigned for Robert's capture (investing her character with a certain dangerous will and strength), in general she seems a pleasant and pliable figure who poses no threat to masculine power. As in other fantasy films of the period, Shangri-La appears to be largely devoid of a female population, and indeed there is only one other important woman in the narrative. Maria is a Russian who was brought to Shangri-La in the nineteenth century at the age of twenty. In the film, she has a rather exotic aura which is explained by the fact that Capra conceived her as "of mixed parentage" and cast a Mexican actress for the role (Capra 1971:193, 196). Unlike Sondra, she is a negative, disgruntled, and forceful figure who seems marked by the kind of discontent that Chang associates with the corrupt outside world. She complains of being a virtual prisoner in Shangri-La and, like George, actively pursues an escape. While Sondra allows Robert to take the lead in courting her and acts with "proper" modesty and discretion, Maria chases George, pleading with him to come to visit her. It is, in fact, to assure their bond that she choreographs their getaway together. It seems significant that it is Maria whose age is specifically noted (and revealed as supernatural), while Sondra's is left ambiguous and unstated. Moreover, one of the most horrific scenes of the film is that in which Maria suddenly becomes (like Hash-A-Mo-Tep in the 1935 *She*) a wizened hag (along with appearing inexplicably more "Asian" in her decrepitude). Hence, Maria (the aggressive woman) seems the "witch" of paradise, while Sondra (the pliant one) seems its fairy princess. Clearly, in Maria's disturbing preternatural demise (and her responsibility for George's death), she is the ultimate femme fatale and "the villain of the piece" (Capra:193). Furthermore, the denouements of both *Lost Horizon* and *She* would seem to indicate that Woman's greatest crime is to grow old. As Eddie Cantor told them: "Keep yourself young and beautiful if you want to be loved."

Shangri-La's bipolar mix of modernity and antiquity gives the space its requisite sense of timelessness. As Mandelbaum and Myers point out, this aura was in part

MADAME SATAN

achieved because the sets were built to be only ephemeral edifices—"well-planned fantasies designed for a limited run" (170). This impermanence allowed their creators to use lightweight and innovative construction materials in conceiving them. Ironically, it was the sets' very temporary status that led to their seeming to be eternal structures. As Mandelbaum and Myers note, "There's no need [in cinematic set design] for the inhibiting dignity that comes with delusions of immortality" (170).

If *Lost Horizon* offered a surrogate universe to the world-weary adult viewer of the late 1930s, *The Wizard of Oz* (1939) proposed one to the youth. While Capra's film assumes that events experienced by Robert Conway are "actually" happening, Victor Fleming's movie presupposes that Dorothy is merely dreaming, having been knocked unconscious by a Kansas tornado. As we well know, the reason that Dorothy (Judy Garland) suffers this fate is that she has been out looking for her dog Toto, whom the misanthropic Miss Gulch (Margaret Hamilton) has snatched away for his misbehavior. Had Dorothy not been traumatized by the old woman's actions, she would have been safe in the storm cellar along with Aunt Em, Uncle Henry, and the farmhands. Obviously, when Dorothy loses consciousness, she transposes the characters of her daily life into protagonists within a fantasy: Miss Gulch becomes the Wicked Witch of the West, Aunt Em becomes the benevolent Glinda; the three farmhands become the Scarecrow (Ray Bolger), the Lion (Bert Lahr) and the Tin Man (Jack Haley); and an itinerant carnival man becomes the Wizard.

Like Shangri-La, Oz is an equivocal space, but it does have its utopian elements. As Salman Rushdie writes: "In its most potent emotional moment, this is unarguably a film about the joys of going away, of leaving the greyness and entering the colour, of making a new life in the 'place where there isn't any trouble.'" Thus, rather than laud the superiority of Home, Rushdie sees the film's narrative as "a grand paean" or "hymn . . . to Elsewhere" (1999:23).

What is significant for our purposes is that Elsewhere is an Art Deco cosmos—linking Oz's Emerald City to Shangri-La's Blue Valley (fig. 8.9). As Paul Nathanson notes, in a rather extended passage:

> The Emerald City, in fact, is a fantastic variation on the kind of architecture considered avant-garde in 1939. At first glance, it looks like a forest of skyscrapers. Its dynamic verticality (notable in the elevation as seen from the field of poppies, and in the vaulted corridor leading to the Wizard's audience hall), its "streamlined" lighting fixtures and indirect illumination (seen in both corridor and audience hall), its ornamental lettering (which identifies the Wash and Brush Up Company), its glittering, sparkling, highly polished surfaces (seen everywhere), and many other details owe as

much to the *Exposition internationale des arts décoratifs et industriels modernes* (Paris 1925) and the Century of Progress Exposition (Chicago, 1933–34) as they do any unique fantasies of William Horning, Cedric Gibbons, or others involved in creating the sets at MGM. (1991:37–38)

To the Deco details that Nathanson enumerates, we might add Oz's use of silver accents to its green color scheme, its penchant for geometric ornaments (triangles and rectangles on door façades), and its predilection for mechanical tropes (the star-shaped wheels that decorate Oz's floors). Similarly, Nathanson sees the costumes worn by Oz's women (and, significantly, created by Adrian) as high-styled and futuristic. As he remarks: "Some female residents, for example, wear long, flowing gowns with elaborate hats, . . . exaggerated versions of all the elegant and sophisticated gowns Adrian designed for Hollywood stars. . . . Other female residents . . . look as if they have just been recruited straight from the Cocoanut Grove or the Ziegfeld Follies" (39).

While Salman Rushdie may see Oz as the Promised Land, conventional wisdom deems it a disturbing space where a sham wizard rules (with smoke and mirrors), where bizarre "little people" dwell, and where a malevolent witch unleashes her fury on an innocent girl. So, again, as in *Lost Horizon* as well as the Buck Rogers and Flash Gordon films, an Art Deco space (while whimsically attractive) is also a realm of potential derangement and terror.

In *The Wizard of Oz*, the poles of good and evil are clearly best represented in the battle between the kindly spirit Glinda (Billie Burke) and the vile Witch of the West (Margaret Hamilton). Again, reading against the grain, Rushdie prefers the latter. He asks: "Of the two . . . can there be anyone who'd choose to spend five minutes with Glinda?" (42). One sees his point but, in truth, most audiences prefer her, despite her clichéd fairy-princess getup and her bland, insipid manner. While I would not want to argue that, in any literal way, the Wicked Witch of the West is another Art Deco diva (and her medieval castle, her shrouded garb, her ancient magic all speak against it), she nonetheless *is* a femme fatale in a decidedly modernist space — a landscape that contrasts sharply with the farm on which Dorothy lives and the forest through which she passes. Hence, as water melts the witch at the end of the saga, we are reminded of *Metropolis* and the fiery dissolution of the false Maria, as well as the disintegration of Maria in *Lost Horizon*.

Nathanson has seen *The Wizard of Oz* as an American cultural myth whose theme is articulated through Dorothy's geographic journey from heartland to city and back again. Once more, this confirms the import of the spatial parameter in the fantasy mode. As he writes, Dorothy moves "from paradise, through history,

FIGURE 8.9

The cityscape of Oz as Art
Deco urban skyline in *The
Wizard of Oz* (1939).
(Courtesy British Film
Institute)

and back to paradise," saying, "in effect, that for Americans to 'grow up' as a nation . . . they must also 'go home' (recapture their innocence in the original garden paradise)" (173). Of course, this message duly reflects a "traditional, rural utopianism of the agrarian, or populist, world view"—one that was prevalent at the time (173).

Released in 1939, at the end of the Depression, *The Wizard of Oz* arrived at a moment when the modernist interventions of the twenties and thirties (and, perhaps, their excesses) are questioned and on the wane. With the film's claim that there is "no place like home," it proposes a certain skepticism about the adventures and advances of urban contemporaneity—of what lies over the modernist (and capitalist) "rainbow." To do so, it chronicles the demise of yet another Deco-era femme fatale. "Ding-Dong! The Witch Is Dead"!

As we know, however, this dangerous woman will not be moribund for long but, rather, will rise again—transformed (like She-Who-Must-Be-Obeyed)—to thrill and haunt us as she lures men into the moral miasma of film noir in the 1940s.

AFTERWORD

This book, *Designing Women*, has sought to bring new perspectives to the study of Art Deco and the cinema—seen both as separate and interrelated subjects. When I began writing it, there was no concentrated scholarly text on the topic. *Screen Deco* by Howard Mandelbaum and Eric Myers provided lush illustrations of the style (as practiced in the movies) in conjunction with much useful commentary, but was primarily a gorgeous "coffee table" volume. While Donald Albrecht's *Designing Dreams: Modern Architecture in the Movies* illuminated the area of Deco set design, it failed to engage the movement's broader influence. Even such groundbreaking work on cinematic mise-en-scène as Charles and Mirella Jona Affron's *Sets in Motion* contained only passing reference to the Art Deco mode. When *Designing Women* was completed, a book emerged more consonant with my own approach: Anne Massey's *Hollywood Beyond the Screen: Design and Material Culture*. While a section of that study focuses on the American context, the work concentrates on the British incarnation of the Art Deco made through an examination of advertising, home design, and personal history. While Massey mentions in passing a few of the same films I consider (e.g., *The Kiss* and *Metropolis*), only one receives an in-depth analysis: *Our Dancing Daughters*. Finally, half of Massey's volume examines periods beyond the heyday of the Style Moderne: post–World War II culture and post–classical Hollywood. Thus, even now, a full cultural reading of Art Deco and the cinema is in its initial stages.

Designing Women has sought to bring a variety of new frameworks to the topic. First, it has tried to acknowledge the complexities of defining American Art Deco by underscoring its relation to the broader international Style Moderne, whose artistic lineage involves Expressionism, Art Nouveau, Cubism, Constructivism,

Secessionism, and the Bauhaus. Second, rather than staying within a formalist, art-historical framework, the book offers a wider perspective by taking a cultural studies stance on the Art Deco style. For example, instead of seeing Deco's interest in the Exotic and the Primitive as a matter of mere influence or aesthetics, it views these predilections in terms of the era's Orientalist and colonialist fantasies. Likewise, this study, while acknowledging that the image of Woman is ubiquitous in Art Deco material culture (chryselephantine sculptures, figural pottery, glassware, and lamps), asserts that the phenomenon has not been duly noted. In recognition of that lacuna, *Designing Women* (as the title indicates) attempts to interpret this female fixation as a "symptom" of societal anxieties about the emergent New Woman, a challenging figure on the American scene in the 1920s and 1930s. In a sense, the book argues that the Art Deco style became a kind of "trademark" for the modern woman of the era—aligning her with certain cultural myths for which the movement stood. One author of such allegories was the French illustrator Erté, whose vision of Woman is discussed in the book as interpreted by Roland Barthes. To some degree, *Designing Women* argues that the Art Deco Woman, as screen protagonist, was at her most radical in the mid- to late-1920s—as embodied by European actresses like Greta Garbo or Brigitte Helm. As the thirties progressed, the Art Deco female in such American genres as the musical, the exotic adventure epic, and the fantasy film became progressively more muted and tamed. Clearly, this chronologically matches the decline in the movement itself (whose cutting-edge elements were gradually appropriated into the mainstream). Furthermore, it is consonant with a growing conservatism regarding women in American culture which, in the Depression era, questioned the feminist advances of an earlier generation.

Designing Women has also sought to contextualize the Art Deco movement within the larger dynamics of American consumerism—revealing how its appeal to women in the era was utilized to sell cosmetics, clothing, home furnishings, housewares, jewelry, and *objets d'art*. Beyond hawking such material goods, the style also peddled a certain mythology of glamour, stylishness, contemporaneity, and youth. All these associations were drawn upon and augmented by the movies, which harnessed the Art Deco style as a "brand name" and "sales pitch" during the 1920s and 1930s.

I have also viewed Art Deco's ties to the movies as part of its wider cultural address. While books have documented the *fact* of the style's impact on Hollywood and have communicated (through the reproduction of illustrative stills) its beauty as visual delight, none has explored the movement's relation to American film in a more extended fashion. While Massey analyzes only one movie in detail in her book on the subject, *Designing Women* scrutinizes a much larger body of work—

in terms of set design as well as costume design. Moreover, this volume, seeing style as more than simple decoration, links the film's visual discourse to how it is used to effect character portrayal, narrative trajectory, and articulation of theme. Further, *Designing Women* approaches Art Deco cinema through a generic lens, questioning how the style is itself affected by generic context—be it the musical, the melodrama, the adventure, or the fantasy film. Thus, in the melodrama, the character associated with the Art Deco mode is often a bold New Woman, whereas in the fantasy film she is frequently a femme fatale. While in the South Seas adventure epic, the Art Deco woman exhibits a Primitive or Exotic mode, in the musical she is frequently just a dazzling ornament—almost coequal with the set!

As part of this exploration of Art Deco and the cinema, *Designing Women* also investigates the movement's implications for the star system. While previous critics have mentioned Joan Crawford and Myrna Loy within this context, no one has discussed Greta Garbo's important role in the era. Here it is crucial that Garbo was a Continental star working in America—a figure whose international image connected her to the modernist mode. In line with this, *Designing Women* discovers an important, though unremarked, link between screen Deco and the European émigré director—be it Feyder, Murnau, Ulmer, Lang, or Whale.[1] Additionally, beyond focusing on particular films, the present volume has sought to extend the conception of the cinematic "text" beyond the borders of the screen by examining the realm of movie theater design. In investigating the architectural rhetoric of the Oakland (California) Paramount, for example, it finds a discourse consonant with that of the exotic adventure film.

Finally, *Designing Women* aspires to add a personal note to the paradigm of distanced academic study—by revealing my own "stake" in the project. Here, I have confessed my long-standing and enthusiastic penchant for collecting Art Deco objects—a habit I have tried to correlate with the "vagaries" of my life. I hope, however, that beyond constituting a personal meditation, this book serves as a contribution to a "collection" of a different order—that of scholarly works on design and the cinema.

---

1. For a discussion of the politics of "Hollywood Modernism" and the role that émigré artists played in the intellectual community of the movie world, see *Hollywood Modernism: Film and Politics in the Age of the New Deal* (Giovacchini 2001).

BIBLIOGRAPHY

ARTICLES AND BOOKS

Abel. 1937. "Lost Horizon" (review). *Variety* (March 10). Reprinted in *Variety Film Reviews, 1907–1980* 5 (no page numbers). New York and London: Garland, 1983.

"Accessories That Denote Discrimination; Costume Details Are of Vast Importance." 1928. *Harper's Bazar* (October): 110–11.

Adrian. 1935. "Adrian Answers 20 Questions on Garbo." *Photoplay* (September), cited in Griffith, ed., *The Talkies* (1971), 10–11, 272.

"Adrian—American Artist and Designer." 1974. *Costume* 8: 13–17.

Affron, Charles and Mirella Jona Affron. 1995. *Sets in Motion: Art Direction and Film Narrative*. New Brunswick, N.J.: Rutgers University Press.

Albrecht, Donald. 1986. *Designing Dreams: Modern Architecture in the Movies*. New York: Harper and Row.

Allen, Frederick Lewis. 1931. *Only Yesterday: An Informal History of the Nineteen-Twenties*. New York and London: Harper.

"America's Interesting People: Margaret Mead." 1935. *American Magazine* (September): 42.

Armitt, Lucie. 1996. *Theorising the Fantastic*. London and New York: Arnold.

Arwas, Victor. 1975. *Art Deco Sculpture: Chryselephantine Statuettes of the Twenties and Thirties*. London and New York: Academy Editions and St. Martin's.

——. 1992. *Art Deco*. New York: Abrams.

Bade, Patrick. 1979. *Femme Fatale: Images of Evil and Fascinating Women*. New York: Mayflower Books.

Banner, Lois. 1974. *Women in Modern America: A Brief History*. New York: Harcourt Brace Jovanovich.

Barrett, Richmond. 1931. "Chic Oases." *Harper's Bazaar* (January): 88–89.

Barry, John F. and Epes W. Sargent. 1927. "Building Theatre Patronage." In Waller, ed., *Moviegoing in America* (2002), 110–15.

Barthes, Roland. 1957. "Myth Today." In *Mythologies*, 109–159. Paris: Éditions du Seuil.

——. 1972. "Literally." In *Erté (Romain de Tirtoff): Text by Roland Barthes with an Extract from Erté's "Memoirs,"* 17–68. Translated by William Weaver. Parma (It.): Ricci.

"Bathrooms Glisten with Cleanliness." 1931. *Harper's Bazaar* (August): 76.

Baudrillard, Jean. 1993. *Symbolic Exchange and Death*. Translated by Iain Hamilton Grant. London: Sage.

——. 1994. "The System of Collecting" (1968). In Elsner and Cardinal, eds., *The Cultures of Collecting*, 7–24.

Baxter, John. 1970. *Science Fiction in the Cinema*. New York: A. S. Barnes.

Belk, Russell W. 1995. *Collecting in a Consumer Society*. London and New York: Routledge.

Benjamin, Walter. 1999. *The Arcades Project*. Translated by Howard Eiland and Kevin McLaughlin. Cambridge and London: Harvard University Press. (Translation of a German book originally published in 1982)

Benson, Susan Porter. 1986. *Counter Cultures: Saleswomen, Managers, and Customers in American Department Stores, 1890–1940*. Urbana: University of Illinois Press.

Bernhard, Lucian. 1929. "*House and Garden's* Modern House: An Original Scheme for a Lady's Bedroom Showing the Contemporary Mode in Furniture and Decoration." *House & Garden* (January): 68–69.

Bernstein, Matthew and Gaylyn Studlar, eds. 1997. *Visions of the East: Orientalism in Film*. New Brunswick, N.J.: Rutgers University Press.

Biery, Ruth. 1932. "The New 'Shady Dames' of the Screen." *Photoplay* (August), cited in Griffith, ed., *The Talkies* (1971), 218–19.

"Blue and White." 1928. *Harper's Bazar* (December): 76.

Borst, R. V. 1992. *Graven Images: The Best of Horror, Fantasy, and Science Fiction Film Art*. New York: Grove Press.

Bowman, Sara. 1985. *A Fashion for Extravagance: Art Deco Fabrics and Fashions*. London: Bell and Hyman.

Brokaw, Clare Boothe. 1932. "The Great Garbo." *Vanity Fair* (February): 63, 87.

Brooks, W. R. 1928 (review of Margaret Mead's *Coming of Age in Samoa*). In *Outlook* 149.717 (August 29).

Bruzzi, Stella. 1997. *Undressing Cinema: Clothing and Identity in the Movies*. London and New York: Routledge.

Buchanan, Lucile. 1927. "Clever Make-Up Is Part of the Ensemble." *Harper's Bazar* (July): 58, 124, 126.

——. 1928. "A Day in a Modern Apartment—How People Manage." *Harper's Bazar* (April): 110–111.

"Bulletin Board." 1929. *House & Garden* (January): 51.

Burnett, Frank. 1923. *Summer Isles of Eden*. London: Sifton, Praed.

Bush-Brown, Harold. 1976. *Beaux Arts to Bauhaus and Beyond*. New York: Watson-Guptill.

Calder-Marshall, Arthur. 1963. *The Innocent Eye: The Life of Robert J. Flaherty*. Baltimore, Md.: Penguin.

Calderon, George. 1922. *Tahiti*. New York: Harcourt.

Calverton, V. F. 1928. *The Bankruptcy of Marriage*. New York: Macaulay.

Capra, Frank. 1971. *The Name Above the Title: An Autobiography*. New York: Macmillan.

Carothers, Alva. 1931. *Stevenson's Isles of Paradise: A True Story of Adventures in the Samoan South Sea Islands*. Santa Barbara, Calif.: Alva Carothers.

"Chinese Clay Figurines." 1929. *House & Garden* (January): 7.

Clement, Russell T. 1991. *Paul Gauguin: A Bio-Bibliography*. New York: Greenwood.

Cleve, Felix. 1931. "Greta Garbo, the Woman Nobody Knows." *Living Age* 340 (June): 369–72.

Coates, Paul. 1991. *The Gorgon's Gaze: German Cinema, Expressionism, and the Image of Horror*. New York and Cambridge: Cambridge University Press.

Condon, Frank. 1931. "Greta and Marlene." *Saturday Evening Post* 203 (May 30): 29–44.

——. 1932. "The Lady Who Lives Behind a Wall." *Saturday Evening Post* 204 (March 26): 31*ff*.

Corliss, Richard. 1976. "Flaherty: The Man in the Iron Myth" (1973). In Richard Meran Barsam, ed., *Nonfiction Film Theory and Criticism*, 230–38. New York: Dutton.

Cresswell, Howell S. 1925. "The Paris Exposition of Modern Decorative Arts." *Good Furniture Magazine* (October): 187–99.

Croce, Arlene. 1972. *The Fred Astaire and Ginger Rogers Book*. New York: Outerbridge and Lazard.

Dadoun, Roger. 1986. "Metropolis: Mother City—Mittler-Hitler." *Camera Obscura* 15 (Fall): 136–63.

Daggett, Helen M. 1935. *Interior Decorating*. Richmond, Va.: Leisure League of America.

Dailey, Victoria. 1990. "The Posters of Sven Brasch." *Journal of Decorative and Propaganda Arts* (Summer): 4–21.

Daniel, Robert L. 1987. *American Women in the 20th Century: The Festival of Life*. New York and London: Harcourt Brace Jovanovich.

Dant, Tim. 1999. *Material Culture in the Social World*. Buckingham (Eng.) and Philadelphia: Open University Press.

Doane, Mary Ann. 1991. *Femmes Fatales: Feminism, Film Theory, Psychoanalysis*. New York and London: Routledge.

Doctorow, E. L. 1985. *World's Fair: A Novel*. New York: Random House (cloth ed.); New York: Fawcett Crest (paperback).

Donovan, Frances R. 1929. *The Saleslady*. Chicago: University of Chicago Press.

Dorsey, G. A. 1928. "Books" (review of Margaret Mead's *Coming of Age in Samoa*). *New York Herald Tribune* (September 2): 4.

Dowd, Maureen. 2002. "A Blue Burka for Justice." *New York Times* (January 30): A27.

Draper, Muriel. 1928. "Modern Modes in Furniture: The Multiform Shapes of Machinery Influence Our Newest Furniture." *Harper's Bazar* (March): 98–99, 128.

Duncan, Alastair. 1986. *American Art Deco*. New York: Abrams.

——. 1988a. *Art Deco*. London: Thames and Hudson.

——. 1988b. *Encyclopedia of Art Deco*. New York: Dutton.

——. 1993 (rev. ed.). *Art Deco*. London: Thames and Hudson.

Eckert, Charles. 1990. "The Carole Lombard in Macy's Window" (1978). In Gaines and Herzog, eds., *Fabrications: Costume and the Female Body*, 100–121.

Eisner, Lotte. 1964. *Murnau*. Berkeley and London: University of California Press.

——. 1977. *Fritz Lang*. New York: Oxford University Press.

Ellis, Havelock. 1921. *Little Essays of Love and Virtue*. New York: Doran.

Elsner, John and Roger Cardinal. 1994. *The Cultures of Collecting*. Cambridge: Harvard University Press.

Encyclopedia Brittanica (online version). For entry on "Art Deco," *see* www.search.eb.com.

Endres, Kathleen L. and Therese L. Lueck. 1995. *Women's Periodicals in the United States: Consumer Magazines*. Westport, Conn., and London: Greenwood.

Erté. 1926. "Frocks and Faces." *Harper's Bazar* (May): 112.

——. 1972. "From Erté's Memoirs" (trans. William Weaver). In Barthes, *Erté (Romain de Tirtoff)*, 71–154.

Evans, Sara M. 1989. *Born for Liberty: A History of Women in America*. New York and London: Free Press.

Fales, Winnifred. 1927. *A Simple Course in Home Decorating*. New York: Dodd, Mead.

——. 1936. *What's New in Home Decorating*. New York: Dodd, Mead.

"Felt or Velvet for Winter Hats." 1929. *Good Housekeeping* (October): 70–71.

Ferris, Hugh. 1929. *The Metropolis of Tomorrow*. New York: Ives Washburn.

Fischer, Lucy. 1976. "The Image of Woman as Image: The Optical Politics of *Dames*." *Film Quarterly* 30.1 (Fall): 2–11.

——. 1979. "The Lady Vanishes: Women, Magic, and the Movies." *Film Quarterly* 22.1 (Fall): 30–40.

——. 1989. *Shot/Countershot: Film Tradition and Women's Cinema*. Princeton: Princeton University Press.

——. 2001. "The Eye for Magic: Maya and Méliès." In Bill Nichols, ed., *Maya Deren and the American Avant-Garde*. Berkeley and London: University of California Press.

Flaherty, David. 1959. "A Few Reminiscences." *Film Culture* 20: 14–16.

Flash Gordon: Space Soldiers (1936). 1996 (DVD). Hearst Entertainment. (Liner Notes: Sources given as "Alex Raymond's Flash Gordon," *Films in Review* [April 1988] and *Filmfax* #45 [June–July 1994].)

Flash Gordon's Trip to Mars (1938). 1996 (DVD). Hearst Entertainment. (Liner Notes: Sources given as "Alex Raymond's Flash Gordon," *Films in Review* [April 1988] and *Filmfax* #45 [June-July 1994].)

Florescu, Radu. 1998. *In Search of Frankenstein: Exploring the Myths Behind Mary Shelley's Monster*. New York: Robson Books/Parkwest.

"Folio of New Fabrics, A." 1927. *Harper's Bazar* (September): 67.

"For the Dressing Table of Today." 1929. *House & Garden* (March): 102.

Forry, Steven Earl. 1990. *Hideous Progenies: Dramatizations of Frankenstein from Mary Shelley to the Present*. Philadelphia: University of Pennsylvania Press.

Frankenstein (1931). 1999 (DVD). Universal.

Franklin, Harold B. 2002. "Motion Picture Theater Management" (1928). In Waller, ed., *Moviegoing in America*, 116–17.

Freeman, Derek. 1999. *The Fateful Hoaxing of Margaret Mead: A Historical Analysis of her Samoan Research*. Boulder, Colo.: Westview.

"French Decorative Art on Exhibition." 1926. *New York Times* (February 26): sec. 4, pp. 10–11.

Freud, Sigmund. 1958. "The Uncanny" (1919). In *On Creativity and the Unconscious: Papers on the Psychology of Art, Literature, Love, Religion*, 122–61. New York: Harper and Row.

Fromm-Reichman, Freida and Virginia Gunst. 1977. "On the Denial of Women's Sexual Pleasure." In Jean Baker, ed., *Psychoanalysis and Women*, 86–93. New York: Penguin.

"Furniture in the Modern Manner." 1927. *Vogue* (March 15): 84.

Gabbard, Krin. 1996. *Jammin' at the Margins: Jazz and the American Cinema*. Chicago and London: University of Chicago Press.

Gaines, Jane. 1989. "The *Queen Christina* Tie-Ups: Convergence of Show Window and Screen." *Quarterly Review of Film and Video* 11.1: 35–60.

Gaines, Jane and Charlotte Herzog, eds. 1990. *Fabrications: Costume and the Female Body*. New York and London: Routledge.

Gaines, William. 1934. "Hollywood Snubs Paris." *Photoplay* (April), cited in Griffith, ed., *The Talkies* (1971), 192.

Gallagher, Fiona. 2000. *Christie's Art Nouveau*. New York: Watson-Guptill.

Gauguin, Paul. 1920. *Noa Noa*. Translated by O. F. Theis. New York: Brown.

Gelman, Woody. 1974. *Flash Gordon*, vol. 1: *The Planet Mongo*. New York: Nostalgia Press and King Features. (*Note:* This book has no page numbers.)

Giovacchini, Saverio. 2001. *Hollywood Modernism: Film and Politics in the Age of the New Deal*. Philadelphia: Temple University Press.

Glover, Margaret. 1931. "A Seasonal Potpourri from the Little Shops." *Harper's Bazaar* (June): 10.

Glut, Donald F. 1984. *The Frankenstein Catalog*. Jefferson, N.C., and London: McFarland.

Greenhalgh, Paul. 1988. *Ephemeral Vistas: The Expositions Universelles — Great Exhibitions and World's Fairs, 1851–1939*. Manchester: Manchester University Press.

Greenhalgh, Paul, ed. 2000. *Art Nouveau: 1890–1914*. New York: Abrams.

Grey, J. R. and B. B. Grey. 1927. *South Sea Settlers*. New York: Holt.

Griffith, Richard. 1959. "Flaherty and *Tabu*." *Film Culture* 20: 12–13.

Griffith, Richard, ed. 1971. *The Talkies*. New York: Dover.

Grove Dictionary of Art (online version). For entry on "Art Deco," *see* www.groveart.com.

Gunning, Tom. 2000. *The Films of Fritz Lang: Allegories of Vision and Modernity*. London: British Film Institute.

Haggard, Henry Rider. *She* (1887) in *The Works of H. Rider Haggard*. Reprinted in Roslyn, N.Y.: Black's Readers Service Company, 1928.

Hall, James Norman. 1928. *Mid-Pacific*. Boston: Houghton Mifflin.

Hall, James Norman and Charles Bernhard Nordhoff. 1921. *Faery Lands of the South Seas*. New York and London: Harper.

Hall, Leonard. 1930. "Garbo-Maniacs." *Photoplay* (January), cited in Griffith, ed., *The Talkies* (1971), 4–5, 270.

Hansen, Miriam [Bratu]. 1991. *Babel and Babylon: Spectatorship in American Silent Film*. Cambridge: Harvard University Press.

——. 2000. "The Mass Production of the Senses: Classical Cinema as Vernacular Modernism." In Christine Gledhill and Linda Williams, eds., *Reinventing Film Studies*, 332–50. New York: Oxford University Press.

Harvey, Stephen. 1975. *Fred Astaire*. New York: Pyramid.

Heisner, Beverly. 1990. *Hollywood Art: Art Direction in the Days of the Great Studios*. Jefferson, N.C., and London: McFarland.

Hershfield, Joanne. 1998. "Race and Romance in *Bird of Paradise*." *Cinema Journal* 37.3 (Spring): 3–15.

Hiller, Bevis. 1971. *Art Deco*. Catalog for an exhibit at the Minneapolis Institute of Arts (July 8–September 5).

Hilton, James. 1936. *Lost Horizon: A Novel* (1933). New York: Morrow.

Howard, Kathleen. 1931. "White Accents." *Harper's Bazaar* (August): 35.

Howard, Marjorie. 1926. "Paris Keeps on Shingling; Our Monthly Paris Article." *Harper's Bazar* (June): 80–87.

——. 1927. "Color Makes the New Clothes New." *Harper's Bazar* (August): 46–61.

——. 1929. "Modern Ornament." *Harper's Bazar* (September): 93.

Hudson, W. H. 1904. *Green Mansions: A Romance of the Tropical Forest*. Rpt., New York: Heritage Press, 1944.

Hungerford, Edward. 1922. *The Romance of a Great Store*. New York: Robert McBride.

Huyssen, Andreas. 1986. *After the Great Divide: Modernism, Mass Culture, Postmodernism*. Bloomington: Indiana University Press.

"In the Manhasset Residence of Mrs. Charles S. Payson." 1929. *Harper's Bazar* (May): 114–15.

Internet Movie Data Base (IMDB). *See* us.imdb.com/search.

"Japanese Garden Created in the Catskill Mountains, A." 1929. *House & Garden* (October): 106–107.

"Jewels on Your Christmas List." 1926. *Woman's Home Companion* (December): 85.

"Joseph Urban's Urban Apartment." 1929. *Harper's Bazaar* (November): 108–109.

Kaplan, Wendy, ed. 1995. *Designing Modernity: The Arts of Reform and Persuasion, 1885–1945*. London: Thames and Hudson.

Katz, Ephraim. 1998. *The Film Encyclopedia, Third Edition*. New York: HarperCollins.

——. 2001. *The Film Encyclopedia, Fourth Edition*. New York: HarperCollins.

King, Edith Morgan. 1929. "Modernism?" *Vogue* (May 11): 104, 162–72.

Knight, Marion A., Mertice M. James, and Matilda L. Berg, eds. 1929. *The Book Review Digest: Books of 1928*. New York: H. W. Wilson.

—, eds. 1930. *The Book Review Digest: Books of 1929*. New York: H. W. Wilson.

Koues, Helen. 1929. "*Good Housekeeping* Studio Builds an Apartment in the Modern Feeling." *Good Housekeeping* (December): 60–65, 236.

——. 1930. "Fashion: Paris Establishes the Silhouette." *Good Housekeeping* (February): 66.

Kracauer, Siegfried. 1966. *From Caligari to Hitler: A Psychological History of the German Film* (1947). Princeton: Princeton University Press.

Kron, Joan. 1977. *Home-Psych: The Social Psychology of Home and Decoration*. New York: Clarkson N. Potter.

Krützen, Michaela. 1992. *The Most Beautiful Woman on the Screen: The Fabrication of the Star Greta Garbo*. Frankfurt and New York: Peter Lang.

Lane, W. Robert. 1980. *In a Glamorous Fashion: The Fabulous Years of Hollywood Costume Design*. New York: Scribner.

Laver, James. 1937. *Taste and Fashion from the French Revolution to the Present Day*. London: Harrap.

——. 1995. *Costume and Fashion: A Concise History*. London: Thames and Hudson.

Lawrence, D. H. 1920. *Women in Love*. New York and London: Bantam, 1969.

Leigh, Helena. 1930. "This Ageless Era." *Harper's Bazaar* (March): 70–71, 122, 126, 132.

Levin, Steven, ed. 1991. *The Oakland Paramount*. Theater Historical Society Annual 18. (Based on 1976 study [HABS no. CA 1976] prepared by Luch Pope Wheeler, HABS [Historic American Buildings Survey] Writer/Editor.)

Lippmann, Walter. 1929. *A Preface to Morals*. New York: Macmillan.

"Little Revolution in Negligees, The." 1925. *Harper's Bazar* (March): 81.

Lost Horizon (1937). 1999 (DVD). Columbia Tristar Home Video.

Lucie-Smith, Edward. 1990. *Art Deco Painting*. Oxford: Phaidon.

Macquarrie, Hector. 1920. *Tahiti Days*. New York: Doran.

Maland, Charles J. 1980. *Frank Capra*. Boston: Twayne.

Mandelbaum, Howard and Eric Myers. 1985. *Screen Deco: A Celebration of High Style in Hollywood*. New York: St. Martin's.

Marchand, Roland. 1985. *Advertising the American Dream: Making Way for Modernity, 1920–1940*. Berkeley and London: University of California Press.

Margolies, John and Emily Gwathmey. 1991. *Ticket to Paradise: American Movie Theaters and How We Had Fun*. Boston and London: Little, Brown.

Massey, Anne. 2000. *Hollywood Beyond the Screen: Design and Material Culture*. Oxford and New York: Berg.

McClinton, Katharine Morrison. 1986. *Art Deco: A Guide for Collectors*. New York: Clarkson N. Potter.

McCracken, Grant. 1988. *Culture and Consumption: New Approaches to the Symbolic Character of Consumer Goods and Activities*. Bloomington: Indiana University Press.

Mead, Margaret. 1928. *Coming of Age in Samoa*. New York: Morrow.

——. 1929. "South Sea Hints on Bringing Up Children." *Parents' Magazine* (September): 21–22, 49–52.

——. 1930. "Water Babies of the South Seas." *Parents' Magazine* (September): 20–21, 61.

——. 1931. "Standardized America vs. Romantic South Seas." *Scribner's Magazine* (November): 486–91.

——. 1932. "South Sea Tips on Character Training." *Parents' Magazine* (March): 13, 66.

Menten, Theodore, ed. 1972. *The Art Deco Style in Household Objects, Architecture, Sculpture, Graphics, and Jewelry*. New York: Dover.

Meyer, Baron de. 1928. "Novelties of the Paris Season." *Harper's Bazar* (November): 93.

Mitias, Michael H. 1994. *Philosophy and Architecture*. Amsterdam and Atlanta: Rodopi.

"Mode Becomes More Formal, The." 1929. *Good Housekeeping* (April): 76–77.

"Modern Furniture Reflects the Changing Habits in Daily Living." 1928. *Woman's Home Companion* (April): 135.

"Modern Room for a Boy, A" and "A Modern Room for a Girl." 1929. *House & Garden* (April): 100–102.

"Modern Housekeeper Selects Up-to-Date Gifts, The." 1928. *Good Housekeeping* (December): 80–81.

"Modernism Enters the Nursery." 1929. *House & Garden* (April): 123.

"Modernist Art Applied to Painted Fabrics" (sketch). 1925. *Vogue* (February 15): 56.

"Modernistic Exhibitions in New York Shops." 1929. *Good Housekeeping* (January): 52–53.

"Modernistic in Color and Design." 1929. *Woman's Home Companion* (July): 64.

Moholy-Nagy, László. 1932. *The New Vision: From Material to Architecture*. Translated by Daphne M. Hoffman. New York: Brewer, Warren, and Putnam.

Moonan, Wendy. 1997. "The Hunt for Art Deco Jewelry." *New York Times* (December 5): E35.

Morley, Sheridan. 1995. *Shall We Dance: The Life of Ginger Rogers*. New York: St. Martin's.

Morris, William. ed. 1978. *American Heritage Dictionary of the English Language, College Edition*. Boston: Houghton Mifflin.

Muensterberger, Werner. 1994. *Collecting—An Unruly Passion: Psychological Perspectives*. Princeton: Princeton University Press.

Münsterberg, Hugo. 1970. *The Photoplay*. New York: Arno.

Murnau, F. W. and Robert Flaherty. 1959a. "*Tabu (Taboo)*: A Story of the South Seas." *Film Culture* 20: 27–38.

——. 1959b. *"Turia*: An Original Story." *Film Culture* 20: 17–26.

Nathanson, Paul. 1991. *Over the Rainbow: The Wizard of Oz as a Secular Myth of America.* Albany: State University of New York Press.

Naylor, David. 1981. *American Picture Palaces: The Architecture of Fantasy.* New York and London: Van Nostrand and Reinhold.

Neuhaus, Eugen. 1939. *The Art of Treasure Island.* Berkeley: University of California Press.

"New and Decorative." 1929. *Harper's Bazar* (March): 119.

O'Brien, Frederick. 1919. *White Shadows in the South Seas.* Garden City, N.Y.: Garden City Publishing.

——. 1921. *Mystic Isles of the South Seas.* New York: Century.

——. 1922. *Attols of the Sun.* New York: Century.

"Ornaments Strange and Exotic from Darkest Africa Influence Paris Jewelry." 1931. *Harper's Bazaar* (August): 50–51.

Ortner, Sherry B. 1974. "Is Female to Male as Nature Is to Culture?" In M. Z. Rosaldo and L. Lamphere, eds., *Woman, Culture, and Society*, 66–87. Stanford, Calif.: Stanford University Press.

Otey, Elizabeth. 1935. "Modern Art Influences in Our Houses." *Good Housekeeping* (September): 72–73.

Ott, Frederick W. 1979. *The Films of Fritz Lang.* Secaucus, N.J.: Citadel Press.

"Pajama-Negligee Has a Promising Future, The." 1925. *Harper's Bazar* (March): 87.

Palmborg, Rilla Page. 1930. "Chapter Two of the Private Life of Greta Garbo." *Photoplay* 38.5: 36–39, 60–61, 141.

Paris, Barry. 1995. *Garbo: A Biography.* New York: Knopf.

"Paris Makes These Smart Clothes." 1927. *Good Housekeeping* (January): 52.

"Paris Paints Its Frocks in Cubist Patterns." 1925. *Vogue* (May 15): 88–89.

Parsons, Frank Alvah. 1926. "An Analysis of Modernism: As It Is Found Exemplified in the Furniture and Fabrics of the Latest Innovations Presented in Paris." *House & Garden* (February): 72–73, 134.

Patterson, Curtis. 1930. "A Summer Living-Room on a Penthouse Terrace." *Harper's Bazaar* (July): 94–95, 105.

Peak, Mayme Ober. 1932. "Study the Stars and Dress Your Line." *Ladies' Home Journal* 49 (June): 8–9, 105.

Pearce, Susan M. 1995. *On Collecting: An Investigation into Collecting in the European Tradition.* London and New York: Routledge.

Peters, Sally. 1991. "From Eroticism to Transcendence: Ballroom Dance and the Female Body." In Laurence Goldstein, ed., *The Female Body: Figures. Style, Speculations*, 145–158. Ann Arbor, Mich.: University of Michigan Press.

"Picture Section." 1928. *Woman's Home Companion* (April): 133.

Pildas, Ave. 1980. *Movie Palaces: Survivors of an Elegant Era.* New York: Clarkson N. Potter.

Pinchot, Gifford. 1930. *To the South Seas.* Philadelphia: John C. Winston.

"Play Clothes from Paris." 1930. *Good Housekeeping* (June): 76.

Poe, Edgar Allan. 1976. "The Black Cat" (1843). In *The Short Fiction of Edgar Allan Poe: An Annotated Edition*. Edited by Stuart and Susan Levine. Urbana: University of Illinois Press.

"Precious Jewels Mark the Subtle Lines and Modern Note of Exquisitely Charming Femininity." 1930. *Harper's Bazaar* (October): 100–101.

Puxley, W. Lavallin. *Green Islands in Glittering Seas*. New York: Dodd.

Raley, Dorothy, ed. 1934. *A Century of Progress: Homes and Furnishings as Exhibited at the World's Fair, Chicago 1934*. Chicago: M. A. Ring.

Rankin, Ruth. 1935. "Who is Your Husband's Favorite Actress?" *Photoplay* (February), cited in Griffith, ed., *The Talkies* (1971), 196.

Raulet, Sylvie. 1985. *Art Deco Jewelry*. New York: Rizzoli.

"Really Desirable Oriental Garments for Negligees Are the Fine Old Pieces of Antiquity, The." 1925. *Harper's Bazar* (March): 82.

"Renovating the Old Fashioned Bathroom." 1933. *Good Housekeeping* (May): 53.

Ricci, Franco Maria. 1972. "The Publisher to the Reader" (trans. William Weaver). In *Erté*, 13–14. Parma (It.): Ricci.

"Rising Tide of White Decors, The." 1931. *Harper's Bazaar* (August): 74.

Robbins, Athena. 1929. "Saks Fifth Ave., Chicago." *Good Furniture and Decoration* (August): 91–92, 94.

Rogin, Michael. 1996. *Blackface, White Noise*. Berkeley: University of California Press.

Ross, Virgilla Peterson. 1931. "Profiles: American Pro Tem." *The New Yorker* (March 7): 28–31.

Rushdie, Salman. 1999. *The Wizard of Oz*. London: British Film Institute.

Rydell, Robert W., John E. Findling, and Kimberly D. Pelle. 2000. *Fair America: World's Fairs in the United States*. Washington, D.C.: Smithsonian Institution Press.

Sanford, Nellie C. 1926. "The Loan Exhibition from the Paris Exposition Shown in the Metropolitan Museum of Art." *Good Furniture Magazine* (April): 185–88.

Scarlett, Frank and Marjorie Townley. 1975. *Arts Décoratifs 1925: A Personal Recollection of the Paris Exhibition*. New York: St. Martin's.

Schmalhausen, Samuel D. 1929. "The Sexual Revolution." In V. V. Calverton and S. D. Schmalhausen, eds., *Sex in Civilization*, 349–436. New York: Macaulay.

Shayo, Alberto. 1993. *Chiparus: Master of Art Deco*. New York and London: Abbeville Press.

Shelley, Mary. 1996. *Frankenstein* (1818). Rpt., New York and London: Norton.

"Shoes by Saks Fifth Avenue." 1929. *Vogue* (March 2): 48.

Slater, Don. 1997. *Consumer Culture and Modernity*. Cambridge, Eng.: Polity.

Solomon, Deborah. 2002. "Is the Go-Go Guggenheim, Going Going . . ." *New York Times Magazine* (June 30): sec. 6, pp. 36–41.

Spencer, Charles. 1970. *Erté*. New York: Clarkson N. Potter.

Spiegel, Ellen. 1973. "Fred and Ginger Meet Van Nest Polglase." *The Velvet Light Trap* 10 (Fall): 17–22.

Stewart, Susan. 1993. *On Longing: Narratives of the Miniature, the Gigantic, the Souvenir, the Collection*. Durham and London: Duke University Press.

Stickney, Rebecca. 1928. "The Cosmetic Urge." *Harper's Bazar* (December): 182.

"Stitch That Saves Time, The." 1932. *Harper's Bazaar* (September): 34–35.

Stock, Ralph. 1921. *Cruise of the Dreamship*. Garden City, N.Y.: Doubleday.

Stone, Susannah Harris. 1991. *The Oakland Paramount*. Oakland, Calif.: Oakland Paramount Theater.

Stote, Dorothy. 1935. *Making the Most of Your Looks*. Philadelphia: Lippincott.

"Striking Examples of Modernist Decoration in Paris." 1925. *Vogue* (December 1): 72.

Striner, Richard. 1994. *Art Deco*. New York and London: Abbeville Press.

Strout, Cushing. 1963. *The American Image of the Old War*. New York and London: Harper and Row.

"Studio Builds a Bedroom in the Modern Feeling, The" (by "The Director"). 1929. *Good Housekeeping* (September): 56–57.

Susman, Warren I. 1984. *Culture as History: The Transformation of American Society in the Twentieth Century*. New York: Pantheon.

Taylor, Demetria M. 1935. "Toast the Toaster." *Good Housekeeping* (March): 85.

Teall, Gardner. 1928. "Screens and Furniture by Jean Dunand." *Harper's Bazar* (April): 114–15.

"That Extra Touch." 1926. *Woman's Home Companion* (December): 91.

Thomas, Tony and Jim Terry, with Busby Berkeley. 1973. *The Busby Berkeley Book*. New York: New York Graphic Society.

Tierney, Tom. 1978. *Glamorous Movie Stars of the Thirties Paper Dolls*. New York: Dover.

Tobing Rony, Fatimah. 1996. *The Third Eye: Race, Cinema, and Ethnographic Spectacle*. Durham, N.C.: Duke University Press.

Todd, Dorothy. 1929. "Some Reflections on Modernism: What It Is, Here and Abroad, and What It Is Not." *The House Beautiful* (October): 416–17, 470, 472, 474.

Torgovnick, Marianna. 1990. *Gone Primitive: Savage Intellects, Modern Lives*. Chicago and London: University of Chicago Press.

"Trends of the Day in Modern Decorating." 1935. *Good Housekeeping* (February): 69.

Troy, William. 1934. "Films: Garbo and Screen Acting." *The Nation* (January 24): 112

Tyler, Parker. 1947. *Magic and Myth of the Movies*. New York: Holt.

"Useful Christmas Suggestions in Trade-marked Lingerie and Hosiery Which You Can Find in Variety in Your Own Shops." 1928. *Good Housekeeping* (December): 66.

Walker, Nancy. 2000. *Shaping Our Mother's World: American Women's Magazines*. Jackson: University Press of Mississippi.

Waller, Gregory, ed. 2002. *Moviegoing in America*. Malden, Mass., and Oxford, Eng.: Blackwell.

Ware, Susan. 1982. *Holding Their Own: American Women in the 1930s*. Boston: Twayne.

Watts, Stephen, ed. 1938. *Behind the Screen: How Films Are Made*. London: Arthur Barker.

Weber, Eva. 1985. *Art Deco in America*. New York: Exeter.

West, Myrtle. 1926. "That Stockholm Venus" *Photoplay* 29.6: 36.

"What Makes An Ideal Husband?" 1919. *Cumberland (Md.) Evening Times* (October 29): n.p.

Wilcock, Arthur. 1925. "A New York Decorator's Opinion of the Paris Exposition." *Good Furniture Magazine* (November): 260.

Williams, Linda. 1984. "When the Woman Looks." In Mary Ann Doane, Patricia Mellencamp, and Linda Williams, eds., *Re-Vision: Essays in Feminist Film Criticism*, 83–99. Frederick, Md.: University Publications of America.

Wilson, Christina Kathleen. 1998. "Cedric Gibbons and Metro-Goldwyn-Mayer: The Art of Motion Picture Set Design." Ph.D. diss., University of Virginia (Department of Architectural History).

Winokur, Mark. 1996. *American Laughter: Immigrants, Ethnicity, and the 1930s Hollywood Film Comedy*. New York: St. Martin's.

World Almanac Knowledge Source (online version). For entries on "Diving" and "French Polynesia," *see* www.oclc.org/firstsearch/databases.

Wright, Richardson. 1925. "The Modernist Taste: At the Exhibition des Arts Décoratifs in Paris, Modernism Concentrated Its Latest Experiments." *House & Garden* (October): 77–79, 110, 114.

Yellis, Kenneth A. 1980. "Prosperity's Child: Some Thoughts on the Flapper." In Esther Katz and Anita Rapone, eds., *Women's Experience in America: An Historical Anthology*, 367–88. New Brunswick, N.J. and London: Transaction.

Young, Stark. 1932. "Film Note: Greta Garbo." *New Republic* (September 28): 176–78.

Zim, Larry, Mel Lerner, and Herbert Rolfes. 1988. *The World of Tomorrow: The 1939 New York World's Fair*. New York: Harper and Row.

MAGAZINES AND CATALOGUES: ADVERTISEMENTS AND PHOTO SPREADS

[Alfred Dunill advertisement]. 1928. *Harper's Bazar* (March): 151.

[American Standard Plumbing advertisement]. 1924. *Good Housekeeping* (October): 192.

[Armand Cold Cream Powder advertisement]. 1928. *Good Housekeeping* (April): 191.

[Associated Tile Manufacturing Company advertisement]. 1929. *House & Garden* (August): 41.

[B. Altman & Co. advertisement]. 1929. *House & Garden* (September): 5.

[Belding's Silks advertisement]. 1928. *Good Housekeeping* (September): 277.

[Bergdorf Goodman advertisement]. 1928. *Harper's Bazar* (November): 61.

[Black Starr & Frost advertisement]. 1929. *House & Garden* (January): 107.

[Bon Ami advertisement]. 1933. *Good Housekeeping* (July): 162.

[Bon Ami advertisement]. 1933. *Good Housekeeping* (May): 53.

[Bonwit Teller advertisement/Vingtieme Shops]. 1928. *Harper's Bazar* (November): 4–5.

[Cammeyer advertisement]. 1929. *Vogue*. (April 13): 22.

[Cannon Towels advertisement]. 1928. *Good Housekeeping* (January): 94.

[Cannon Towels advertisement]. 1931. *Harper's Bazaar* (February): 52.

[Coty advertisement]. 1925. *Harper's Bazar* (January): 101.

[Crane Plumbing and Heating advertisement]. 1926. *Woman's Home Companion* (December): 111.

[Cunard Anchor Lines advertisement]. 1930. "The Great . . . African Cruise." *Harper's Bazaar* (June): 170.

[Cutex advertisement]. 1929. *Good Housekeeping* (July): 171.

[D. H. Gipsy [*sic*] Moth advertisement]. 1930. *Harper's Bazaar* (March): 52.

[Delman Shoe Salon advertisement]. 1926. *Vogue* (November 1): 114.

[Dollar Steamship Line advertisement]. 1929. *House & Garden* (March): 59.

[Drew Arch Rest advertisement]. 1928. *Good Housekeeping* (September): 289.

[Dynamique Creations advertisement]. 1928. *Harper's Bazar* (October): 159.

[El Encanto Department Store advertisement]. 1929. *Vogue* (January 19): 19.

[Elizabeth Arden advertisement]. 1931. *Harper's Bazaar* (February): 107.

[Fisher Car Body advertisement]. 1932. *Good Housekeeping* (March): 125–26.

[Foot Saver Shoes advertisement]. 1929. *Woman's Home Companion* (May): 92.

[Ford Motor advertisement]. 1926. *Woman's Home Companion* (May): 12.

[Fostoria advertisement]. 1929. *Good Housekeeping* (October): 260.

[French Line advertisement]. 1928. *Harper's Bazar* (March): 39.

[General Electric advertisement]. 1934. *Good Housekeeping* (June): 121.

[General Electric/Hotpoint advertisement]. 1934. *Good Housekeeping* (December): 151.

[Guerlain advertisement]. 1929. *House & Garden* (November): 4.

[Guerlain advertisement]. 1930. *Harper's Bazaar* (January): 21.

[Guerlain advertisement]. 1931. *Harper's Bazaar* (February): 111.

[*Harper's Bazar* advertisement]. 1928. *Good Housekeeping* (September): 246.

[*Harper's Bazar* advertisement]. 1929. *Good Housekeeping* (July): 224.

[*Harper's Bazaar* Fashion Services advertisement]. 1932. *Harper's Bazaar* (February): 26.

[*Harper's Bazaar* advertisement]. 1931. *Harper's Bazaar* (February): 37.

[Helena Rubinstein advertisement]. 1928. *Harper's Bazar* (December): 128.

[Houbigant advertisement]. 1926. *Harper's Bazar* (April): 187.

[Houbigant advertisement]. 1927. *Harper's Bazar* (August): 4.

[Houbigant advertisement]. 1928. *Harper's Bazar* (December): 125.

[Houbigant advertisement]. 1929. *Harper's Bazar* (February): 137.

[Houbigant advertisement]. 1929. *Vogue* (June 8): 141.

[Houbigant advertisement]. 1931. *Harper's Bazaar* (May): opposite page 176.

[Houbigant advertisement]. 1932. *Harper's Bazaar* (May): 103.

[I. Miller advertisement]. 1926. *Vogue* (June 1): 8.

[I. Miller advertisement]. 1927. *Vogue* (June 1): 14–15, 18.

[International Silverplate advertisement]. 1929. *Good Housekeeping* (June): 302.

[International Silverplate advertisement]. 1929. *House Beautiful* (November): 627.

[Isabey of Paris advertisement]. 1927. *Harper's Bazar* (July): 8.

[J. E. Caldwell advertisement]. 1928. *Harper's Bazar* (December): 147.

[J. E. Caldwell advertisement]. 1928. *Harper's Bazar* (November): 139.

[J. E. Mergott Co. advertisement]. 1929. *Harper's Bazar* (February): 13:

[Jeanne Lanvin advertisement]. 1928. *Harper's Bazar* (October): 57.

[Kirsch Drapery advertisement]. 1929. *Good Housekeeping* (January): 207.

[Kohler advertisement]. 1929. *Good Housekeeping* (June): 281.

[Lentheric Parfums advertisement]. 1929. *House & Garden* (September): 169.

[Listerine advertisement]. 1929. *Woman's Home Companion* (July): 46.

[Lovely Linen advertisement]. 1929. *House & Garden* (March): 144.

[Lucite advertisement]. 1928. *Good Housekeeping* (December): 178.

[Lucite advertisement]. 1928. *Harper's Bazar.* (November): 153.

[Lux Toilet Soap advertisement]. 1929. *Good Housekeeping* (May): 197.

[Macy's advertisement for China Department]. 1929. *House & Garden* (May): 7.

[Macy's advertisement for Chinese Figurines]. 1929. *House & Garden* (January): 7.

[Marcus & Company advertisement]. 1927. *Vogue* (March 13): 123.

[Margot Landberg Cosmetics advertisement]. 1929. *Vogue* (March 16): 191.

[Martha Washington Footwear advertisement]. 1928. *Good Housekeeping* (September): 235.

[Mary Ann Shell Pans advertisement]. 1929. *Good Housekeeping* (March): 241.

[Mauboussin advertisement]. 1928. *Harper's Bazar* (November): 54.

[Modess Sanitary Pad advertisement]. 1929. *Good Housekeeping* (October): 269.

[Mohawk Rug advertisement]. 1927. *Good Housekeeping* (January): 189.

[Monel Metals advertisement]. 1929. *Good Housekeeping* (February): 127.

[Mosaic Tile Company advertisement]. 1929. *House & Garden* (September): 64.

[New Mix Toothpaste advertisement]. 1929. *Good Housekeeping* (October): 231.

[Onyx Hosiery advertisement]. 1926. *Vogue* (October 1): 2.

[Photo Spread]. 1928. *Good Housekeeping* (December): 66.

[Photo Spread]. 1928. *Good Housekeeping* (December): 72.

[Photo Spread]. 1929. *Woman's Home Companion* (July): 52.

[Photo Spread]. 1929. *Good Housekeeping* (September): 54–55.

[Photo Spread]. 1932. *Good Housekeeping* (November): 75.

[Photo Spread]. 1933. *Good Housekeeping* (December): 69.

[Ponds advertisement]. 1930. *Woman's Home Companion* (March): 53.

[Poudre de Fioret advertisement]. 1927. *Good Housekeeping* (January): 110.

[Rayon advertisement]. 1929. *Good Housekeeping* (February): 179.

[Rayon advertisement]. 1929. *Good Housekeeping* (May): 296.

[Rogers Brothers Silverplate advertisement]. 1929. *Good Housekeeping* (September): 102.

[Rogers Brothers Silverplate advertisement]. 1929. *House & Garden* (October): 149.

[Rogers Brothers Silverplate advertisement]. 1929. *Good Housekeeping* (June): 148.

[Rogers Tinted Lacquer advertisement]. 1929. *Good Housekeeping* (May): 285.

[Roseville "Futura" Pottery advertisement]. 1928. *Good Housekeeping* (December): 193.

[Roseville "Futura" Pottery advertisements]. 1928. *Harper's Bazar* (November): 166. (See also issues for December 1928:108 and March 1929:160.)

[Saks Fifth Avenue advertisement]. 1926. *Harper's Bazar* (April): 13.

[Saks Fifth Avenue advertisement]. 1926. *Vogue* (August 1): 28.

[Saks Fifth Avenue advertisement]. 1926. *Vogue* (October 1): 50.

[Saks Fifth Avenue shoe advertisement]. 1926. *Harper's Bazar* (April): 12.

[Saks Fifth Avenue shoe advertisement]. 1926. *Harper's Bazar* (June): 10.

[Saks Fifth Avenue shoe advertisement]. 1927. *Harper's Bazar* (July): 7.

[Saks Fifth Avenue shoe advertisement]. 1927. *Vogue* (March 15): 11.

[Schumacher & Co. advertisement]. 1927. *Vogue* (February 1): 109.

[Schumacher & Co. advertisement]. 1929. *House & Garden* (July): 77.

[Sears Roebuck advertisement]. 1930. *Good Housekeeping* (January): 185.

Sears Roebuck Catalogue (Fall 1925).

Sears Roebuck Catalogue (Spring/Summer 1926).

Sears Roebuck Catalogue (1927).

Sears Roebuck Catalogue (Fall 1929).

Sears Roebuck Catalogue (Winter 1930–1931).

[Simmons Chains and Necklaces advertisement]. 1930. *Good Housekeeping* (June): 276.

[Standard Plumbing Fixtures advertisement]. 1929. *House & Garden* (April): 241.

[Standard Sanitary Manufacturing Company advertisement]. 1930. *Harper's Bazaar* (April): between pp. 160 and 161.

[Steinway and Sons advertisement]. 1928. *Good Housekeeping* (December): 255.

[Steinway and Sons advertisement]. 1929. *House & Garden* (February): 185.

[Stewart advertisement]. 1929. *Harper's Bazaar* (December): 43.

[Stewart advertisement]. 1929. *Harper's Bazaar* (November): 49.

[Stunzi Sons Silk Company advertisement]. 1929. *Harper's Bazar* (October): 193.

[Telechron advertisement]. 1933. *Good Housekeeping* (December): 174.

[Valspar Finishes advertisement]. 1929. *Good Housekeeping* (May): 244.

[*Vanity Fair* advertisement]. 1929. *Vogue* (January 2): 14.

[Vitrolite advertisement]. 1929. *House Beautiful* (September): opposite 244.

[Vollrath Ware advertisement]. 1929. *Good Housekeeping* (September): 286.

[Wallpaper Association of the United States advertisement]. 1929. *Good Housekeeping* (February): 275.

[Wallpaper Association of the United States advertisement]. 1929. *House & Garden* (September): 18.

[Whittall Rugs advertisement]. 1929. *Good Housekeeping* (March): n.p.

[Whiting and Davis advertisement]. 1931. *Good Housekeeping* (June): 181.

[Williams Ice-O-Matic Refrigeration advertisement]. 1929. *House & Garden* (April): 57.

[Worth advertisement]. 1927. *Vogue* (May 15): 35.

INDEX

Page numbers in **bold** indicate an illustration.

Production Code influence on, 128; set design, 25, 109–110, 225–27, 254; silent films vs. talkies, 164–65; South Seas films, 151–83; style and, 254–55; vernacular modernism in, 24–25

movie theaters, 185–202; architecture, 25, 186, 189–95, 189n1; demise of picture palaces, 187; as experience, 186–87; illusion and, 201; musical imagery in, 145; Oakland Paramount, 186–90 (*see also* plates 10–13); as populist spaces, 187; romance of, 185–86, 191; sound and, 187; as theme park, 200–201

Mucha, Alphonse, 29

Muensterberger, Werner, 5, 7

Munch, Edward, 216, 219

Münsterberg, Hugo, 26

Murnau, F. W., 25, 156–63, 206, 226

musical films: African influence on, 131–37; Art Deco in, 123–49; Astaire/Rogers films, 124–31; "Big White Set," 131; chryselephantine sculptures and, 147; costumes, 127, 130–31; dance in, 123, 124, 137; elegant Deco in, 124–31; exotic Deco in, 131–37; flamboyant Deco in, 137–47; lighting in, 144; nightclubs in, 142; production numbers, 126–27; set design, 125, 126, 128–29, 138–41. *See also* dance

musical imagery, 124, 145

music halls, Parisian, 123

Myers, Eric, 135–36, 226n6, 253

The Mysterious Lady (1928), 96

Mystic Isles of the South Seas (O'Brien), 151–52

Nagel, Conrad, 105

Nanook of the North (1922), 157, 166, 169

Nathanson, Paul, 249–50

nature, 12, 191

Naylor, David, 190, 200

Negro Woman (sculpture), 132

neoclassicism, 198

Neuhaus, Eugen, 246

"Never Gonna Dance," 126, 127

Newman, Bernard, 125

newsreels: fashion marketing in, 67

New Woman, 33–35, 175

New York World's Fair (1939), 242–43

nightclubs, 142

Noa Noa (Gauguin), 154

"No More Love," 146

Nordhoff, Charles Bernhard, 152

Nosferatu (1922), 157

nostalgia: collecting and, 5

Novarro, Ramon, 100, **101**

Nowlan, Phil, 238

nudes and nudity: female, in advertising, 74–75; in South Seas films, 163–64, 168; statues, 26–27

Oakland (California) Paramount Theater: abstract/linear Art Deco, 199–200; aquatic themes, 194; as "Art Deco paradise," 186, 187–90; Auditorium, 198–99, **199**; bas-reliefs, 196–97, **197**, 198–99; Exotic/Primitive in, 190–95; as feminized space, 195–200; floral motifs, 193–94; "golden maidens," 196 (and plate 13); marquee, 189, 189n1; music imagery, 145; mythological imagery, 196–97, **197**; nature symbolism, 191, 193; restoration, 201–202; South Seas motif, 156, 190–91, 194–95; tile mosaic,

195–96; tropical rain forest theme, 191–93. *See also* plates 10–13

O'Brien, Frederick, 151–52, 170, 172, 176, 195

Odeon Dancer (sculpture), 143

Odette, Mary, 217

Olympia (Florida), 186

Olympia (Paris), 123

Orientalism: in Art Deco, 18–19; in clothing, 68; in fantasy films, 228, 230–31; in furnishings, 79; in Garbo films, 96, 97f, 98–100; in interior decoration, 76–77; in objects, 78; in science fiction films, 234–35

ostrich feathers, 70, 131, 141

O'Sullivan, Maureen, 181

Otey, Elizabeth, 18, 76

Our Blushing Brides (1930), 54–58, **58**

Our Daily Bread (aka *City Girl*; 1929), 157

Our Dancing Daughters (1928), 54, 148, **149**, 253

Our Modern Maidens (1929), 54

Page, Anita, 54

The Painted Veil (1934), 96, 98, **98**, 113, **114**, 151

Pallas Athene (painting), 216

Paris, Barry, 95, 100, 104

Paris Exposition (1925): European focus of, 20; fashion show, 66; female image in medal, 30, **30**; frozen fountain motif, 139; magazine coverage of, 51; public reaction to exhibition, 21; theatricality of, 16. *See also* Exposition Internationale des Arts Décoratifs et Industriels Modernes,

Paris Exposition Coloniale (1931), 132